THE DEFINITIVE
WHERE TO FISH
NORFOLK AND SUFFOLK

by
JOHN WILSON

John Wilson
July
2002.

BARNWELL'S TIMESCAPE PUBLISHING LIMITED

THE AUTHOR

Following careers in hairdressing, the Merchant Navy and printing, John Wilson ran his own well known tackle shop 'John's Tackle Den' in Norwich for over 25 years before selling up to concentrate purely on angling journalism, video production and television presenting. He currently writes regularly for *Angling Times, Sea Angler* and foreign magazines with a weekly specialist angling column in the *Sunday Express*. John has written over 30 hard back specialist books on angling, 20 of these for Boxtree/Macmillan.

For 16 years during the screening of 102 programmes, John's face has become familiar to millions as presenter and co-producer of the highly acclaimed *Go Fishing* for Anglia and Meridian Television which, when shown nationwide on Channel 4, regularly attracted an audience of between two and three million viewers. *Go Fishing* has been the most successful and longest running series ever of television angling programmes, featuring species and techniques both in the UK and abroad, and has been screened in over 20 countries around the world.

A full time angler in every way, John is also senior tackle consultant for one of the UK's largest tackle companies, Masterline International Limited, and when his wife, Jo, and assortment of family pets permit, John travels in search of big fish to exotic locations all over the world. Despite having caught sharks from the beaches of South West Africa, huge white sturgeon from Canada's Fraser River and most species in between in over 60 countries, much of John's enthusiasm still relates to angling in and around the UK, particularly East Anglia where he lives west of Norwich in his own lakeland setting close to the River Wensum.

John's impressive list of British specimen fish includes dace 1 lb. 2 oz., grayling 3 lb. ½ oz., roach 2 lb. 14½ oz., rudd 3 lb. 8 oz., perch 4 lb. 8 oz., pike 30 lb. 13 oz., bream 13 lb. 14 oz., barbel 12 lb. 12 oz., zander 11 lb. 3 oz., tench 9 lb. 4 oz., chub 6 lb. 7 oz., golden orfe 6 lb. 6 oz., grass carp 21 lb. 5 oz., mirror carp 33 lb. 1 oz., sea trout 9 lb. 4 oz., brown trout 11 lb. 12 oz., rainbow trout 15 lb. 10 oz., bass 12 lb. 0 oz., cod 26 lb. 12 oz., coalfish 17 lb. 0 oz., pollack 18 lb. 12 oz., tope 42 lb. 0 oz. and conger eel 76 lb. 0 oz.

John's list of foreign sports fish topping that magical 100 lb. barrier includes Nile perch, wels catfish, white sturgeon, stingrays, big eyed tuna, tarpon, plus oceanic, bronze whaler, hammerhead and lemon sharks. He still rates his greatest achievements ever, however, being an 81 lb. and 92 lb. mahseer caught two hours apart one morning from South India's Cauvery River, and a day's catch of six monster perch from Buckinghamshire's Upper Great Ouse, weighing an ounce less than 24 lb. No less than four weighed over 4 lb., the best 4 lb. 7 oz.

John with tench of 9 lb. 4 oz. and 7 lb. 2 oz.

DEDICATION

For John (Jinx) Davey of Bungay, Suffolk. A friend of over 40 years' standing who first showed me where to fish in East Anglia.

Published by
Barnwell's Timescape Publishing
Barnwell's Printing Works,
Penfold Street, Aylsham, Norfolk. NR11 6ET.
Telephone: +44(0)1692 404042

ISBN 0 9531851 8 4

Printed in England by
Barnwell's Print Ltd, Barnwell's Printing Works,
Penfold Street, Aylsham, Norfolk. NR11 6ET.
Telephone: +44(0)1263 732767

CONTENTS

INTRODUCTION

Little did I envisage, when preparing the copy for this book's first edition, that I would be still at it exactly 30 years later. Yet the purpose of this book is the same now, in this completely revised and updated seventh edition, as it was in the first way back in 1973. And that is to help the angler in his choice of venues from the vast amount of water in Norfolk and Suffolk. Whether he prefers game, coarse or sea fishing in East Anglia, and whether he is local or just visiting the area, I sincerely hope that the following pages may help his fishing.

There is such an array of available fishing in East Anglia that much of it is little known, especially by the coarse angler who often tends only to think in terms of the Norfolk Broads and their accompanying tidal rivers. However, quite apart from the clean flowing upper reaches of the big rivers, several interesting mini-rivers and many streams, there is so very much more available sport now to be found in the unlimited acres comprised of ponds, lakes, meres and particularly in clay, gravel and sand pits.

Naturally as time marches on the cost of both day and season tickets is bound to increase and no doubt numerous venues within the following pages will either cease to be available as fisheries, or simply change hands and revert to being strictly private. So I ask the reader's indulgence in this and hope that perhaps he might even inform me of any important changes as they occur.

To those who have already freely given information and assisted with the preparation of this book I should like to express my gratitude. These, unfortunately, are too numerous to name but my particular thanks go to George Alderson, Chris Newell, the late Len Head, Neville and Marge Bailey, Dave Batten, John Nunn, Mike Grief, Geoff Baker, Terry Houseago, Brian Finbow, John Easdown, Roy Webster, Chris Turnbull, Christine Shipp and the late Bill Cooper of Norwich. I should also like to thank Paul Kerry for his invaluable help with the sea section and my typist, Jan Carver.

Tight lines.

John Wilson
Great Witchingham
2002

Left: The River Bure at Wroxham is the busiest spot in the whole of Broadland. However sport with roach and pike can prove most consistent, especially during the winter months. Bridge Broad West is situated in the middle of the photo

NORFOLK RIVERS

THE RIVER ANT

The Ant is unique as it is the only Broadland river which actually feeds a broad. It enters at the northern end of Barton Broad, where one may follow the course upstream by boat to Honing Lock and floods in and out at the southern end, giving the broad colour and an ever-changing circulation of fish.

The Ant's watercourse is actually born in the village of Antingham where, from a large lake (private), it flows in a south-easterly direction through Swafield and on to the market town of North Walsham. The fishing in these upper reaches has greatly deteriorated over the years and almost everywhere one finds cases of silting and dilapidation at the mills and around the bridges and locks. From North Walsham where the Ant is canalised, it meanders down to Ebridge Mill. It is perhaps rather difficult for the visitor to accept that such large vessels as Norfolk wherries did actually sail upriver along the Ant here, when one considers the present state of silting and the fact that a wherry, when fully laden, must have drawn 3 feet of water, for the average depth here nowadays is about the same and, in many parts, even less. It is all actually known as the North Walsham – Dilham Canal downriver to the confluence with Taylor's Cut.

Two miles downstream from Ebridge Mill is Briggate Mill and then a one mile stretch leading to Honing Common which can offer good roach fishing. There are also tench, bream, eels, pike, perch and ruffe. From Honing Lock to Tonnage Bridge at Dilham one finds the

Left: A visiting angler enjoys superb sport with specimen-sized Norfolk Chub. Where? In the Wensum of course

same species with bream and roach predominating. It should be noted that motor cruisers cannot pass beyond Tonnage Bridge. Fishing here can be rewarding during the winter months but sessions in summer time should be kept to late evening or early morning as the boat traffic may prove frustrating even this far upriver, bank access being extremely limited.

About half a mile downriver from Tonnage Bridge, Dilham Cut joins the main stream from the southern bank. There is good fishing all the way up this navigable channel to Taylers at the top end, where navigation ceases at the road bridge carrying the Honing to Dilham road. Species to be found here are shoals of medium sized bream to 4 lb., rudd, perch, fair roach and numerous pike.

A little further downstream from the Ant's junction with Dilham Cut, Wayford Bridge spans the river, carrying the A149 road to Stalham, an excellent winter spot. Boats can be hired here from Urwins Day Boats (Tel: 01692 582071) and there is a public slipway close by. Pike fishing is excellent (though most are small) from here down to Barton Broad. One mile downstream from Wayford Bridge, Stalham Dyke enters from the left bank. This leads up to the boatyards at Stalham where one may hire dinghies or day launches from Stalham Yacht Services (Tel: 01692 580288). These must be booked well in advance and are available all year round.

Fishing can prove very rewarding from the boatyards, especially at the tail end of the season and the boatyard of R. Richardson issues day permits to fish from its property (Tel: 01692 581081). There is also a certain amount of free fishing from the public staithe. Stalham

Angling Club have sole fishing rights to certain basins within Richardsons Boatyard complex. Enquire at reception for details. Halfway along Stalham Dyke, a short dyke leads in from the staithe at nearby Sutton where the fishing is entirely free from the roadside. But one requires a boat to fish the dyke itself as the banks are privately owned. Access to the north bank of the Ant between Wayford Bridge and Stalham, along which one finds lovely Hunsett Mill, is via Chapel Field Farm, off the A149 road, a little west of Stalham. This entire area offers excellent coarse fishing for bream, roach with some perch, tench, plenty of eels and often (among lots of jacks) a really good pike. As with much of the Ant, sport improves from October onwards, or at dusk and dawn during the summer.

Following on from the confluence of Stalham Dyke with the mainstream, there is just half a mile of reed-fringed river before the Ant enters Barton Broad (see 'The Broads'). After furrowing down the length of Barton, the Ant emerges from its southern end as a river of changed character. The average depth has increased to around 6 feet with a good colour, over a silty bottom. The flow is often strong at times from here on, as the Ant passes through the famous Irstead Shoals. There is superb bream fishing from the bank along the public staithe at Irstead, particularly at night when the boats are dormant. Bream here run to over 5 lb. and roach average between 4 and 8 oz. Best tactics when night fishing are ledgering flake or maggots and utilising a quiver-tip if bites prove delicate. Daytime sport improves from late October with mixed catches of sizeable roach and bream falling to anglers who trot or lay-on maggots anywhere along the three and a half mile course from Irstead through How Hill,

Johnson Street and finally to Ludham Bridge. Fishing is free on the left bank when walking upstream from Ludham Bridge with access for one and a half miles until a dyke stops progress. The entire area of Ludham Bridge becomes a hive of activity during high summer and, as with much of the Ant, only night and early morning sessions are worthwhile.

Alan Green from Clacton enjoys the pike fishing on the River Ant at Hunsett Mill

To concentrate on the bream, ledgering is best using flake, paste, maggots or redworms, rolled down on the bomb or stationary in conjunction with a block end swim feeder. Small roach and bream, together with many eels, can nearly always be caught but this is little consolation for the serious angler. The fishing drastically improves when the boats tie up for the winter, which is characteristic nowadays of most of the tidal rivers in Norfolk and Suffolk. However, for those wishing to boat fish, dinghies with or without motors and day launches are for hire at reasonable rates from Ludham Bridge Services (Tel: 01692 630486). Bait and tackle are available and the manager, Mr. Robert Paul, will give additional information and is only too pleased to advise anglers (Tel: 01692 630322).

Leaving Ludham Bridge and the wide water, the Ant courses on its last half mile before joining forces with the Bure at Ant Mouth, just above St. Benet's Abbey. The swims at this junction offer some of the best tidal river fishing in Norfolk, particularly during the summer and autumn for quality roach, hybrids and bream. Best tactics are to ledger on the bomb with a quiver-tip and baiting with maggots or breadflake or trotting through with maggots or casters.

The northern bank from Ant Mouth by St. Benet's Abbey down to Thurne Mouth is controlled by Norfolk and District A.A., with £2 day tickets available to non members from Throwers Stores in Ludham or Ludham Bridge Stores. Practically opposite the remains of the Abbey, some of which lie encrusted with tackle at the bottom of the Bure, Fleet Dyke leaves the Bure's southern bank to feed South Walsham Broads (see 'The Broads'). This is a wonderful stretch to trot from a boat during the autumn and boats may be hired (the closest spot) with or without motors from Ludham Bridge Services (Tel: 01692 630486).

THE BABINGLEY RIVER

This miniature, narrow river rises just nine miles inland from the Wash. It appears to obtain most of its water from the ponds in the grounds of Flitcham Abbey and makes its way due west through Flitcham and on to Babingley where the A149 crosses its path just two miles south of Royal Sandringham Park. The Babingley offers rather difficult coarse fishing for dace, some trout, pike, roach and, rather strangely for such a limited water, bream up to the 4 lb. mark. Upstream of the A149 road bridge, fishing is private but below the polite enquiring angler is rarely refused permission. The river here is not over-fished which stands to reason really for the fishing is frustrating because of ridiculously clear water running between high banks which bear little vegetation. One needs to crawl about a little in order to present a bait without scaring the ultra-shy fish. The Babingley ends at the Wash where it spills its water through the marshes and into the North Sea.

THE BLACKWATER STREAM

Rising in the villages of East Bilney and Gressenhall from an amalgamation of brooks, the Blackwater winds its way north-easterly for just three miles before joining the River Wensum at Worthing. It is a delightful mini-river holding some jumbo-sized dace, chub, roach and brown trout. Access throughout is limited and privately controlled, although there are one or two spots where the polite, enquiring angler will find sport.

Just before it joins the Wensum at Worthing, there is a super but short stretch available on a day ticket. These cost £3 (season permits at £35) from Mr. Eve of Tannery House, Worthing (Tel: 01362 668202) and includes fishing in an adjacent one acre lake (see 'Tannery Lake' under Stillwaters). The river fishery starts at Worthing road bridge, running upstream on the southern bank for about 200 yards and include a lovely little deep pool plus some slow, wider water above the Mill holding good roach, dace, chub, perch and a few trout. Below the road bridge on much of both banks the fishing is controlled by Worthing

Fisheries (Tel: Mr. T. Houseago on 01362 869122). In addition to fine dace and chub there is also the chance of a barbel in this twisting, overgrown stretch before the Blackwater's junction with the Wensum.

THE RIVER BURE

If one studies an Ordnance Survey map of north-east Norfolk and in particular the area of Broadland, it will become apparent that the major river is the Bure. With its tributaries the Ant and Thurne, together with the vast complex of broads and dykes that they collectively feed, the Bure is indeed a mighty waterway. But this river is also two-faced because its deep tidal, broad-connecting reaches bear little resemblance whatsoever to the peaceful and comparatively tiny upper reaches which start high up in mid north Norfolk, near Melton Constable.

The Bure is predominantly a highly reserved trout fishery in these narrow, streamy upper reaches as it flows through the miniature, most picturesque mills of Corpusty and Itteringham in an easterly direction. Nearly all the fishing is private but the individual can do no harm by asking permission, especially if he possesses a fly rod and shows interest (see also under 'Trout Fishing – Syndicate waters').

The first actual accessible part of the river is immediately downstream of Ingworth Bridge which carries the old A140 road from Norwich to Corpusty (see 'Salmon and Trout Association Waters'). The Bure here is a most enchanting and challenging venue, being an almost miniature replica of the famous Itchen and holds numbers of large dace in addition to brown trout.

From Ingworth, the Bure courses south-easterly towards Aylsham where, just above and below the town, the banks are

The picturesque and meandering River Bure half a mile downstream from Buxton Mill

privately owned. However, there is a stretch worth exploring for big dace in the area of where the Aylsham by-pass crosses the river. Local farmers are usually sympathetic to the serious angler if permission is asked first. The river bed is constantly changing character with a depth variation of between 2 and 8 feet. The deepish runs between weed beds generally hold the better sized fish but the water is absolutely crystal clear in the summer and fishing is painfully difficult. A stealthy approach is always advisable even when rain colours the stream.

The Upper Bure is probably the most difficult to fish of all Norfolk's rivers. Per acre of water this river has very limited fish stocks, although individual fish are often of specimen size. Two miles down from Aylsham the Bure flows beneath the tiny humpbacked road bridge at Burgh and divides around the old mill. There is little access above this area but below the mill on the northern bank – stretching all the way down to Oxnead road bridge – the fishing is owned by Mr. T. Colchester (Tel: 01603 279274) who gives anglers free access providing they telephone beforehand.

From Oxnead Mill to Buxton Mill a syndicate of the Norfolk Anglers Conservation Association (N.A.C.A.) has the fishing rights along the right hand (southern) bank looking downstream. Anglers wishing to join the syndicate should contact John Nunn (Tel: 01692 671949). The N.A.C.A. fishery also extends above Oxnead Mill to the first bend upstream of Brampton Bridge. The Bure in these winding two miles starts narrow but widens and deepens as it nears Buxton. It is very much a specialist's water holding small shoals of bream in the 4 – 10 lb. range, plus the odd tench to 7 lb. A 9 lb. 6 oz. bream was caught here in 2001 by Alan Burgess.

There are also pike including occasional specimens over 20 lb., plus odd dace, trout, roach and chub.

Below the mill at Buxton chub really start to feature with numerous fish over 3 lb. plus the odd specimen to 6 lb. along with a few quality roach, dace and odd big bream. Bob Jackson caught a 6 lb. 2 oz. chub here in 2001. There are some nice dace and chub runs immediately above and below the old railway bridge where the N.A.C.A. fishery starts again (around the mill fishing is private) extending downstream for half a mile on the downstream (southern) bank to opposite the beck.

Immediately below Mayton Bridge is an excellent dace run and one or two large brown trout inhabit this stretch. The river now twists and turns between banks lined with beds of tall reeds for a distance of two miles down to Horstead road bridge. There is a lovely overgrown wooded part with free access along the southern bank via a footpath behind Horstead church on the B1354 road. Here there are numerous chub, some quality roach and odd good bream and pike. Access to the opposite (northern) bank starts at Horstead road bridge where fishing is free from the public footpath all the way upriver to the first dyke. The wide double 'S' bend 400 yards above the bridge is known as Bream Corner, where bream to 8 lb. have been caught in past seasons. The shoals are numerically nowhere near so strong today but the chance of taking just one or two slabs to 7 lb. plus is still there. Fishing into darkness with ledgered breadflake takes some beauties and occasionally produces a big roach. A few specimens to 2½ lb. still exist here, along with some nice dace. Locate a double figure pike, of which there are several in this stretch, and its feed will not be far away.

Four hundred yards below the road bridge which carries the B1150 from Norwich lies Horstead Mill, the boundary line between the Bure's upper and tidal reaches. The pool is deep and much of the bottom is strewn with large boulders and discarded rubbish. This terrain provides shelter to the many huge eels but makes any attempt to extract a sizeable specimen almost impossible on standard equipment. Good shoals of quality roach exist here plus a few whoppers at the tail end of the flush, together with odd large perch, chub and brown trout. Dace and gudgeon are numerous in all the fast, shallow water and between the cabbage patches live some pike well into double figures. There is always a chance of specimens over 20 lb. here.

At certain times throughout the summer shoals of sizeable bream enter the pool from downriver. These bronze beauties run to a good size and, in the mid 1960s, a local angler, the late George Woods, amassed an incredible 140 lb. of fish to 4 lb. Such numbers do not exist nowadays, however, but individual fish are much larger. Access to anglers is from the roadside adjacent to the pool's south bank and fishing is free.

The Bure divides below the pool around a long island for about 400 yards and then meets again to pursue its course towards Coltishall Common, a popular holiday spot and an excellent winter fishery when the summer boats have been put away. However, small 'bream flats' and roach are taken here during the summer, even when things are in full swing, but for better sport and quality fish one concentrates on either early morning or evening sessions. Fishing dinghies can be hired on the Common during the summer months only. Fishing from the towpath on the Common is free.

The fishing in these now tidal reaches is far easier than in the upper reaches, due mainly I think to the permanently coloured water. Another plus factor is that actual shoals of most species, except dace, are so much larger. One may fish the same swim all day and accumulate a bag which many consider an impossible task upriver.

From Coltishall to Belaugh and on to Wroxham there are four miles of fishing, which is largely inaccessible from the banks, due mainly to surrounding marshland and private controls. However, one may navigate upriver from Belaugh or even put a small car-top dinghy in from Coltishall Common and Horstead Mill (no slipways) and enjoy sport with good concentrations of roach, plus a few bream and numerous pike which are to be found in this reach. In the village of Belaugh there are two public staithes. One is adjacent to the house on the left of the boatyard and to the right is the mooring staithe where one can park the car. The river then meanders slowly down towards Wroxham through beautifully wooded marshes. Belaugh Broad, the small badly silted broad on the northern bank, one and a half miles upstream of Wroxham, is private although it is reputed to contain numbers of tench, bream and even carp.

One mile upstream from Wroxham there is around 500 yards of free fishing on the south bank along Caens Meadow, adjacent to the school. Access is from the Norwich - Wroxham road via Castle Street. Cars must be left at the top of the lane.

At Wroxham the Bure is the busiest spot in Broadland, especially during summer. However, small 'bream flats' and young roach are caught among the hustle and bustle. River craft, large and tiny, plough down the river with parties of tourists attracted to the local sights. Boats hibernate from November onwards, however, and until the season ends Wroxham becomes a mecca for anglers. Incidentally, bait and local advice are available from Wroxham Angling Centre in Station Road (Tel: 01603 782453). The Bure here offers easily accessible fishing from comfortable bankside swims where good roach, bream, perch, ruffe and even odd tench are taken most of the winter through. If the mainstream doesn't pay dividends then there are usually some concentrations of medium-sized fish to be found in the now deserted boatyards. Favourite tactics are light float fishing with casters or maggots or worms, with light cereal groundbait for added attraction. Extremely stable, aluminium boats may be hired from Fineway Leisure of Riverside Road (Tel: 01603 782309). The pike fishing here is really excellent with hordes of fish in the 4 – 12 lb. range and fish over 20 lb. are taken regularly throughout the winter. The river record was taken in 1980 quite close to Wroxham Bridge by Roger Westgate and weighed 32 lb. 13 oz. Bridge Broad (west) also known as Little Bridge Broad (see 'The Broads') is worth a try, particularly during the winter for pike. Its entrance is half a mile upstream of Wroxham via the southern bank.

Travelling immediately downriver from Wroxham, one passes numerous dykes and quay headings which offer good roach and bream fishing, especially during winter. Numbers of decent-sized pike lurk around the entrances to these boat dykes. The angler should note that nearly all the banks here are privately owned and boat fishing is the only means of transportation to the most productive swims. In recent years trotting the stream with casters and maggots has produced some cracking bags of quality roach up to and sometimes over the 1½ lb. mark plus the odd nice perch. There is over half a mile of the Bure harbouring these dykes and cuts with interesting swims all the way along, as it channels through picturesque woodlands.

From the southern bank two navigable dykes lead to Wroxham Broad (see 'The Broads') a mile below Wroxham Bridge, while on the opposite bank lies the first of five dykes which feed Hoveton Great Broad. This is the largest of the Bure-fed broads but, being a nature reserve and private, it is out of bounds to anglers.

The Bure bends slowly between Wroxham and Hoveton Broads for almost two miles before the first of two entrances to Salhouse Broad is visible (see 'The Broads'). The fishing during winter time is both uninterrupted and rewarding but is best forgotten during the summer daylight hours. The course winds downstream with Hoveton Marshes on the northern bank and Woodbastwick Marshes on the southern. As the Bure skirts Decoy Broad (see 'The Broads') it bends very sharply and continues down towards the village of Horning. On the northern bank lies the entrance to Little Hoveton Broad (private) while on the southern is Woodbastwick Staithe and the second of two entrances to Decoy Broad. The river is quite wide and often has a strong pull. Summer boat traffic at its peak has to be seen to be believed with very little serious fishing until darkness, when the river craft cease. Then from dusk until dawn, the Bure opens its arms to keen anglers and offers large nets of sizeable bream in the 2 – 6 lb. range. Breadflake or paste are the baits to tempt the larger bream with maggots running a close second. Much of the waterside in this area is private marshland with little public access. However from

Woodbastwick on the southern bank, going downstream, Norwich and District A.A. controls about one mile of excellent fishing for members only. Access is the same as for Decoy Broad and there are no day tickets (see 'The Broads').

As the Bure channels down towards Horning it bends acutely by the Yacht Club House, close to the Swan Public House. Here the Bure is quite deep and although the whole scene is chaos in summer, from October onwards fishing is first class with quality roach and the odd big hybrid predominating plus some bream to 4 lb. plus. Naturally with such a larder of feed in this area many sizeable pike move in for the pickings. Fish of over 20 lb. are taken every season with countless other fish weighing high into double figures. Mostly the better fish succumb to large livebait trotted close to the bottom and to ledgered deadbaits. There is excellent sport to be found in the numerous boat dykes and yards, particularly during severe weather. But permission should always be obtained first.

Running parallel with the Horning village reach along the north bank is Horning Lower Street which leaves the B1354 from Wroxham and leads to the Horning Ferry public house. Here there is limited bank fishing as far as the first boat dyke downstream. Anglers' dinghies can be launched from the public slipway adjacent to the Swan PH (see 'Boathire and slipways within tidal Broadland'). Exactly opposite Horning Ferry on the Woodbastwick (southern) bank from the Broads Authority mooring downstream to Cockshoot Broad dyke there is half a mile of excellent fishing also controlled by the N.D.A.A. This extends both upstream and downstream of the access road which leads direct from Woodbastwick village. Travelling still further downstream, the Bure bends slowly for two miles through lonely, thickly wooded marshland, until it reaches Ant Mouth. There is little or no access along this stretch because of the soggy nature of the banks. However, one may tie up a boat to a firm piece of bank to fish. Boat fishing is often better during the winter for one is able to float fish and hold out in the fast current.

Halfway between Horning and Ant Mouth, situated on the southern bank, lies Ranworth Dyke, which leaves the main flow to feed Ranworth Broad Inner where boats may be hired (see 'The Broads'). The dyke can fish quite well at times but is obviously prone to heavy boat traffic in summer except at early morning and late evening. The Environment Agency controls fishing on the entire south bank of the Bure, starting from and including Fleet Dyke, stretching downriver past Thurne Mouth and beyond Upton Dyke. This fishery includes both banks of Upton Dyke and offers very attractive fishing. Access points are from South Walsham boatyard, Upton and Acle where the A1064 road spans the Bure. Fishing is of a similar nature along this entire stretch with most anglers content to beat the fast flow by ledgering and using plenty of groundbait. As in the whole of the lower Bure bream and roach predominate.

Below Acle Bridge, where fast tides are common and the water is very deep, there are good shoals of quality roach plus bream to 6 lb. Around three-quarters of a mile downstream, off the northern bank, the Muck Fleet Dyke joins the Bure via a sluice. This tiny drain is weedy and unfishable during the summer but from autumn onwards provides good sport with roach and hybrids. Season permits only are available from N. Jarmey of the George Prior A.C. (Tel: 01493 780531).

Below the Muck Fleet Dyke's junction the Bure roars on past Stokesby and roach and bream can often be taken but like the other tidal rivers such as the Yare and Waveney, as they in turn near the sea, salt tides are the over-governing factor to whether sport is worthwhile or not, especially in winter. The very last point of access as far as viable summer fishing is concerned is the Stracey Arms public house, which can be seen dividing the River Bure from the Yarmouth A47 road in the middle of the Acle Straight, a fast six mile length of road bordered by shrub willows and marshland leading into Great Yarmouth. This crosses the Bure a little upstream from Breydon Water, before it makes its way to Gorleston Harbour and out into the North Sea.

THE RIVER BURN

This tiny, shallow trout stream rises near South Creake and completes just six miles before it flows beneath the A149 north Norfolk coast road and into the estuary at the top end of Overy Staithe, via Burnham Overy Mill. It hold stocks of brown trout, and the fishing is mostly private.

THE RIVER CHET

The Chet rises in the village of Poringland, near Norwich, and for the following eight miles that it takes to reach Loddon is of little interest as a fishery, although there are a few trout, dace, roach and pike present. It is for the most part narrow, shallow and quite overgrown. In Loddon, however, it quickly changes into a tidal channel with a wide marina and staithe. This has been enlarged in recent years and during the summer months the entire area is a hive of activity and most popular with the boating fraternity. However, during the winter months, particularly in spells of high water when floods spoil sport throughout the area, roach, bream and large hybrids pack into the marina and sport is excellent. From Loddon until the Chet joins the Yare via its southern bank at Hardley Cross, there are three miles of river which offer somewhat patchy fishing.

There is a terrific circulation of fish movement from the Yare into the Chet, especially on the flood tide and for the very best results one should become acquainted with the tides. Generally the best results are obtained in winter when the pleasure boats are tied up, when good bags of sizeable roach along with some bream can be expected. Trotting or dragging bottom is favoured near Loddon with the ledger paying dividends in the deeper, faster water lower down close to the Yare, where there is accessible bank fishing from the south bank via the B1140 road leading to Reedham Ferry.

THE RIVER DELPH

Although born in Earith where the Great Ouse divides its waters, the Norfolk boundaries of the Delph start just above Welney Bridge carrying the A1101 Outwell to Littleport road. The Delph here is between 40 and 60 yards wide with a depth of between 10 and 14 feet and the banks like all fenland drains are very open. It fishes well in summer for roach, rudd, bream and even the occasional carp into double figures, with specimen zander and pike for those wishing to specialise. Peter Redman caught a 20½ lb. carp from the Delph here in February 1989. It is prone to autumn flooding by the farmed washes and thus is a rather temperamental river to fish. It even becomes unfishable during the winter due to an excess of water, but when in trim and on form zander to 14 lb. and pike over 25 lb. can be taken. Fishing is controlled by Welney Angling Club, the secretary is Mr. Booth (Tel: 01354 610247) and day tickets cost £2.50 on the bank. This covers over four miles of the Delph from Welney Bridge to Welmore Lake Sluice where it empties into the Hundred Foot. Access is from the bridge at Welney. Anglers should note there is a wildfowl reserve between the Delph and the Hundred Foot Drain, of about one mile in length which is out of bounds to fishing.

THE RIVER GLAVEN
See 'Trout Fishing – Syndicate waters'.

THE GREAT OUSE
The southern Norfolk boundary crosses the Great Ouse at Ten Mile Bank where the Little Ouse runs in. The Ouse is wide and deep here with raised banks and contains tremendous bream shoals with fish from 1 to 4 lb. and large stocks of roach. There are, of course, hordes of eels, some perch, dace, good tench, which are not regularly caught, plus plenty of pike and zander. Ledgering tactics usually pay good dividends when seeking the bream which at times will accept any baits, though flake and worms often account for the better quality fish when presented over groundbait. This should be mixed stiffly for throwing, or loosely when used in swim feeders, when maggots can be laced in if using them on the hook. Roach often fall to the ledger too with some specimens up to the 1¾ lb. mark and there are some very much larger. Winter fishing generally offers

the best prospects. However, float anglers generally account for the largest bags of roach, with wheat, punched bread, maggots, casters and hemp all proving effective at times. When the water is on the clear side a deadly method of presentation is to loose-feed with hempseed and to fish a single caster, a grain of hemp or an elderberry on the hook. Trotting proves effective but when the water is 'dead' lay-on for the quality fish though bites may prove spasmodic.

Fishing along the Ouse here is controlled by the London Anglers' Association (L.A.A.) on both banks from Littleport High Bridge, downstream to Low Farm on the west bank, and Modney Drove on the east bank – some 14 miles of bank where day tickets are available from the bailiff who calls round. From these two points downstream to Denver Sluice, where the Ouse pours its water into the sea-going tidal channel, there is six and a half miles of river on both banks controlled by the King's Lynn Angling Association. Day tickets cost £3.50 on the bank. Only King's Lynn members can night fish. Anyone may join the King's Lynn A.A. which has an open membership with club cards costing £28.00 (£14.00 senior citizens and £5.00 juniors) from all local tackle shops or the secretary, Mr. M. Grief, 67 Peckover Way, South Wootton, King's Lynn, PE30 3UE (Tel: 01553 671545). The club controls a wealth of local fishing in both rivers and lakes.

THE GREAT OUSE
CUT OFF CHANNEL
This tremendous length of water stretches due south from the sluices at Denver where it is separated from the Relief Channel and travels nearly 30 miles to Mildenhall. It seems, in fact,

almost a replica of the Relief Channel and holds an identical stock of fish, though it is nowhere near so wide and impersonal. The banks are rarely more than 50 yards apart with a depth varying between 8 and 10 feet.

There are good shoals of quality roach spread throughout the Cut Off with numerous specimens topping 1½ lb. and isolated shoals of bream between 3 and 6 lb. The Cut Off contains a strong head of zander in all size ranges from schoolies of 2 – 4 lb. up to huge double figure fish. And many specialists expect a 20 pounder to one day come from this prolific fishery. Pike fishing is also good with numerous fish in the 6 – 12 lb. range plus whoppers of over 20 lb.

During the 1980s and 1990s both the Cut Off and the Relief Channel suffered badly from run-off where the water was purged from the system at an alarming rate. This certainly upset the fish and consequently sport became very patchy.

Today, however, when on form, some marvellous catches of quality roach are taken from this man-made drain. Day tickets cost £3.50 on the bank or from local tackle shops who also sell club cards of the King's Lynn A.A., who control the Cut Off Channel. Although 30 miles in length actual fishing access is limited to an 11 mile section along both banks from the sluice at Denver to Wretton Fen road bridge.

THE GREAT OUSE RELIEF CHANNEL

This channel, which is up to 100 yards wide, does exactly what its name implies and relieves the Great Ouse of its excessive water which is stored in the Channel to run parallel with the Great Ouse for 11 miles before it reaches King's Lynn, where there are exit sluices. It really is a formidable single sheet of water covering in total nearly 400 acres of surface area. Depth varies between

The Great Ouse at Denver Sluice, a favourite location for roach, bream, pike and zander. This is the start of both the Cut off Channel and Relief Channel

10 and 15 feet through the middle with a constantly good depth one rod length out just over the drop off. The banks are naturally very steep, being 15 feet. above water level in some sections, to accommodate any sudden massive injection of floodwater. There are usually enough spots, however, particularly where beds of reeds line the margins, to provide a flat platform just above water level.

The history of this enigmatic water has been very well documented over the years since the introduction of zander in the early 1960s. Many, including of course the Anglian Water Authority, have blamed zander for the fluctuating levels of sport during the last four decades. But if this were true, and the zander had eaten everything in sight including those massive shoals of 5 and 6 lb. bream which used to be around – and this of course is ludicrous – we should have been catching very thin zander with ridiculous ease. Whereas the fact today as I write in 2002, is that both zander and pike are spread just as thinly throughout the 11 miles as the roach and bream.

Prior to the long and heavy flooding of the 1976-7 winter I regularly made the journey from Norwich to enjoy the sport provided by the pike and zander in the Channel. Downham to Stow was my favourite length and funnily enough it is probably still the best bet for contacting roach and bream in the Channel. But in the early to mid 1970s while walking to a favourite zander hot spot I regularly kicked myself for not taking along the other rods. Huge shoals of specimen bream could be seen topping through the middle section as dawn broke. The shoals were hundreds of yards long. There were roach everywhere too, with enormous shoals of quality fish. Naturally there were predators to match

and it was a very healthy balance suiting both the pleasure and specialist angler alike. Then quite suddenly in 1977 it was all gone and much of the stocks had in fact gone – straight through the sluice gates into the tidal Ouse and out into the Wash. Lug diggers were finding heaps of dead zander, roach and bream on Terrington Marshes and local trawlers were netting the corpses of coarse fish.

The Channel once held the record for zander with a monster of 17¼ lb. caught by Dave Litton from St. Germans in 1977 and though limited in numbers, a jumbo sized zander is still on the cards from this mysterious fishery, as are specimen roach, bream and pike on the right day. In their pursuit, however, one must endure endless numbers of blank days. It appears that prolonged run-offs during the winter (now unfortunately a regular policy with our river authorities) have done more harm particularly to fry, which cannot tolerate the force of continual heavy flow, than zander ever will. But then the Relief Channel was not designed for somewhere to fish but to get rid of floodwater off the land. So in truth we anglers have little say.

However, in the past there have been massive injections of quality bream and roach into the Channel from Grafham Reservoir with the result that some good yet isolated catches have been made. So what of the future? Well we shall simply have to wait and see. The jury is still out. Those who enjoy boat fishing for pike and zander may now take their craft on to the Relief Channel between Denver and Magdalen Bridge from 16 June to 31 October only. Access is via a slipway immediately above Denver Sluice adjacent to the Environment Agency's car park – and a new lock system within the Denver complex. The lock opens between April and October only for navigation. Boat anglers must be in possession of a King's Lynn A.A. club book or a day ticket. For additional information telephone the lock keeper at Denver Sluice complex, Mr. Mike Fairweather on 01366 382340. Fishing along the entirety of the Relief Channel is controlled by the King's Lynn A.A. who issue day tickets costing £3.50 (full membership is £28.00) on the bank or through local tackle dealers. Contact Howletts Cycles and Fishing (Tel: 01366 386067) in Downham Market, and Geoff Baker of The Tackle Box in King's Lynn (Tel: 01553 761293) who will advise visiting anglers.

THE HUNDRED FOOT (NEW BEDFORD) DRAIN

This tidal channel originates at Earith with surplus water from the Great Ouse and flows for over 25 miles through Welney, Denver and King's Lynn, gathering drainage water pumped off the land from numerous dykes and channels, finally dumping it all into the Wash.

From its Norfolk boundary just upriver from Welney where it runs parallel with the River Delph and the Old Bedford, fishing is entirely free and the width about 30 yards, although it widens considerably as it moves seawards through Denver. Depth fluctuates between 4 and 12 feet, depending on the state of the tide and the current is naturally very fast at times, necessitating heavy leads. It is always thickly coloured and although there are numbers of roach, bream, eels, pike, zander and numerous flounders, sport is anything but consistent. With such excellent fishing available close by on the River Delph and the Old Bedford, few anglers bother with the patchy rewards offered by this tidal drain. The odd good bag of bream is taken, however, and as far downstream as Denver, where it really rockets through and looks more like the estuary it really is than a fenland drain.

THE LITTLE OUSE

The source of the Little Ouse starts where the Waveney also begins its life at Redgrave Common, just six miles due west of Diss. It flows west throughout its lengthy 40 miles and is, in fact, the county boundary between Norfolk and Suffolk almost all the way. Passing through Garboldisham Common, just three miles downstream from Redgrave, it navigates the villages of Riddlesworth, Rushford and on to Euston where a stream called Black Bourne enters from the Suffolk bank. There is a little fishing in the Bourne itself up to as far as Ixworth (10 miles) where the A143 Bury St. Edmunds road spans its course. Angling in these narrow, shallow upper reaches to beyond Euston is nearly all private, with numbers of dace, roach and odd chub over 4 lb. This part of the river was ravaged by pollution early in 1989 but it has since been restocked.

From Barnham the river runs for three miles until it enters Thetford, where it joins forces with the River Thet. But the Ouse retains its title and leaves Thetford to hide for seven miles within the huge expanse of Thetford Warren, the largest pine forest in East Anglia. In Thetford itself along the haling (towpath) path where the river winds within the town boundaries, there is free fishing along the southern bank down as far as the Staunch. The river runs very clear and fast, with excessive weed during the summer, and it also generally fishes better from October onwards with long-trotted maggots or casters producing the best results. The Thetford and Breckland Club control two short stretches in Thetford. Anyone can join by contacting the Chairman, John Reeves (Tel: 01842 753895). From the by-pass bridge carrying the A11 for about one and a quarter miles on the northern bank downstream to the sewer works is free fishing. Dace of a large average size between 6 and 10 oz. are to be found in this town reach together with one or two nice roach and bream to 7 lb. plus. A popular spot is by the Staunch (sluice) where the water deepens considerably.

As the Little Ouse winds through beautiful Thetford Warren it reaches Santon Downham where, from the road bridge going downstream for about a mile and a half on the southern bank, past the camp site and almost to Brandon, there is a super length controlled by the Bury St. Edmunds A.A. Again, as they do throughout this lovely river, big dace predominate, with roach, chub and pike also present. Numbers of fish are not large but individual size is usually well above average. Seven hundred grayling were stocked here in 1986.

Going upstream from Santon Downham road bridge along the northern bank fishing is free up to the second staunch. A barbel is not unlikely in this part of the river having been stocked as a joint effort between the Environment Agency and the Bury club, two thousand being introduced in 2001. The very best sport starts from October onwards when the summer weed starts to ease and the normally gin clear water colours a little. Favourite baits are casters, maggots and redworms which, if long-trotted on light float tackle, will soon sort out the kind of dace for which this river is so justly famous.

The British record dace of 1 lb. 4½ oz. was caught in the Little Ouse by J. L. Gasson in 1960. The average size was once so high that the late Bill Clarke regularly took pound-plus dace. Nowadays, however, any dace between 8 and 10 oz. is considered a specimen. The roach are taken to 1½ lb. with odd 2 lb. plus fish, while the chub exceed 5 lb., though they are quite isolated in many parts of the Little Ouse, with one or two real monsters still uncaught. There are some quality dace, roach and big bream in the river at Brandon where the local club, the Brandon and District A.C., has a mile of the Little Ouse. The club has an open membership with extra fishing on two local lakes (see 'Stillwaters – Members only – Playingfield Lakes', p.139). Apply to Paul Macloughlin (Tel: 01842 812979) or to the Leisure Centre in Brandon (Tel: 01842 813748) who also issue club season permits. These cost £15 adults, £10 senior citizens and £5 juniors. The club stocked 300 barbel into the river in 1999.

From Brandon the river bends for six miles down to Lakenheath Holt (with little access along the way) and then flows beneath Wilton Bridge once it has crossed the Cut Off Channel. From Wilton Bridge downstream for a distance of four miles on the Norfolk bank to Redmyre, fishing is controlled by Bury St. Edmunds A.A. There are no day tickets but anyone may join the club. Yearly membership costs £38 for adults and £15 for juniors, available from the general manager, John Easdown (Tel: 01284 753602). The local tackle shop, Tackle Up, in Bury St. Edmunds (Tel: 01284 755022) will advise visiting anglers.

The Little Ouse changes somewhat in the Wilton Bridge area, where depth increases to around 6 feet, but the water although often slightly coloured can just as easily be gin clear. The current is much slower than in the upper reaches and predominant species are fine roach up to the 2 lb. mark with bream averaging about the same, although specimens in excess of 5 lb. are sometimes taken. There are also dace, of course, perch, chub and pike which can provide a nuisance in the warmer months including fish to 20 lb. plus. A monster of 32 lb. was taken in 2001. Favourite local tactics are to lay on with flake or maggots during the early mornings or late evenings in conjunction with just a little groundbait, if quality roach or bream are sought. This works well during the summer but for winter tactics light float fishing, casters and maggots are preferred.

Three miles downstream from Wilton Bridge, Stallode Wash (a tiny drain) enters from the south bank at Botany Bay. From here down to where this wonderful river loses its identity by entering the Great Ouse at Brandon Creek by the Ship Inn public house, a huge network of dykes criss crosses its path. The fishing in these last four miles is similar in that the pace is slow and species are roach, dace, bream, perch and pike. The King's Lynn A.A. control one and a half miles of single bank above the iron bridge in Little Ouse village and one mile upstream of Brandon Creek Bridge on the eastern bank. Day tickets cost £3.50 on the bank.

THE MIDDLE LEVEL DRAIN

This super fishery starts its life at the junction of Pophams Eau and the Sixteen Foot by the bridge at 'Three Holes' which carries the A1101 Outwell to Littleport road. It averages around 50 yards wide and between 10 and 16 feet deep throughout the middle with deep water close in over dense beds of reed. The water is usually nicely coloured with next to little flow, unless it is being run off, and it fishes consistently well throughout its 11 miles, particularly during the summer and autumn before emptying into the tidal Ouse at King's Lynn.

There is a good stock of roach of all sizes, including some over the pound, with

John caught this 5 lb.plus chub from the diminutive reaches of Norfolk's River Nar

shoals of bream up to 4 lb. Pike fishing is excellent from October onwards and among a horde of lesser fish there are some nice doubles plus a sprinkling of enormous fish approaching the 30 lb. mark. The Middle Level probably offers the best zander fishing in England. It contains shoals of schoolies in the 2-4 lb. range in addition to chunky specimens from 6 lb. upwards to 20 lb. The British record zander weighing 19 lb. 6 oz. was reputedly caught from the Middle Level in 1998 by David Lavender. David caught another monster of 18 lb. 9 oz. just six months later. If there is one thing wrong with this drain it is that there is an awful lot of it and the bigger fish cannot be everywhere. The best way of latching on to these bigger zander is to ledger deadbaits at night or when the drain is heavily coloured coinciding with a spell of mild winter weather. During September and early October is the best time when eels are less active. During daylight a paternostered livebait takes a lot of beating and sport can suddenly switch on whenever it starts to run off. All the fishing on the Middle Level is controlled by the King's Lynn A.A., with £3.50 day tickets on the bank.

THE RIVER NAR

The little River Nar rises just west of Litcham village and flows through the lake (private) at nearby Lexham Hall. It is a narrow shallow river in these upper reaches as it winds its way through the villages of Castle Acre and West Acre covering some 10 miles before it runs alongside the huge lake at Narford Hall (private). Most of the fishing in these upper reaches is privately owned and really excellent trout fishing. As the Nar progresses steadily downstream it unfortunately suffers badly from water abstraction, which is a sad state of affairs because this wonderful little river once produced numbers of roach in excess of 2 lb. and really huge dace. Nowadays quantity is very limited throughout much of the river although quality is still high, particularly with dace. In Narborough the Nar divides around Narborough Trout Fisheries (see 'Trout Fishing – Day ticket – Stillwaters') passing through a beautiful old mill and beneath the old King's Lynn to Norwich road. Below the bridge stretching for two miles downstream to the waterworks at Marham is an excellent stretch holding trout controlled by the Salmon and Trout Association (see 'Trout Fishing'). From Wormegay High Road bridge all the way downriver to King's Lynn access points are from the road bridges as the Nar winds down through Wormegay and on to Setchey and vary from bank to bank following the public footpaths. There are isolated groups of large bream up to 8 lb. in this part of the river with some really large pike plus lots of small roach and chub from below Wormegay Bridge down to the A47 King's Lynn ring road. During the spring good numbers of smallish sea trout make their way upriver. There are some very large pike over 20 lb. in this area. But the banks here are dangerously slippery. A monster bream of 13½ lb. was found in the throes of dying in this area several years ago and now rests mounted in a case in the King's Lynn Museum. One mile below the pool the Nar then spews its water into the tidal Ouse. All the

---

Top Right: Brian Ward from Southampton caught this splendid 12 lb. plus barbel from the River Wensum at Costessey

Bottom Right: An angler fishes for pike at Hellesdon Mill on the River Wensum

fishing in these tidal reaches is free.

THE OLD BEDFORD RIVER

Although originating from the Great Ouse at Earith in Cambridgeshire, the Norfolk boundary line of this narrow drain commences at Welney where the River Delph and the Hundred Foot (both drains) run side by side below its southern bank and like the Old Bedford eventually shed their water into the Wash. The Old Bedford varies between four and 8 feet deep and contains some nice roach and rudd plus tench, bream, perch, pike and the odd zander. It is an excellent summer fishery for quality roach and bream, while during the winter it may turn up a really big pike among numerous fish into double figures. The first mile upstream to Welney Hotel and the first three miles down from Welney Bridge to the pylons (on both banks) are controlled by the Welney A.C., the following three miles down to the sluice at Salters Lode being controlled by the Downham Market A.C. Day tickets for all this water are available on the bank. Access is from the A1101 crossing the bridges at Welney.

THE PULVER DRAIN

This narrow channel is just two miles long and empties into the Great Ouse Relief Channel opposite Wiggenhall St. Peter. Depth varies between 4 and 6 feet and during the summer weed can prove rather troublesome, but some bream and tench to 3 lb. are there for the

Top Left: This 5 ¼ lb. chub from The Upper Reaches of the River Yare succumbed to a surface lure. Great summertime sport on a baitcasting outfit

Bottom Left: John caught this superb brace of zander from The Great Ouse at Ely

catching. Sport from autumn onwards is perhaps best when water from the drain is regularly pumped into the Relief Channel; trotting then produces some quality roach and for the pike enthusiast there are some nice doubles plus the odd whopper. A stealthy approach is often rewarded on this drain.

Season permits for the Downham A.C. which controls the fishing, are available from Howletts Cycles and Fishing in Downham Market (Tel: 01366 386067). Access to the fishery is then from the road running parallel to the Relief Channel between Watlington and St. Germans.

THE RIVER STIFFKEY

This charming little river rises near Fulmondestone in mid-north Norfolk and takes 16 miles to reach the sea at Blakeney Harbour. Throughout its length it is not much more than a stream but does contain numbers of brown trout. Travelling downstream through East Barsham, Walsingham, Wighton and on to Stiffkey much of the fishing is available to the polite angler who will find local landowners generally obliging when asked permission. The trout average on the smallish side with any fish exceeding the pound a specimen.

THE RIVER TAS

This charming, intimate mini-river rises two miles east of New Buckenham, near Carlton Fen, gathering strength from countless brooks and streams as it meanders on its course through some 20 miles of Norfolk's quietest countryside until it joins forces with the Yare at Norwich. From its source and for the initial eight miles the Tas is but a stream until it reaches the mill at Tasburgh where rivulets from Hempnall and Wreningham join up with the mainstream, adding width and depth. These side streams are worth exploring for dace and the odd trout. So too in fact is the entire river above Tasburgh, but numbers of fish should not be expected. One must, of course, always obtain permission to fish from the respective landowners who, if approached politely, will generally oblige, and this rule applies to much of the fishing along this little river for there is little day ticket or club water. Where, however, the fishing is obviously private and reserved for trout only, the angler must show respect. From Tasburgh Mill the Tas gradually improves in depth and width until it reaches the mill at Newton Flotman. Between these two points most of the river is inaccessible, except for a length which runs beside Taswood Lakes in Flordon. Telephone 01508 470919 for information about these excellent carp waters (see 'Stillwaters'). The river here runs fairly shallow with odd deep holes containing some nice dace and a few roach. Part of the Grove Water Trout Fishery (see 'Trout fishing – Day ticket – Stillwaters') is a nicely restored three-quarters of a mile of the river here providing excellent fly rod stalking for brown trout. Contact the bailiff, Tony Smith on 01508 471786 (mobile 07767 811007).

At Newton Flotman Mill the Tas runs beneath the A140 Ipswich road and meanders down to Shotesham. There is no access around the mill but below on the eastern bank there is around 400 yards of 'streamy' water where 'thoughtful' anglers are allowed to fish along Smock Mill Common. Access is from the Saxlingham road opposite Duffields Mill and fishing is from behind the houses down to the wood, which is the boundary line.

At Shotesham Park the stream splits into two channels and links up again just upstream of the ford, where a deep pool forms holding some cracking roach, dace, trout and one or two pike. Fishing in the pool is free. From the ford downstream the water level is obviously low and this is due, so it seems, to the removal of the old water mill. But there are shoals of dace about and for the fly fisherman this type of water is indeed an irresistible challenge. The river deepens again as it flows down to Swainsthorpe with some glides and undercut banks at many of the bends which harbour quality roach in addition to numerous dace and several trout. Unfortunately there is no public access here.

Downstream from Swainsthorpe is the mill at Stoke Holy Cross which was converted into a restaurant (highly recommended) many years ago. The mill pool and within the mill grounds is strictly private but the owner, Mr. Rio, does issue the occasional day ticket to the serious fisherman. Telephone the Old Mill on 01508 493337. Upstream of the mill for a distance of about half a mile on the eastern bank fishing is allowed. In this slow stretch depth averages around 5 feet and there are some good sized shoals of quality roach topping the pound.

Going still further down this pretty little river the Norwich to London railway line can be seen high on the hills above the western bank and it does in fact run parallel with the Tas all the way into Norwich. There are some nice dace and roach along this stretch and from here on downstream chub start to become evident.

At Caister St. Edmunds, just a mile off the A140 Ipswich road, the Tas flows beneath an old bridge next to a farm. Here, once again, polite anglers who ask first are usually granted permission and this covers a good mile of the river above the bridge and a long way downstream into Old Lakenham. At a spot known as Six Arches where the railway line spans the adjacent River Yare, there is an interesting oblong-shaped piece of water belonging to the farm at Caistor, which is in fact an old 'dead' piece of the Yare. It holds a few tench and one or two large carp in addition to roach, etc.

The largest roach ever from the river was taken by local angler Bill Coleman in 1972. It weighed 2 lb. 10 oz. Actual shoals of roach are never huge, though, and one generally sees upwards of a dozen to 30 varying sized fish in a glide which they occupy all year through. It is possible to creep up on such a shoal with the aid of polarised sunglasses, and to cast a freelined bait such as a lump of breadflake or a lobworm, etc., in their direction and a little upstream of the largest fish. If they are unaware of your presence then they may well accept it. But if they do, the moment one gets hooked or is lost the rest become agitated and exceedingly difficult to tempt. This, of course, is due to the crystal-clear water of the Tas, where even during the winter, unless there has been an appreciable rainfall, most species behave cautiously and one must long-trot a long way to encourage bites.

It has been my experience that high water after several days of hard rain is the ideal time to fish this river, especially when the water is fining down and is coloured but not dirty. It is on such occasions that an actual bag of fish is possible and the largest of the dace start to show themselves. The best dace ever thought to come from the Tas was taken

way back in 1943 by C. Comer and weighed 1 lb. 3½ oz., but few specimens are caught these days. A good average would be around 6 oz. with odd fish exceeding 10 oz. I would, however, rate the Tas in sixth position behind the rivers Wensum, Bure, Thet, Little Ouse and Tud as a big dace water.

Below the road bridges at Old Lakenham which span the River Yare, the railway line and the River Tas, there is just a few hundred yards of the Tas left before it loses its identity and merges with the Yare. There are some sizeable roach, dace and chub in this area, which is well worth exploring during the summer months, when the water is gin clear, to see the lie of the land with winter trotting in mind.

THE RIVER THET

The Thet starts around Attleborough where many tiny brooks join together. However, it is not until one reaches Shropham Fen that something tangible from an angling outlook can be seen. Immediately below the road bridge in Shropham there is a short 300 yard stretch owned by the adjacent carrot factory, where permission is usually given. The river runs fast and quite shallow here and unfortunately has over the past few years suffered from several mild bouts of pollution. This has minimised the chances of latching on to the really large chub for which this part of the upper Thet was once renowned. However, there are still a few chub about, plus some perch, dace and numerous pike.

Travelling downstream, the river flows between the large pits on either side (see 'Stillwaters' for Snetterton and Shropham Pits) and runs through Snetterton, of racing fame. It then flows beneath the road bridge carrying the

A11 at Larling, where one must ask local farmers for permission. Again chub and dace are predominant, with odd roach to the pound. Because the river is so shallow and weedy and in summer runs gin clear, fishing is invariably more fruitful in winter. However, the overgrown banksides do offer cover for the specimen hunter seeking chub when they can be seen in the summer months hiding beneath weed rafts and under low-hanging branches.

Two miles below Larling road bridge the river flows beneath the B1111 in East Harling and then twists down to Bridgham, skirting Harling Conifer Forest along its southern bank. There are some nice dace, roach and chub along this reach and although access is limited there are local farmers sympathetic to the polite angler who likes the roaming style of fishing because shoals are not large (although individual specimens are). Fishing on the northern bank starting a mile above the Diss A1066 Thetford roundabout is controlled by the Thetford and Breckland A.C. Here there are a few nice chub to 4 lb. plus with roach, rudd, pike and specimen dace. Again winter long-trotting sorts out the better fish, particularly after a good flood when the river is fining down but still holds some colour. As the river enters Thetford it tumbles over a weir and flows beneath Nuns Bridges adjacent to the neighbouring Little Ouse with which it amalgamates some 600 yards further on. But the Thet loses its name in the process. Nearly all the fishing rights in these last few miles of the Thet are private though one is quite at liberty to ask permission from local landowners who can only say no.

THE RIVER THURNE

Although this tidal river is Norfolk's shortest, with an overall length of just five miles, it is nevertheless of paramount importance both as a connecting vein to several famous broads and a really first rate fishery in its own right. Moreover the Environment Agency controls such an enormous amount of the Thurne's bank space that there are indeed very few parts where the angler cannot find comfortable free fishing in a truly Broadland setting.

The Thurne starts as a river in the village of West Somerton with a network of feeding dykes and streams adding their water in the area of nearby Martham Broad (sometimes called Somerton Broad) (see 'The Broads'). The Thurne actually runs through the middle of this shallow water and then winds slowly downstream between thick reed beds towards Martham Ferry (also see 'The Broads'). This length is perhaps the nicest, quietest part of the Thurne and compared to other tidal rivers in Norfolk it is quite sluggish. The fishing is thus comparatively more relaxed, nearly all float fishing in a depth of around 4 to 5 feet of water, which at the Somerton end only is incredibly weedy and crystal clear. However, the tidal influences can still dictate how the river will fish and, at certain times, quite without apparent reason, it just seems to switch off. Summer boat traffic can also prove a menace in the Thurne's limited width and only early or late sessions are recommended during the winter months.

Half a mile below Martham Broad there is a double 'S' bend at Dungeons Corner (a good pike and bream spot) below which the river often becomes heavily coloured due to a drainage discharge. Anywhere along this part of the Thurne can throw up a massive pike, like the 37½ pounder taken by A. Cottrell in the summer of 1982 and the 42 lb. 2 oz. ex-record caught by Derrick Amies in 1986. These monsters in all probability do most of their feeding in Martham Broad but wander into the river whenever there are sufficient concentrations of roach and bream close by. One usually needs to wade through numerous jacks, however, before a big one turns up. There are some nice shoals of quality bream and roach all the way along the river down to Martham Ferry and during the summer night fishing is recommended for the bream. But for mixed catches mild spells during the winter can produce some really good bags on trotted maggots or casters. The Environment Agency controls most of the Thurne and the entire reach on both banks from Martham Broad to the ferry swing bridge is free fishing with access from Martham Ferry only.

Four hundred yards below Martham Swing Bridge Ferry, Candle Dyke, which is the link between Hickling, Heigham Sound and Horsey Mere, enters from the northern bank (see 'The Broads'). This wide junction often fishes well in the late autumn as the bream shoals leave Hickling and the Sounds on their down-river migration through Candle Dyke, into the Thurne. Fishing is entirely free in this section save that from the privately owned chalets and bungalows which front the Thurne's southern bank immediately down from the ferry. Boats may be hired with or without an engine, at Martham Ferry to fish the area from Thurne Boat Building (Tel: 01493 740303). Situated close to the ferry on the opposite side of the dyke are Martham Pits which are excellent alternative venues, particularly in the summer (see 'Stillwaters – Day ticket'). From Candle

Dyke's junction downstream the flow increases somewhat with the extra push of the water from Hickling and one finds a greater depth, though only 6 inches of water drops between tides. Preferred and well proved winter tactics for this length of the Thurne are to trot down casters or maggots, along or just off the bottom and to loose-feed with the same. It is in fact wonderful stick float fishing. Occasionally one needs to offer a static bait and ledgering is widely used along the Thurne here. Quiver-tipping is much favoured and can prove a deadly efficient method of hitting those delicate bream bites which occur in very cold temperatures. At such times a tiny red worm will often render more positive bites as opposed to bread or maggots.

One mile further downriver one reaches Potter Heigham where the A149 from Stalham to Great Yarmouth spans the now slightly wider Thurne. Access is from the bridge with free fishing on both banks both upstream and downstream except for a few areas where private businesses and chalets front the water's edge. As far as summer angling is concerned the entire area around Potter Heigham is at best very poor, although fish are about if one night fishes certain locations. In any event winter fishing, or at the earliest from October onwards, is a far better bet, with roach and bream predominating. Boats can be hired at Potter Heigham from Phoenix Fleet Boatyard (Tel: 01692 670460). Between the old and new bridges is a popular winter spot where the roach and hybrids pack in tight. A distance both above and below the bridges of 100 yards also offers excellent pike potential and the odd specimen between 20 and 30 lb. is not unlikely.

A mile and a half below Potter Heigham, with accessible free fishing on both banks along most of the way, Womack Water leads off from the mainstream on the northern bank (see 'The Broads'). Here one may fish on both banks of Womack Dyke and the river and also from a strip opposite on the Thurne's southern bank, access to this part being from Thurne village. Returning to the north bank and a little way downriver from the Environment Agency's holding around Womack Dyke, the Norwich and District A.A. controls a slice of the bank known as Cold Harbour with £2 day tickets available from Throwers Stores at Ludham (Tel: 01692 678248). In these last two miles, as the Thurne nears the River Bure, it widens and tidal currents are more pronounced with ledger taking over from the float. One also requires a substantial amount of groundbait to hold fish in the swim, with worms, paste, flake and maggots all proving effective, quiver-tip ledgering being the favoured method.

THE RIVER TIFFEY

This tiny river rises in Wymondham at the confluence of several streams. It flows down to Kimberley Park and into the 30 acre lake which is now badly silted, although years back, before water abstraction became a problem, it held a fine head of fish and was very deep. From the lake the Tiffey makes a four mile journey until it feeds the Yare at Barford. There are dace, roach, rudd, perch and pike to be found en route, along with an ever increasing population of chub and permission to fish is sometimes given by local farmers.

THE RIVER TUD

This enchanting river starts life a little south of East Dereham by obtaining water from three separate sources and rambles in an easterly direction through sleepy farmland for some 14 miles until it reaches the suburbs of Norwich. Unfortunately it never really gains in stature in all its length and as it passes through the villages of North Tuddenham, Hockering, Honingham, Easton, Costessey and finally to Hellesdon Mill where it merges with the Wensum below the pool, one may wade across at almost any point. However, its shallowness and lack of width make no difference to the stamp of fish it produces. For the Tud's water is crystal clear, fast flowing and has lush weed beds full of aquatic life, including lampreys, bullheads, freshwater shrimps and stoneloach. All are superb natural baits.

Species to be found in the Tud, some of which can be taken with the above baits, are dace, roach, chub, trout, perch and a few grayling. Dace and trout are the predominating species especially in the upper reaches. Tud dace are most prolific and renowned for their high average size, being beautifully coloured and proportioned. I spent countless hours in their pursuit during the 1970s and 80s accounting for many fish from 14 oz. to 1 lb. 1 oz. Most were taken on long-trotted maggots in winter when the water had some colour to it. However these larger dace can sometimes be tempted during the summer months by the fly fisherman, especially at the early part of the season before the weed becomes too thick. Slow sinking nymphs work well, especially the black beetle and mayfly variations. A tiny, dark, dry fly fished at dusk will also take its fair share. The largest dace recorded was caught by Andy Davidson in January 1972 and weighed 1 lb. 2½ oz. Andy had another of an ounce less on the very same day. Unfortunately the river has suffered rather badly during the past two decades from odd bursts of pollution caused by careless farmers and in places the stocks of dace and trout are still rebuilding. A specimen from the Tud nowadays is anything over 8 oz. Although much of the fishing is privately owned there are still accessible spots where the polite enquiring angler will find landowners sympathetic.

WELL CREEK

This narrow and steeply banked drain runs adjacent to the A1122 road for seven miles from Outwell to Salters Lode near Downham Market, where its water empties into the tidal Great Ouse. It is free fishing all the way wherever the banks are accessible (which is almost throughout) and because the water is always well coloured sport is excellent for roach, bream, zander, pike and some fine tench topping 4 lb. Occasionally there is even a small run of sea trout. Depth varies between 4 and 6 feet and the banks are heavily lined with reeds and sedges.

THE RIVER WENSUM

This, the loveliest of Norfolk's rivers, begins its life above the village of Raynham, where several small streams amalgamate and flow through the lake at Raynham Park. The Wensum is then joined by the tiny River Tat along Tatterford Common as it trundles downstream to Shereford and on to the market town of Fakenham. The Wensum is a very attractive little river flowing clean and fast through lush countryside holding dace of a very high average size. Dace over 8 oz. are common and specimens from 12 oz. upwards are taken each winter when the weed has gone and the river is nicely coloured. There is also a sprinkling of quality roach, pike and brown trout, plus the occasional big perch. Although much of these high

upper reaches are privately controlled by fly fishing syndicates, the Fakenham Angling Club controls around two miles of the southern bank, starting from the first bridge upstream of the mill (see map of river under 'Trout Fishing', p.154). To join the Fakenham Angling Club anglers must live within a 10 mile radius of the town. Apply to Dave's Tackle Shop, Millers Walk, Fakenham (Tel: 01328 862543) who also issue day tickets costing £5 for a two fish limit.

Immediately above the mill there is comfortable fishing free to all from the anglers' staging installed by the Environment Agency. Below the mill there are two miles of free fishing along Fakenham Common stretching down to the three brick arches, all good fly water during the summer and super long-trotting during the winter for dace especially, plus the odd good roach. Travelling downstream much of the fishing is in private hands as the river slowly increases in both depth and width.

Between Guist and Bintree the fishing is unfortunately now all inaccessible to anglers and again immediately below Bintree Mill fishing is private, except for a delightful fly only beat immediately downstream of Bintree Mill controlled by the Salmon and Trout Association (see 'Trout Fishing') who have an open membership. Contact Membership Secretary/Branch Organiser Mr. N. Hammond (Tel: 01362 691510). For day tickets contact Mr. Terry Lawton (Tel: 01603 872393). These cost £10 for a two fish limit. A major river habitat restoration project was started here in 2000 as a joint effort between the Environment Agency and the S.A.T.A. Bintree Mill Fishery. The result is a now rapidly improving trout fishery containing both stocked and a natural head of wild brown trout.

Winding through Bintree Hills the Wensum reaches North Elmham and flows beneath the B1145 towards Billingford Common. Much of the river in these high upper reaches is under private control with little access.

Starting 200 yards below the B1145 bridge spanning the River Wensum at North Elmham at the junction of the tiny Blackwater Stream there is a lovely streamy three-quarters of a mile of the Blackwater and half a mile of the Wensum both controlled by Worthing Fisheries. This winding, overgrown shallow fishery holds some good dace, roach, barbel, chub and odd trout and runs behind Worthing gravel pit, also controlled by Worthing Fisheries. The syndicate has an open membership and is run by Mr. Terry Houseago (Tel: 01362 869122).

Half a mile downstream from Worthing the Dereham and District Club control fishing at Swanton Morley Fisheries. This comprises over half a mile of the river's southern bank and five adjacent gravel workings with day permits available (see 'Stillwaters') at £5 from the bailiff who calls round. Season permits are also available costing £30 from Myhills Tackle Shop of Church Street in Dereham (Tel: 01362 692975). Here there are really good specimen chub, dace and roach in the Wensum with some trout, odd barbel and pike spread along the shallow runs, glides and in the deep holes on the bends. Excellent trotting in winter. Exceptionally weedy during the summer, but surface plugs sort out the chub which run to 5 lb. plus.

At Swanton Morley the Wensum divides and flows over two attractive sluice pools, one large and called locally 'The Falls' where the B1147 road passes over its tail-end and a smaller one situated

further upstream which runs alongside and beneath the same road. Really large dace are numerous, together with an occasional good roach or brown trout but only the small pool and the narrow stretch of side stream running beside the road are publicly accessible. Two hundred yards below these road bridges, the Wensum links up again and flows down to Elsing Mill. Much of the land between these two points runs through Castle Farm where fishing is available to Dereham A.C. members only. This one and a half mile stretch of the river runs slowly and it is quite deep in parts, holding limited numbers of specimen sized roach, bream, pike, perch, chub and dace. At Elsing Mill all immediate parts of the river and for a distance downstream of over a mile are strictly private. With access via the southern bank however, midway between Elsing and Lyng Mill, there is a three-quarter mile stretch holding roach, big bream and chub, perch and pike, available to members of the Kingfisher Fishing Club Lakes complex (see 'Stillwaters – Members only'). Telephone Cyril or Paul Rogers of 01603 873333 or 870400 for details. There is then a short quarter-mile narrow piece controlled by Lyng and District A.C. with access on the southern bank via Richmond Place in the village of Lyng. Day tickets are available from the secretary, Mrs. Julie Stevens (Tel: 01603 872530) and cost £2.50.

The last mile of the northern bank between Elsing and Lyng Mill is controlled on a syndicate basis (Sparham Hall Reach) by the Norfolk Anglers Conservation Association (N.A.C.A.). Contact Mr. Tim Ellis, 19 Mallard Close, Salhouse, Norwich. Members of N.A.C.A. can obtain day tickets from syndicate members to fish the above section and a superb one and a half mile length called 'Sayers Meadow Reach' starting at and including the two mill pools at Lyng Bridge going downstream towards Lenwade. Prolific fishing for dace, roach, chub and barbel which were introduced by N.A.C.A. following their habitat improvement programme. It was in this vicinity that my good friend Jimmy Sapey took on fly one of the largest brown trout to come from the Wensum. It weighed 7 lb. 15 oz. and fell to a large wet fly in July 1971. Anglers wishing to join N.A.C.A. should first contact Malcolm Hitchens, Woodside Home, 5 The Meadows, Aylsham, NR11 6HP (Tel: 01263 732752). Only then can they apply for the Association's syndicate waters on the Wensum. There is a waiting list, however. Graham Gamble caught a 3 lb. roach from the river at Lyng in 1997.

Continuing from the N.A.C.A. boundary on the northern bank there is a one mile stretch controlled by the Lenwade Country House Hotel available to guests only (Tel: 01603 872288), plus a one acre lake (see 'Stillwaters – Hotel accommodation'). As the Wensum flows further downstream through Lenwade there is access to the northern bank at Lenwade Common via Common Lane in Lenwade directly from the A1067 Fakenham to Norwich road. Day tickets cost £5 from the bailiff who calls round and in addition to three-quarters of a mile of the Wensum this includes excellent stillwater fishing in the three 'Common Lakes' (see 'Stillwaters – Day ticket'). Concessionary tickets available for senior citizens and juniors.

On the opposite (southern) bank of the river day tickets costing £3.50 on the bank are available from the Catch 22 Fishing Centre, a two lake carp complex. This is for three-quarters of a mile of the Wensum only. (Telephone manager David Wilby on 01603 872948.) Some nice chub and roach fishing spots here.

In Lenwade Mill pool (private) a brown trout weighing 9 lb. 12 oz. was taken in 1964 by the mill's owner and is, to date, the heaviest Wensum trout to be grassed although double-figure fish are known to exist. Unfortunately the river around Lenwade is now mostly trout syndicates or under private control. There is, however, a short (600 yard) fast streamy piece of the Wensum containing chub, bream, roach, carp and barbel immediately below Lenwade Road Bridge on the northern bank available on a £5 day ticket from the adjacent Bridge Public House (Tel: 01603 872248) which includes fishing on a five acre lake (see 'Stillwaters – Day ticket') for Bridge Fishery Lake. The Bridge Pub specialises in anglers' accommodation.

From Lenwade the Wensum winds its way for four miles to Ringland Road Bridge with just two points of access. The first is a one and a half mile syndicate stretch at the farm of Mr. and Mrs. Oram. For details about their beat, which holds numbers of chub, dace and pike plus a few trout and includes fun fishing in a one acre irregular shaped lake beside the river for roach, tench and carp, telephone 01603 867317. No day tickets. The second is a super one and a half mile long beat bordering the Wensum Valley Hotel, Golf and Country Club in Taverham. Only anglers staying in the hotel for a minimum of two nights can gain access to the river here and it is fabulous chub fishing. I have caught several chub in excess of 6 lb. from this stretch which also contains some nice brown trout (Tel: 01603 261012 for additional information).

Upstream of Ringland Road Bridge on the southern bank it is common land for the first two meadows, with access down a track in the village close to the Post Office. For a short 200 yard stretch on the northern bank, above the bridge, and on both banks for about 100 yards below the fishing is open to all. Here the Wensum runs clear and shallow between huge flowing weed beds over a gravel bottom, where roach, dace, trout, chub, huge gudgeon and the occasional grayling are caught on trotted baits or with fly tackle. Back in 1996 100 grayling were introduced by the Environment Agency into the river at Attlebridge where the A1067 Fakenham to Norwich road spans the Wensum. The Wensum at Ringland Bridge is an excellent training ground for fly fishermen because it always contains a fair head of brown trout. One of the best ever caught here rests in a glass case in the public bar of The Swan, adjacent to the bridge. It weighed exactly 6 lb. and was caught by Mr. Cyril Bullard in 1960 not on a fly but a minnow.

Half a mile below the bridge the Wensum starts to slow in pace and deepens as it flows through beautiful Ringland Hills towards Taverham, where most of the fishing is privately owned. However, there is a quarter mile length containing pike, roach and dace available on the northern bank controlled by RMC Angling, together with seven pits. Day tickets cost £4 and must be purchased in advance from Tom Boulton's Tackle Shop (Tel: 01603 426834) in Norwich (see Ringland Lakes under 'Stillwaters – Day ticket',p.118).

A short length (around 80 yards) of the southern bank is public fishing where it runs alongside Ringland Road and then everything is inaccessible down to Taverham, except for a superb stretch of around three-quarters of a mile immediately upstream of Taverham Mill on the southern bank which includes the Mill pools and downstream on the same bank to Taverham Road Bridge. This is all syndicate water and part of the

Carp like this 21½ pounder taken by John from the River Wensum on the outskirts of Norwich at Hellesdon, are regular catches even during the winter months

Taverham Mills Fishery (see 'Stillwaters – Day ticket') owned by Anglian Water. Only a limited amount of yearly tickets are issued for this fabulous piece of river, which contains big roach, numbers of chub to 6 lb. plus, pike, dace, barbel into double figures and even a few carp (Tel: Taverham Mills Fishery Lodge on 01603 861014 for details). Largest barbel caught here weighed 16 lb. 13 oz. to the rod of John Fulton in 1998.

Below Taverham Road Bridge the river winds for two miles down to Costessey Mill with three access points. The first stretch is a lovely twisting three-quarter mile piece full of quality 3 – 5 lb. chub, plus the odd good roach, dace and pike, controlled by the Norwich and District A.A. This lies behind Costessey Pits on the southern bank and forms part of the Wensum Fisheries complex, including three well stocked lakes (see 'Stillwaters – Members only'). For entrance to the club, which has much fishing in local pits, broads and rivers, contact local tackle dealers or the secretary, Mr. C. Wigg, 3 Coppice Avenue, Norwich (Tel: 01603 423625). Continuing on from the N.D.A.A. stretch on the same (southern) bank with access via West End in Old Costessey, is a half mile yearly syndicate beat controlled by Mrs. Mann (Tel: 01603 743877 for details).

The third and final access to fishing between Taverham and Costessey is a short (one meadow only) length of the northern bank immediately upstream of Costessey Mill. This is available only to N.D.A.A. members and anyone may join through local tackle dealers. Some nice roach and chub here.

At Costessey Mill there are three separate sluice pools, all holding fish including dace, roach, perch, chub, barbel, pike, eels and the odd bream, carp and brown trout. Some of the fishing (around the big pool only) is free from the roadside and during the winter months when the river is high and coloured, good numbers of chub between 3 and 4 lb. pack into the big deep pool along with odd big roach and barbel. From here on downstream for the next mile or so is where some of the Wensum's largest barbel live. The old River Authority, now the Environment Agency, first stocked the river below Costessey Mill in 1971 with over 150 barbel although a couple of dozen were introduced several years before. These fish are now well established, in this particular reach, due to the fast water over gravel which suits them well and they seem to reproduce no more than is sufficient to keep up their numbers. Hence the reason for their maintaining such a high average size, between 6 and 8 lb. There is also a sprinkling of double figure fish to 15 lb. Chris Turnbull caught a barbel of 14 lb. 12 oz. here in 2001. Most of these are 'well known' individual fish which are recognisable to those who fish the Wensum regularly. I have records and many photos of one particular fish being caught nearly 20 times and on each occasion it blessed its captor with a 'double figure barbel'. So the entire river is far from being one big barbel swim, as much of the angling press would suggest.

With the stockings of barbel into several locations along the Wensum in recent years it is plausible they will spread throughout the river's upper reaches. Or perhaps their distribution will be restricted (and this is my guess) to fast water over gravel swims only. Either way, they offer superlative sport for the specialist, together with chub of a high average size. Throughout these last four miles of the Wensum until it reaches Norwich, there is a splendid head of chub in the 3 – 5½ lb. range with specimens topping 6 lb. plus a limited number of mirror carp running to nearly 30 lb. which escaped during floods a few years ago from the then N.R.A. fish farm at Hellesdon Mill and several gravel pit carp fisheries along the Wensum Valley. Roach are nowhere near so thick on the ground as they once used to be due to cormorant predation, but whoppers over the 2 lb. mark are still there for the taking in the deeper, slower swims along with occasional bream in the 4 – 9 lb. range. A big tench is also not unlikely.

Immediately below the 'point' at Costessey where the main river meets the mill stream the Norfolk Anglers Conservation Association (N.A.C.A.) control half a mile of the southern bank down to Drayton Railway Bridge. This is called 'Ketteringhams Syndicate' fishery and extends along the opposite (northern) bank from the Low Road, downstream to Drayton Green Lanes, a distance of about three-quarters of a mile. One thousand young barbel were introduced here in 2001 at the upstream end of the fishery which will undergo much habitat restoration work on behalf of N.A.C.A. by the Environment Agency. For syndicate details (open to N.A.C.A. members only) contact Mr. Chris Turnbull (Tel: 01603 630187).

The next accessible fishing is a lovely half mile winding stretch and completely free fishing on the northern bank known as Drayton Green Lanes, with access through a steep spinney from the Low Road linking Drayton to Hellesdon. The Wensum is a most secluded spot here, where great willows overhang the water as it narrows into a double 'S' bend before flowing down to Hellesdon. In this part of the river almost anything can happen, as it did for me during an unbelievable evening session in October 1984. I had just four bites on breadflake presented after dark while laying on with a luminous float in a five foot deep swim. The first produced a mirror carp of 10½ lb., the second a barbel of 12¾ lb. the third a roach of 2 lb. 7 oz. followed by a chub of 4 lb. 6 oz, and all in an hour's fishing. But that's what the Wensum is capable of producing when it feels like it and for optimum results it is worth trying to catch the river just when it's starting to fine down after a flood. There is no better time for latching on to a whopping great roach, chub or barbel.

At Hellesdon Mill one finds most species including roach, dace, big perch, pike, carp, some barbel, very good trout, chub and eels. A brown trout of 6¼ lb. was taken from the pool in 1971 by local angler, D. Hewitt, on a minnow. To dive this famous pool is quite educational for although the surface current is fierce where it pours over the sluice, down below things are very much quieter. Huge shoals of gudgeon move hungrily over all the gravel bars with chub lingering within pouncing distance. The perch and trout hang below the sluice within the undercut gorged out by years of running water while hordes of eels hide among the accumulation of rubbish, including bottles, bedsteads, tree roots and bicycle frames. The angler bent on catching any large fish here might bear these facts in mind.

Above the mill on the south bank is the Environment Agency's fish farm, the first publicly owned fish farm in Great Britain. At the tail end of Hellesdon Pool the tiny River Tud enters and there is a nice swim at this confluence close to the Tud's south bank where the water deepens somewhat. But from here down to the road bridge the Wensum is quite shallow, with a gravely bottom with dace, roach and chub. From the road bridge downstream the stream deepens, especially on the bends, and offers good sport. An occasional tench or carp is not unlikely in this vicinity as the river, now all free fishing (coming within the boundaries of Norwich) flows down to the Gate House Public House where it passes under the Norwich ringroad. Some 400 yards below the bridge the river skirts the waterworks, holding numerous pike and some cracking roach, perch and tench, as it deepens on the many bends. There are also good numbers of bream to 8 lb. here, plus a head of carp to over 30 lb.

As the Wensum enters the city of Norwich it passes beneath Mile Cross road bridge and then becomes quite wide, mostly shallow and extremely weedy in summer before it flows under Dolphin Bridge. However, below the bridge is a deep length where good roach and sizeable pike are taken. There are also very elusive bream in excess of 9 lb. and still more carp to 20 lb. plus. A quarter of a mile below Dolphin Bridge the Wensum runs alongside the large inner ringroad roundabout and flows down to the City Mills, being the last of the upper reaches. This last mile, after extensive dredging in 1983, produces excellent bags of roach up to 1½ lb. along with sizeable chub and carp.

At New Mills Yard the Wensum is actually tidal with quite a drop in level between tides but the pool is generally quite clear and exceptionally weedy in summer. There is only minimal bank fishing here as town houses and factories sit along the waterfront for the following mile. But anyone may boat fish as they are able to do on any tidal channel in Norfolk and Suffolk. In fact boat fishing is the best way of getting results from these tidal reaches. There are none for hire but anglers may launch their own dinghies from the public slipway at Friars Quay halfway between St. George's Street Bridge and Fye Bridge; or from further downriver (and motor up) via the slipway of the Red Lion Public House at Bishopgate Bridge (Tel: 01603 620154). New Mills tidal pool is deep and

The picturesque River Wensum at Pulls Ferry in Norwich

37

holds a fair head of quality roach and many pike into double figures, especially in winter. There are also some perch, barbel, plenty of medium sized dace and often in residence is a huge shoal of bream running from 4 lb. to 7 lb. plus. These move upriver from the lower reaches, attracted by the well oxygenated water of the sluice. Stuart Moir caught a massive mirror carp from the pool in 1986, weighing 31 lb. exactly.

Also present in the Wensum along this stretch are some huge brown trout. They have been taken up to 6 lb. but could possibly reach the double figure mark. In any event if the brown trout do not, there are many sea trout which migrate up the Wensum each year and these most certainly do. I have seen several fish up to at least 14 lb. in this area as early as Easter and as late as September. However, catching them is far from easy for although one may occasionally snap at a small plug or livebait they are generally shy and difficult to tempt. The last creature which inhabits this length of river I would not usually associate with tidal waters. It is the crayfish. So at any rate at least the Wensum must be fairly clean in Norwich.

As the Wensum passes through the city of Norwich it widens and flows down to Fye Bridge where limited free fishing for some cracking roach and bream exists at the three sets of steps. Lovely stick float fishing here. Further on it bends around an ancient Norman water tower called Cow Tower, where there is a deep bend and roach fishing is really good. Maggots or casters for quantity and breadflake for quality is a good point to remember. The Wensum flows quite straight now as it runs adjacent to Riverside Road and approaches the Yacht Station just up from Foundry Bridge which is a mere stone's throw from Norwich Railway Station.

Fishing is free from all the accessible bank space here and although boats may prove troublesome in summer, the whole length fills up choc-a-bloc with roach in the winter. Below Foundry Bridge the Wensum increases its width and the angler will always find a good average depth under his rod tip. The water has a nice tinge of colour too and often a strong pull to it, particularly on the ebb tide. This stretch is popular with angling matches and is a known caster water with quality roach and bream showing up from October onwards along with numerous pike, including specimens over 20 lb. A hundred yards below Carrow Bridge bank access ceases and there is just another half mile of the Wensum before it joins forces with the Yare. This last section can fish particularly well during the winter for pike, roach and bream. But angling is by boat only.

THE RIVER WISSEY

From its source near Shipdham the little River Wissey travels but a few miles before it becomes a trout stream. It navigates between the villages of Bradenham, North and South Pickenham, Hilborough, Ickleburgh, Mundford and on to Northwold, growing in stature and nearly all the way a private trout reserve. There are large chub and other coarse fish present however. In fact the Wissey has the distinction of producing the largest chub ever taken from a Norfolk water on rod and line, a fish of 8¼ lb. taken near Stoke Ferry in 1960 by Mr. M.J. Roberts. Moreover most of the chub introduced into other rivers such as the Waveney etc., were obtained by the river authority from the Wissey.

From Hilborough to Northwold the river passes through deeply wooded countryside and flows through lovely Didington Park where it runs alongside the lake (private). In this area the river holds really monstrous brown trout, possibly into double figures, with 2 – 4 lb. fish in good numbers. There are also numbers of rainbow trout introduced by the respective owners.

The Wissey is an ever-changing little river, with narrow shallow, sandy parts, deep holes especially at the bends, where most of the fish lurk, and is full of weed in summer. It can change from a narrow stream to a fairly wide channel in the course of a few yards and all the time the water is crystal clear. The fishing is consequently most difficult.

From Northwold the river winds down to Foulden, through Borough Fen and on to Whitington. This four mile stretch contains a prolific head of quality chub, some bream and isolated shoals of roach, including specimens approaching 2 lb. Unfortunately it is all in private hands, although the polite enquiring angler will find sympathetic farmers provided permission is asked first. From

Whitington to Stoke Ferry where the river passes beneath the A134 the course has widened a little and the depth is greater. From the A134 bridge Whitington A.C. control around half a mile upstream to Sampson's Hole. The Wissey offers really good mixed fishing here, with dace, roach, perch, tench, good bream and some thumping great chub. There are also some extra large pike and even the occasional sea trout. Travelling further downstream the Wissey actually passes beneath the Cut Off Channel via some sluices.

In the mainstream of the Lower Wissey boats may prove troublesome during the summer and early fishing sessions invariably produce better results, especially for bream. Some good bags are taken, together with the odd large roach to bread baits hard on the bottom. Bread takes some beating in the warmer months with maggots, caster or worms as alternatives. But from October when the weed disappears, and the water has a little more push to it, right through until

The River Wissey flows through scenic Wissey Pools, adjacent to the Sugar Beet Factory

the season ends maggots or casters reign supreme for good bags of quality roach. Fish over the 2 lb. mark are not uncommon in this section as the river meanders down through the famous Wissey Pools to Wissington road bridge. Above the road bridge starting from the stile and including one pool on the southern bank is controlled by the L.A.A. Day permits from the bailiff who calls, with access from the car park at Five Mile Home Farm on the southern bank. Immediately upstream of the bridge the choicest northern bank (including the island) is controlled by the British Sugar Corporation's social club with season tickets from the Secretary. This entire area of the Wissey Pools contains specimen roach, bream into double figures, big tench and numerous pike into double figures with a good sprinkling over 20 lb. There is also a good head of quality zander between 6 lb. and 10 lb. and the odd large brown trout. In fact Norfolk's largest wild brownie was caught here in 1949 by Mr. G. Mays and tipped the scales at 12 lb. 14 oz. Others from around the 8 lb. mark and running into double figures have also been taken. Immediately downstream from the road bridge to the disused railway bridge is strictly private. The Wissey then winds down through Hilgay Fen and beneath the A10. The King's Lynn A.C. controls these last two miles of the Wissey (on both banks) before it joins the Great Ouse just one and a half miles upstream from Denver Sluice. Day permits cost £3.50 and are available from local tackle dealers or on the bank. This stretch of the river offers marvellous sport with roach, including occasional specimens over 2 lb., plus bream and pike very much in evidence at the Ouse confluence. Winter fishing is particularly productive.

THE RIVER YARE

One of the most under-rated and under-fished of all Norfolk's rivers is the Yare, which rises close to the village of Shipdham, just one mile from the source of another famous river, the Wissey. But unlike the Wissey which flows west, the Yare which in its infant stage is but a brook, winds east for 20 miles towards Norwich. For several miles it is fed by other brooks and so by the time it passes beneath the B1135 road to East Dereham, it has materialised into a delightful little river holding some nice dace among other coarse fish.

The Yare is fed below the road bridge by a stream from nearby Thuxton and flows downstream on a narrow course through spinneys and hedgerows to the villages of Barnham Broom, Barford and on to Marlingford. Nearly all of the Yare in this region is privately controlled by local landowners. However, there are a few spots where permission to fish is often granted to polite anglers who ask first.

From Marlingford Mill the river snakes downstream to Bawburgh and much of the fishing is controlled by Marlingford Estates with yearly permits available. Telephone enquiries to Marlingford Estates on 01603 810269. This is a lovely reach, wooded in parts, with deep holes on the many bends and long straights which provide excellent mixed catches on the float during the winter months. There are some cracking dace, roach and chub to 5 lb., plus the occasional large perch and numerous pike. There is about one and a half miles of bank accessible each side of the river except where cottages front the water. It stretches from Marlingford Mill pool to the small pumping station half a

Right: To catch chub from the overgrown reaches of Suffolk's River Stour, a stealthy approach is essential

mile upstream of Bawburgh.

In Bawburgh Mill pool (private) depth exceeds 16 feet but quickly tails off to where one is able to wade across through just 12 inches of water. A sad thought and proof to the extent to which silting due to water abstraction is slowly strangling Norfolk rivers, is that at this very point large barges once passed, taking coal to the mill and returning with flour. Colossal eels live within the decaying woodwork of the loading pylons alongside the mill with odd perch and many ruffe present. There are also dace of an exceptionally high average size along with barbel, roach, chub and smallish pike. Fishing is free from beside the road for a short distance above Bawburgh road bridge and for the following three-quarters of a mile downstream where access can be gained. Good bags of quality roach are caught here during the winter when there is colour in the river. Duncan Holmes caught a 10 lb. 5 oz. barbel from the river here in 1999.

Travelling downstream towards Norwich the Yare is spanned by the A47 southern bypass before bending between large gravel pits on either side and contains a good head of specimen chub, roach and dace, plus some barbel and perch. The only access here is along a three-quarter mile beat running between these large gravel pits controlled by the Norfolk Anglers Conservation Association (N.A.C.A.). Apply to the secretary, Mr. Malcolm Hitchings, Woodside Home, 5 The Meadows, Aylsham, NR11 6HP (Tel:

Top Left: John's wife Jo nets a nice double figure pike she hooked on ledgered deadbait from the tidal Waveney below Beccles

Bottom Left: Float fishing for roach, hybrids and bream from an anchored dinghy in the River Bure at Horning

01263 732752) or enquire at local tackle shops who sell N.A.C.A. membership and permits for the Bawburgh Lakes and river fishery (see 'Stillwaters – Members only'). Norwich City Council own the last one and a half miles along the northern bank with free fishing to within 500 yards of Earlham Bridge. Access to this stretch is through the housing estate in West Earlham. The narrow dyke coming in at the first bend when walking upstream affords good sport with roach when the Yare is hopelessly in flood. Below Earlham Road bridge, where the B1108 Watton Road spans the Yare, fishing is free from the northern bank through Earlham Park for a distance of around two miles, all the way to Cringleford, the boundary being where the A11 crosses the river. High up on the hill sits the University of East Anglia, which has its own University Broad (see 'Stillwaters – Members only) offering excellent sport adjacent to the river. One may walk either downstream or upstream from the road bridges, or gain access from Bluebell Road which runs parallel to the river along the northern bank. This entire stretch is excellent fishing for dace, roach, some specimen chub, plus the odd bream, carp and pike. Depth varies between 2 and 5 feet along the straights, going down to 8 feet on at least a couple of the numerous acute bends. During the summer weed growth can be rather heavy and it's usually a case of presenting baits like breadflake in the holes, preferably at dawn or dusk, to tempt the better quality roach which run to over 2 lb. After the first frosts, however, and especially when the Yare holds some colour, mixed catches, with roach to over the pound predominating, are taken trotting with casters or maggots.

At Cringleford the river divides into two large pools. The mill pool is private but the picturesque sluice pool may be approached from the north bank only. It contains some large roach, some dace, perch, chub and perhaps a large trout or two. Only part of the one and a half miles of river from Cringleford Bridge to the next mill downstream, which is Keswick, can be classed as free fishing, with access via Church Lane which starts at the traffic lights on the old A11 road. One hundred yards below the old bridge the Yare divides around a long narrow island where access is somewhat limited but where it converges again there are some super swims. This section is rather silted up in part but because of this irregularity there are deep, undercut bank swims holding many perch, roach, good sized pike and just the occasional really large chub. These swims are in the vicinity of the railway line which bisects the river some 400 yards upstream of Keswick Mill. Below Keswick Mill pool (private) the Yare winds its way down to Harford Bridge, offering one or two nice swims on the way containing roach to 1½ lb., a small shoal of bream to 7 lb., plus the odd good chub and carp. Anglers may walk upstream on the southern bank from Harford Bridge which carries the main A140 Ipswich Road. Below the bridge the Yare skirts Harford dump. It is now on its last two miles of non-tidal river before it is joined by the River Tas and they both flow into the pool at Trowse Mill. Access is limited above the mill, especially as it winds through Old Lakenham, but the angler who politely asks permission will inevitably find good fishing and within the Yare here there are some cracking roach. Shoals may be isolated but find one and you could latch on to fish well in excess of 2 lb. A really big chub over 5 – 6 lb. is not unlikely here, along with occasional perch, bream and numerous pike.

The Yare can be seen from the new A146 road which links to the A47 southern bypass, some three-quarters of a mile upstream of Trowse Mill, and in these final stages of the Upper Yare some big roach, chub and carp to over 20 lb. are to be found. Where the River Tas merges with the Yare beneath the A47 bypass bridge a 300 yard long stretch is available on a syndicate basis (Tel: Mr. Blackman 01603 712510). Trowse Mill pool, although gin clear in summer and rather weedy, is nevertheless tidal and from here on the Yare quickly changes its character from a quiet stream to a full bodied Broadland river. One may, of course, row upstream into the pool to fish but the banks are privately owned. There are some quality roach in the pool together with numerous dace, a prolific stock of chub, plus the odd huge brown trout, several barbel and the odd carp. I enjoyed the company of the pool's inhabitants on many occasions during the 1970s and 80s while scuba diving and can only assume that the barbel arrived in the pool by coming down the Wensum from Costessey where they were stocked by the old River Authority in 1971. Other visitors to the pool include migratory sea trout at varying times throughout the summer and an ever present horde of flounders which, at times, pinch a single maggot all too readily. A really big pike is not unlikely towards the latter part of the season but throughout most of the year there are few pike of any size from the pool downstream to the road bridge. A massive carp of 31 lb. 6 oz. was taken by Mark Pye from the river here in 1992.

Another piece of the Yare passes beneath the old A146 road 200 yards away and joins in with the flow from Trowse Mill pool close by Trowse church, 300 yards downstream from the road bridge. This weedy channel is actually the old bed of the River Tas, which no longer feeds it, and was once a flowing sluice stream before water abstraction stopped its flow from above Trowse Mill. Now its level rises and falls with the tidal influences of the Yare which three-quarters of a mile below Trowse merges with the River Wensum. But the Yare, which at this stage is a narrow channel compared to the Wensum, quite unfairly becomes the major river. This last intimate length of the Yare can afford good roach fishing with the chance of an odd specimen and produces numbers of pike during winter, though most are small. There are also dace, perch, eels and odd shoals of bream, plus a head of carp in the 15–30 lb. range.

Half a mile downriver from the junction of the Wensum and Yare, the New Cut separates from the old course which flows along by Thorpe Green, creating a huge island (private). On the north bank it can be seen running parallel with the old Yarmouth Road and offers excellent fishing in winter when the pleasure cruisers are tied up. Roach are the main species but bream appear frequently in many swims together with some jumbo-sized hybrids. There is around a half a mile of bank space at Thorpe Green with a varying depth of 5 to 7 feet. Anglers may launch their own dinghies from a short public slipway. Boat fishing is by far the best way of exploring around the island at Thorpe, as much of the bank is inaccessible, and in addition to roach, bream, pike and tench, numbers of mirror carp running high into double figures are taken in this part of the Yare. From the end of the island downstream on the north bank to as far as one can walk is free fishing, with access via Thunder Lane traffic lights and footbridge from Thorpe Road. Boats to fish this area can be hired at £10 rowing, £20 with engine

(electric or petrol) per day from Griffin Marine (who also sell tackle and bait) (Tel: 01603 433253) or their slipway can be used for £5 by those with their own craft. Starting back again on the southern bank, there is a lovely length accessible from Whitlingham Lane, close to Trowse road bridge. Public access commences at the wide bend where a dyke joins the main river, a favourite pike location with local anglers. There are one or two fish over 20 lb. here, along with a terrific head of pike between 6 and 12 lb. and no wonder, for shoals of quality bream live close by and the concentrations of roach are enormous. Paul Pointer caught a 30 lb. 2 oz. pike here in 1998. Winter trotting can produce some bumper nets of roach and hybrids all along Whitlingham Lane (a popular summer picnic spot) where the river runs parallel to the road. Public access then stops at the sewerage works. There is a wonderful panoramic view of the River Yare valley from the A47 southern bypass where it spans the river at Whitlingham just above Postwick Sewerage Works. The famous Postwick outfall swim can in fact be seen from this long bridge if looking to the right when travelling towards Great Yarmouth. Big perch and pike are found here.

Starting half a mile downriver from the outfall Norwich Oddfellows A.C. control a half mile section of the northern bank which is excellent fishing for roach, perch, bream and pike. Anyone may join the club. Contact Kevin Spalding on 01603 745044. The stretch is in fact shared with the Shrublands A.C.

The next easily accessible free fishing is at Bramerton on the south bank, known locally as Woods End, and lovingly named after the public house which stands next to the water. Anglers wishing to park only should ask permission from the landlord (Tel: 01508 538899) who is usually sympathetic to anglers. Anglers who patronise the pub may launch their own craft from the property's concrete slipway. It is functional only at high stages of the tide however. No fishing directly in front of the pub without prior permission or at peak holiday periods. Fishing here is quite comfortable and bags of roach and dace are not difficult to come by, with the flood tide usually providing better sport. Recent years have shown that fishing casters close to the bottom takes some beating, though maggots still produce fish when trotting with the stream. But the ledger invariably contacts a better class of fish, including bream which run from 2 to 5 lb. Fishing after dark in a baited swim is the best way of taking a real bag of bream along this reach. Fishing is free from the public footpath which stretches from the Woods End Public House downriver for a short distance. A little further downstream in the vicinity of Surlingham Church the highest match weight ever for the River Yare was made by Denis Pratt in 1993 during the Yare Championships, with a staggering 150 lb. of bream that included specimens to 8 lb. Further downstream on the northern (opposite) bank lies the village of Brundall. Access from here to Surlingham Broad (excellent pike fishing) is just across the river where the broad is fed from the Yare via the south bank (see 'The Broads').

Fishing in Brundall can be good around the boat dyke areas and in Brundall Dyke itself. Early morning sessions during the summer can produce quality roach and some average sized bream but from October onwards pike fishing can be particularly rewarding. A really big pike is not out of the question (30 lb. fish have been caught in recent years) especially if roach are numerous at a particular spot,

which they often are, but one often needs to move around a bit to locate them. Tackle and bait may be had from Brundall Angling and Yare Boatique (Tel: 01603 715289) on the riverside who also have anglers' dinghies available. Rowing £15, with engine £30 for two and three man boats. Angling dinghies are also available at £10 per day from Fencraft at Riverside Estate, Brundall (Tel: 01603 715011). To use Fencraft's slipway costs £5. Travelling still further downstream the Yare cuts through Strumpshaw Marshes where there is little access to the waterside. However, on the next slow bend a dyke leading to Rockland Broad (the shorter of two dykes that feed Rockland) marks the start of access on the southern bank controlled by Great Yarmouth and Norfolk County A.A. Season permits cost £15 from the Beauchamp Arms Public House and local tackle dealers. Day tickets cost £3. Biggest bream ever to be caught here was taken by Doug Botley in 1998 and weighed 9 lb. 2 oz. There are nearly three miles of fabulous fishing on this bank down to just beyond Langley Green, with access via the Beauchamp Arms roadway which is off the Rockland St. Mary road from Norwich.

As throughout much of the tidal Yare, roach are of a high average size in these reaches. One seldom takes fish under 6 oz. and yet, rather strangely, few are caught over the 1½ lb. mark; but monster roach do exist and just a sprinkling of 2 lb. fish are recorded each year. Bream are localised and found in numbers mostly where the river bends slowly where, if the angler is lucky, there might be just a few yards of slow water close to the bank provided the tide is flowing the right way of course.

The Yare in these wide deep tidal reaches is indeed a formidable river and the person used to light float fishing venues such as canals and ponds will need to rethink his tackle arrangements. The combination of strong currents and deep water, from 12 to as much as 20 feet, necessitates plenty of lead on the line. Float fishing close to the bank is often possible but the bait should be kept well down. When the tide is at its strongest, even ledger weights of an ounce or more may bounce along the bottom, but this can be remedied somewhat by restricting casting distance and actually casting downstream rather than straight out. This will lessen the angle of drag on the line and keep the bait on the bottom. In any event a certain amount of juggling with end tackle is necessary as the flow increases from slack water to the top of the tide. Bite indicators are generally of little value when the tide is really pulling, except perhaps a fast tapered quiver-tip, which is ideal for tackling the Yare. Mostly though bites are positive and unmistakable if a fish is pulling from downstream. However, if a fish takes the bait upstream it merely dislodges the ledger weight and the rod eases back until the weight catches again. Many anglers ignore these bites thinking that the ledger weight is merely repositioning itself, so to be certain, hit anything questionable once the weight or swim feeder has reached a holding position.

As far as baits are concerned I prefer breadflake, maggots and worm, in that order, because I hate catching tiny eels, of which the Yare in places is choc-a-bloc, but meaty baits do prove effective especially for bream. In any event, and whatever bait one uses, some stiff groundbait will be needed to keep the fish in the swim. It should be used in quantity and thrown well upstream to allow for the time it takes to reach the bottom. I often prefer to use a block end feeder if using maggots, to make doubly certain that my bait ends up close to the groundbait, or bait with breadflake for the quality fish. Play a sizeable fish very carefully in this tidal water and try not to hurry it towards the net. Many a huge bream has been lost in this way, so if a slab-sized beauty won't play ball and come upstream against the flow, go downstream and net it when on the surface.

Opposite Cantley on the south bank side lie Langley Marshes with a neighbouring dyke that runs almost to the road and adjacent public house. Sport can be good in the dyke for roach, bream and occasionally a tench or goodish pike, especially where it enters the Yare. Slowly bending downstream one reaches Hardley Cross where the River Chet joins the Yare, but half a mile upstream from this confluence lies Hardley Dyke, which might be worth exploring. It lies on the south bank with access from Hardley Street. Further downriver one reaches Reedham Ferry, the only operative ferry across the river (there is a slipway controlled by Reedham Ferry Inn (Tel: 01493 700429) where for a charge of £3 anglers' may launch their own craft) and then the deep New Cut joining the Yare and Waveney which flow two miles apart at this point but gradually run together to Breydon Water. Here they enter this huge brackish broad which is four miles long and one mile wide and which enters Great Yarmouth with the River Bure flowing in from the north, to finally spew its waters into the North Sea at Gorleston.

Fishing on these last 10 miles of the tidal Yare from Cantley downstream is solely dependent from October onwards on salt tides and whether or not the sugar beet factory at Cantley is working. Many local anglers leave this area well alone because of this factory, as its waste pipe which flows in the Yare turns the water orange and ruins sport.

SUFFOLK RIVERS

THE RIVER ALDE

Although close on 40 miles long, this little river offers very limited potential. It starts with feeder streams in the Dennington area which amalgamate in Bruisyard. At this stage a tiny river, it then flows south-easterly through Rendham and close by Great Glemham. It holds some shoals of dace and even the odd trout in this area, being mostly under private control with no public access as it trundles down to the bridge at Stratford St. Andrew. From here onwards there are odd shoals of roach in addition to dace but fish density is still quite low. In fact the most productive length is the last one and a half miles of its course from Langham Bridge down to the tidal sluices just upstream from Snape road bridge carrying the B1069 road.

On the northern bank starting from the railway bridge above Langham Bridge and going down to the Holland Sluice, just up from Snape Bridge anglers are usually allowed access provided they ask first. Enquire at the farm adjacent to Langham Bridge. The flow is fairly slow (unless the sluice is in operation, when the water really rockets along) with a depth of around 2 to 3 feet plus the odd hole going to 6 feet. Ideal conditions for stick float fishing in fact and there are some good dace and roach present, winter fishing usually producing more consistent results. Below the bridge at Snape Maltings the Alde, now tidal, grows steadily into a wide estuary and meanders for over 20 miles through lonely marshes until it swaps its name to the Ore and flows out into the North Sea five miles south of Orfordness (see 'Sea Fishing'). Additional information plus freshwater and sea baits may be obtained from Brian Finbow at Saxmundham Angling Centre (Tel: 01728 603443).

THE RIVER BLACK BOURN

This interesting little river starts its life a little south of Ixworth with an amalgam of streams. It flows beneath the A143 in Ixworth and in a northerly direction through Bardwell and on to Honington. Depth varies between 4 and 6 feet and the flow is quite gentle allowing a prolific weed growth throughout. Naturally winter fishing is much favoured and there are some good quality roach to be had on the float along with dace and some nice chub to over 4 lb. Between Ixworth and Honington access is very limited but on the western bank from Sapiston, downstream through Little Fakenham to Euston Weir, a distance of about four miles is controlled by the Bury St. Edmunds A.A. Day tickets are not issued but the club has open membership and boasts a very strong junior membership. Yearly membership costs £38 for adults and £15 for juniors (contact manager, John Easdown, Tel: 01284 753602) and entitles Members to fish in six well stocked lakes, in addition to the Black Bourn (see 'Stillwaters – Members only). Below Euston Hall there is little access for the remaining mile of the Black Bourn before it ends its life by feeding the Little Ouse.

THE RIVER BLYTH

This little river is born from streams which rise to the west of Halesworth near Linstead Parva and Wissett. They flow easterly and pass beneath the A144 Halesworth to Bungay road under the railway bridge and on to Holton. From here on downstream there are numbers of roach, with some topping the pound, plus dace and the very occasional trout. There is a public footpath running with the northern bank starting a little way upstream from Mells road bridge, stretching most of the three miles down to Blythburgh bridge carrying the A12 road from Ipswich. There are some attractive bends below Mells bridge with the occasional deep hole and winter fishing has the edge as the river has a prolific summer weed growth.

At Blythburgh the river opens into a wide estuary which flows through Tinkers and Reydon Marshes and empties into the North Sea at Southwold. There is excellent mullet fishing throughout these tidal reaches with eels, flounders and bass in plenty. Good spinning here from the harbour entrance going inland to as far as Blythburgh church.

THE RIVER DEBEN

The River Deben is of two distinct parts. It has nearly 20 miles of non-tidal upper reaches before it runs to Woodbridge and enters the estuary, whereupon there is a further six miles of wide river until it pours its water into the North Sea a little north of Felixstowe. The course actually begins life in the village of Debenham as a tiny stream but is of little value as a fishery until it reaches the village of Cretingham where, unfortunately, accessible fishing is rather limited despite there being the odd group of nice roach present.

Throughout these upper reaches the river passes between picturesque villages and is very narrow, weedy and continually bending. The water is mostly shallow with a sluggish stream. Consequently laying-on with fine tackle and using such baits as breadflake, maggots or worms, is generally favoured. Species to be expected are predominantly roach and perch in the 4–6 oz. class with some dace, eels and numbers of small pike. There is, however, very little public access as the Deben flows by Kettleburgh, Easton, and onto Wickham Market, although in my experience the enquiring, polite angler is seldom refused a day's fishing. Immediately below the A12 bypass bridge for half a mile along the eastern bank is controlled by the Framlingham and District A.C. Here the flow is also sluggish and in addition to some good quality roach to well over the pound, there are numbers of bream to 4 lb., plus perch and some pike. Good winter trotting here. Membership costs £26 yearly from Saxmundham Angling Centre (Tel: 01728 603443). One mile below Wickham Market the Deben flows into a circular lake called Loudham Decoy (private) and out of the lake's southern end where it is spanned by the Ipswich to Saxmundham railway before it meanders down to Ufford. There is, unfortunately, little public access, although the fishing is quite good in these last couple of miles before the Deben pours into the deep weir pool at the Iron Bridge in Melton and becomes tidal with the fishing free. Flowing beneath Wilford Bridge and on to Woodbridge, where it widens considerably into the estuary, the Deben is now on its last six miles. Fishing is most varied and although species have changed to mullet, bass, sea trout, flounders and eels, many anglers use their freshwater gear to good effect. All worm baits work well in this estuary which finally pumps into the North Sea as the boundary between Bawdsey and Felixstowe (see 'Sea Fishing').

THE RIVER DOVE

The River Dove is of little consequence as a fishery until it reaches the town of Eye, but from here on there are five miles of interesting fishing, suited in particular to the roaming type of angler, until it joins the Waveney one mile north of Hoxne with quality dace and roach predominating. Generally the flow is quite sluggish and during the summer months weed growth can be prolific. Some of the fishing is free to those who show politeness and ask permission from local farmers and for a short stretch immediately down from Oakley bridge to where the Dove joins the Waveney it is controlled by the Diss Angling Club. This last section of the Dove can produce some nice bags of roach, particularly during the winter months whenever the river runs coloured and to fish it anyone may join the Diss and District A.C. which also has four miles of the Waveney, plus a large mere in the middle of Diss and a galaxy of pits at Eye. (See 'Stillwaters – Members only.') Club membership costs £18 annually from P. M. Pegg Angling Supplies of Chapel Street, Diss (Tel: 01379 640430).

THE RIVER GIPPING

The River Gipping rises due east of Stowmarket as a result of two streams merging, and flows in a narrow and winding course, passing beneath the Norwich to London railway line on its way to Stowmarket. Here it is joined by the Rattlesden River and the Gipping becomes a slightly larger course holding predominantly roach and chub, plus some dace and pike. Along the west bank in Stowmarket, for a distance of 400 yards at Greens Meadow, the fishing is controlled by the Gipping Valley A.C. Club membership costs £26 from Bosmere Tackle, Needham Market (Tel: 01449 721808).

Starting half a mile below Stowmarket on the east bank there is over two miles of free fishing from the towpath all the way down to just below Hawksmill. As the Gipping flows down through Needham Market and on to Baylham it passes several excellent stillwaters, namely Needham Lake, Bosmere Lake, Alderson Lake, Causeway Lake and Barham Pits (see 'Stillwaters – Members only'). In Needham Market, a short stretch of the river, running beside Needham Lake is also controlled by the Gipping Valley A.C., holding quality roach, dace, tench, bream, carp, chub, perch and pike. Those desiring maximum access to the River Gipping should note that an enormous length, over 10 miles in fact, is controlled by the Gipping Angling Preservation Society which, under the guidance of its honorary secretary, George Alderson, has transformed much of the river from its pollution-problem days of the 1950s and 1960s into what is now the most prolific running water fishery in the whole of East Anglia. Massive stocking programmes were carried out between 1953 and 1973 which included most species of freshwater fish, among them tench and carp. Anyone may join the society by applying to George Alderson, 37 Heatherhayes, Ipswich, IP2 9SL (Tel: 01473 602828). Yearly subscriptions, which also cover extensive lake and pit fishing, cost £43 with reduced rates for senior citizens, ladies and juniors. Membership can also be obtained from the tackle shops in Claydon, Needham Market and Ipswich.

Going downstream from Baylham the river is still mostly shallow with odd deep holes holding large quantities of roach and chub. It consistently produces good bags of chub to the 4 lb. mark and roach over the pound, with stick float fishing during the autumn to winter months offering the best prospects. Due to a prolific weed growth summer fishing is not easy. The Gipping meanders onwards towards Ipswich, passing beneath the B1113 road in Great Blakenham and then beneath the Norwich to London railway line. On the east bank at Station Road in Claydon a few hundred yards are controlled by the Gipping Valley Angling Club. But nearly everywhere else is in the control of the Gipping Angling Preservation Society. Going below where the A1100 crosses the river down to Bramford is not so prolific as the upper reaches, but at Sproughton road bridge, starting along the eastern bank, following the footpath for two miles down to the first railway bridge, is also controlled by the Gipping Angling Preservation Society and is excellent fishing. Day permits are available for this stretch from all local tackle dealers. Winter roaching on the float is fabulous.

From the railway bridge below Sproughton the river widens considerably with depths between 10 and 15 feet and here is a super one and a half mile length controlled by the Ipswich Borough Council, and managed by the Gipping Angling Preservation Society with day tickets from tackle shops and the warden on the bank. The Gipping has now entered Ipswich and transformed into more of a slow-moving canal than a river, holding a good head of roach and bream plus some tench and even the odd carp. Fishing along this reach is allowed only from the purposely constructed angling platforms. The stretch ends at Yarmouth Road bridge below which sport slowly peters out as the river becomes tidal at West End Sluice and feeds the Orwell estuary. There is still some saltwater sport to be had however from the power station downstream, with flounders, eels, mullet and school bass. A huge thick lipped grey mullet was caught from the Orwell in 1994 by Andy Gallagher weighing 8 lb. 3¼ oz. It accepted free lined breadflake.

THE RIVER HUNDRED

Were it in Lincolnshire this little river would be called a drain and that is exactly what it looks like, being narrow, shallow and a sluggish channel throughout most of its length. Its life starts with an enormous network of drainage dykes, ditches and streams a few miles south of Beccles, to meander easterly towards Kessingland where it is spanned by the A12 Lowestoft to Southwold road. Much of this lower part of the river, which holds numbers of good quality roach to the pound, some rudd, tench, the occasional specimen bream and pike, is unfortunately inaccessible and controlled by local clubs. After passing through lonely marshes for another two miles it finishes its short life by spilling out on to the beach via a pumping station.

THE RIVER LARK

The River Lark rises from a source of numerous streams several miles due south of Bury St. Edmunds, and flows in a north-westerly direction through Bury, Hengrave and Lackford where the West Stow Country Park lies adjacent to the northern bank (see 'Stillwaters – Syndicate waters'). The course then follows the A1101 Mildenhall Road through

Icklingham and on to Barton Mills where it flows beneath the A11 Norwich to London road. Fishing in the high upper reaches is predominantly for trout and dace, although limited numbers of roach also exist. Much is in the hands of trout syndicates with little public access. However, the Lark Angling and Preservation Society, for £100 a year covering a two fish per visit limit, has super trout fishing on a three mile beat. Anyone may join the club and membership fees are £15 yearly. The secretary is Mr. E. West, 8 Arrowhead Drive, Lakenheath (Tel: 01842 861369). During 2000 and 2001 several hundred grayling were introduced downstream from Barton Mills.

Going downstream from the bridge at Barton Mills trout are still in evidence but the predominant stock consists of roach, dace and the odd chub, plus one or two nice carp and pike. With the exception of the Jubilee Sports Field, a half a mile length of free fishing on the northern bank, the Lark Angling and Preservation Society has control issuing £5 weekly permits available from Stebbings Sports of Mill Road in Mildenhall (Tel: 01638 713196).

At the Gasworks Pool in Mildenhall the Lark divides and passes through double lock gates and changes pace to a more sedate river, so typical of fenland roach and bream rivers. The Mildenhall Club controls the cricket field section, followed again by the Lark Angling and Preservation Society almost halfway to the Judes Ferry pub where the West Roe road spans the river. Below this point the Lark Angling and Preservation Society controls the river all the way across the fen at West Roe. Good winter roach and pike fishing.

I used to love fishing this part of the Lark many years ago when in my late teens, and the long drive from North London where I then lived always seemed well worthwhile with quality roach showing in good bags during the winter months. Unfortunately pollution struck the Lark throughout this region some years ago but it is now well on the mend, with some reasonable roach being caught once again, plus dace, chub, perch, bream and pike to over 20 lb. Weekly permits costing £5 cover all the bank controlled by the Lark Angling and Preservation Society. These are available through the club or Stebbings Sports in Mildenhall (Tel: 01638 713196). At Isleham Lock the Isleham Angling Club issues season tickets costing £10 from Isleham Post Office (Tel: 01638 780256) and fishing includes the side stream loop from the footbridge and immediately downstream from the Lock on the western bank, for a distance of around two miles. This length was dredged in 1984 after suffering pollution. The roach however are really showing again and they run to over the pound, in addition to bream up to the 4 lb. mark, plus the odd tench and good pike. It is all float fishing in a slow flow with depths varying between 4 and 6 feet. Below the Isleham A.C. holding there is then a private piece, after which the Lark flows down to Lark Grange where it leaves Suffolk and enters Cambridgeshire to eventually feed the Great Ouse just south of Littleport.

THE RIVER MINSMERE

This river is a tiny but comparatively lengthy river which in its upper reaches is known as the Yox. It flows down through Sibton Park with its adjacent lake (see 'Stillwaters') and holds most species of coarse fish. Access to the river is rather limited and anglers should always ask the permission of local farmers and landowners prior to fishing.

The river finally ends as a maze of dykes and lakes within the nature reserve at Minsmere (private) and enters the sea through the New Cut via a sluice. From the bridge at Eastbridge going towards the sea along the southern bank of the New Cut is worth a try for roach, rudd and bream, although it is prone to odd salt influences.

THE RATTLESDEN RIVER

This river joins the River Gipping at Coombs in Stowmarket, having come just six miles from its birthplace in Rattlesden. It holds predominantly roach and dace, being quite narrow in most parts and apart from the odd hole, rather shallow. Apart from asking local farmers for permission the only public access is a short 300 yard section along the south bank at Coombs Ford in Stowmarket. Adjoining this stretch the Gipping Valley Angling Club have control. Anyone may join for just £26 from Bosmere Tackle, 57 High Street, Needham Market (Tel: 01449 721808). This card entitles members to fish other parts of the Gipping and three lakes controlled by the Gipping Valley Club.

THE RIVER STOUR

For most of its course the beautiful Stour, so wonderfully portrayed by Constable in his paintings, is actually the county boundary between Suffolk and Essex. The Stour flows on a lengthy trail from its source in Cambridgeshire, through the villages of Wixoe, Clare, Cavendish and on to Glemsford where the River Glem enters at the northern bank. All along these reaches the Suffolk Stour breeds specimen dace, with chub and roach predominating.

Between Wixoe and Clare in the village of Stoke-by-Clare the Haverhill A.C. control a short stretch within the grounds of Stoke-by-Clare College. Day tickets cost £5 from Haverhill Angling Centre (Tel: 01440 705011). To fish the weir itself which includes barbel, and half a mile immediately upstream (good chub fishing) contact Alan Pearce (Tel: 01787 238200). Below the weir is controlled by the Haverhill Club downstream to Blackbarn. Day tickets from Haverhill Angling Centre (Tel: 01440 705011). The Long Melford and District A.A. controls a two mile length at Clare with day tickets costing £5. These must be obtained in advance from the secretary, Mr. N. Mealham, 6 Springfield Terrace, East Street, Sudbury (Tel: 01787 377139). Club membership costs £35.

Beginning one mile above the old railway station at Glemsford, just off the A1092 road, and continuing downstream to a point 200 yards below Rodbridge between Long Melford and Sudbury is nearly all double-bank fishing controlled by the Long Melford and District A.A. which also has a six acre pit known as Starfield (see 'Stillwaters'). At Glemsford the Stour skirts three lakes controlled by the London Anglers' Association (L.A.A.) (see 'Stillwaters') which also has two short stretches of the river at Clare and Cavendish. The river here is clean flowing, fairly weedy and predominantly a roach, chub, bream and dace water. Following the stream down from Glemsford the Stour flows through Long Melford and then to Sudbury where the Sudbury and District Angling Association controls over eight miles of the fishing. All sections except the Island and Priory pieces are available on day tickets at £5 from bailiffs on the river. The club also controls a one and a half mile piece at Great Cornard, called Wright's Meadow. Additional information can be obtained from the Sudbury and District A.A. Secretary, Mr. Steve Walker (Tel: 01787 319019) or from the local tackle shop, Sudbury Angling Centre of Acton Square (Tel: 01787 312118). A 10½ lb. barbel was caught from the Stour here in 2002 by Steve Walker.

Within the town limits of Sudbury the Stour offers excellent stick float fishing in a gentle flow for dace, some quality roach to well over the pound, maybe, even over 2 lb., some tench (six-pounders have been caught) and for bream up to 9 lb. Some barbel exist here also. Winter trotting when the river holds colour is particularly rewarding, almost anything can turn up in mild conditions. A massive 29 lb. 6 oz. pike was caught by G. Baxter from the Stour here in 1980. Pike over 20 lb. are not uncommon however. In recent years perch of all sizes have started to appear in numbers, once again throughout the middle reaches of the Stour, with specimens to over 3 lb. The Environment Agency introduced 600 barbel into this part of the Stour in 2002.

Downstream from Sudbury several clubs share control over the next six miles of river, with day tickets available from Sudbury Angling Centre. The Sudbury and District A.A. have the lion's share with stretches at five locations – The Rookery, Bevills, Longmead, Clicketts Farm and Plantations. I have fished most of this section from Middleton, down through Henny, Pitmere Lock (now private) and Lamarsh to Bures itself, but many years ago (over 40 in fact) when the roach shoals were very much stronger than they are today. Chub, however, have spread and are now fairly common around the 2½ – 4 lb. mark with odd fish to over 6 lb., and no doubt have something to do with the demise of the roach. Chub are now to be found throughout much of the middle river from Brundon above Sudbury, to as far down as Wormingford and provide good sport along with the occasional barbel. These were introduced several years back by my old friend the late Len Head, in conjunction with the then N.R.A. (now the Environment Agency) and are faring well. Future sport with barbel is certainly an exciting prospect for the river. Sport with roach including a few whoppers is still to be enjoyed along the famous Rookery stretch in Bures where the water is exceptionally deep in parts.

I can well remember on one cold day in February 1958 at the age of 15 taking nearly 200 roach at one sitting from the Stour here, together with several dace and only a dozen or so fish measured less than 8 inches. The best went to 1½ lb. While catches of this size are now generally out of the question, because the shoals are nowhere near so numerically strong, quality seems not to have suffered. And in the mill pool at Bures (under L.A.A. control) there is a large resident shoal of specimen bream up to 8 lb. Bream of up to this size have always lived in the Stour and during the early 1970s there was an injection of enormous bream from Abberton Reservoir. Many of these fish weighed over 10 lb., and one such fish weighing 12 lb. 14 oz. was caught by Gerry Harper from Great Cornard in 1971 and actually held the British record for several years. Nowadays these giant fish are conspicuous by their absence and we can only assume that the Abberton bream have all passed on. A little way downriver from Bures Mill there is an extensive lake (also L.A.A.) where tench over 8 lb. have been taken. The lake also holds bream, plus the odd carp to 20 lb. (see 'Stillwaters – Bures Lake',p.97). It was in this part of the Stour that the old English record perch was caught (before it was deleted from the list by the present fish committee), weighing just a shade under 6 lb. Before the national perch disease of the late 1960s a big perch was always a possibility from the river at almost any point and in recent seasons three-pounders have been showing again throughout the river. Two miles downstream from Bures the river passes beneath the bridge at Wormingford, where it is rather narrow and nicely streamy, holding good dace and chub along with the roach. The northern bank down to just above the weir (private) at Wiston is controlled by the Colchester Angling Preservation Society (membership secretary, Andy Howard (Tel: 01206 513965)), which also has several more miles (varying from bank to bank) of the river stretching over 10 miles down to Dedham. The Colchester club does not issue day tickets but anyone may join the club through Angling Essentials Tackle Shop, 14 Church Street, Witham (Tel: 01376 512255) or from Haverhill Angling Centre (Tel: 01440 705011). Season permits cost £57 and cover a wealth of local fishing, including the famous Layer Pits and several other stillwaters in Essex including a man-made 20 acre lake at Pedmarsh on the Essex/Suffolk border (see 'Stillwaters – Members only'). Between Wormingford and Dedham the Stour flows through Nayland and then down to Stratford St. Mary. Zander have slowly filtered into the Stour but are in such small groups that, as yet, they have not disrupted the indigenous stocks. If anything the roach fishing actually improves in these lower wider reaches below Stratford, where depth averages around 6 feet

Beautiful Flatford Mill is the last mill on the Suffolk Stour before it becomes tidal.

and the flow is very gentle. There are also a few more bream and barbel, plus one or two good pike with carp to 30 lb. Canoes pose a problem along this part of the river especially at weekends.

At Flatford Mill fishing is controlled by the Elm Park Club with day permits available from the bailiff on the bank. Flatford Mill was once the end of the upper Stour before it became tidal and passed into the estuary down to Harwich Harbour and into the North Sea. However, when the dam was constructed across the estuary at Cattawade, near Manningtree, with the fish pass facilities for the odd sea trout wishing to pass upstream, it provided extra fishing between Flatford and Cattawade. This is controlled for a one and a half mile reach along the south bank by the Lawford Angling Club, which issues day permits from its bailiff on the bank. Immediately below the sluice at Cattawade where the A137 passes over the Stour, it immediately spreads into a mile-wide estuary for 10 miles to Harwich and the sea, providing some first class sport with mullet.

THE RIVER WANG

Although the streams which feed its infancy travel for many miles before finally amalgamating between the villages of Uggeshall and Wangford, the River Wang then flows for just another two miles between the A12 bridge at Wangford and the A1095 bridge at Reydon Marshes before becoming tidal and joining the Blyth estuary to pump out into the North Sea at Southwold. Between Wangford and Reydon the Wang meanders along lined by dense beds of rushes and reeds and holds roach up to the pound. The Wang has suffered catastrophically from pollution during the past two decades and although restocked by the then N.R.A. (now the Environment Agency) even if the fishing was worth attention the once 'club controlled' stretches are now all privately controlled with no access to anglers. One can always ask however.

THE RIVER WAVENEY

The Waveney originates from the fen on Redgrave Common as the county boundary between Norfolk and Suffolk. It flows easterly through Roydon and on to Diss, but is hardly worth consideration in these initial six miles although numbers of dace and roach exist. Just beyond Diss the river is fed by two streams and flows on for one mile to Scole. In this area, and in particular from Scole downstream, the fishing is good, predominantly for roach to over the pound, tench and pike. From Billingford Bridge downstream on the Suffolk bank is controlled by the Diss Angling Club. Anyone may join through local tackle dealer, P.M. Pegg Angling Supplies (Tel: 01379 640430). Season permits cost £18 which includes the local Diss Mere and fishing on a galaxy of pits at Eye (see 'Stillwaters – Members only'). The club's stretch goes through Hoxne where the tiny River Dove joins the Waveney, down to Brockdish - a distance of about four miles. The Waveney begins to mature and becomes more varied in character with the odd deep hole to 10 feet situated on the bends between long, weedy glides. Tench are also to be found here, sometimes topping 4 lb., together with some quality roach, dace, pike and the odd nice chub. Chub do, in fact, start showing up in numbers from Brockdish going downstream. In 1994 Gordon Pierce took one of the best ever match weights for the upper reaches of the Waveney with 106 lb. of bream to 7 lb. 2 oz. from Brockdish.

In the Needham area most of the river is inaccessible but going down to Weybread at Lucks Mill the local Harleston, Wortwell and District A.C. controls around 1000 yards of the Suffolk bank above the mill and also below on both banks down to Shotford Bridge. This is all a lovely part of the river, holding roach, dace, chub, pike and even the odd carp. Day tickets are not issued but anyone may join the club for the cost of a £21 yearly fee from the local tackle shop, Waveney Angling in Harleston (Tel: 01379 854886). It is all Harleston water again on both banks below Shotford for the two miles down to Mendham, with Weybread Pits (fabulous carp etc) running parallel to the Suffolk bank (see 'Stillwaters'). The river varies its course dramatically almost every few yards with chub lurking beneath the overgrown swims where bushes shade the narrow twisting parts. Along the open, more even-paced glides there are roach, real beauties up to 2 lb. or more, and hordes of dace, together with a fair head of perch and pike. A good bream or tench is not unlikely either, though never in numbers. When the Waveney runs clear and weedy during the summer, freelining baits before the sun hits the water will take the chub and better-sized roach but bags are not taken until the river colours and the weed dies. This is the time to sit well upstream of any easy-paced run and to feed in loose maggots or casters followed by light float tackle with the bait just off or trundling along the bottom.

As the Waveney winds downstream through picturesque farmland it passes through a beautifully restored mill at Mendham (private fishing) and on to Wortwell, where it separates into several dykes holding good chub, apart from some excellent dace and a few roach. Around half a mile of the Norfolk bank in Wortwell is available on a day ticket (Tel: 01986 788222). Excellent chub, bream and tench here. The source then channels just south of Waveney Valley Lakes (see 'Stillwaters – Day tickets') and makes its way on to Homersfield where fishing is free between the old and new bridges. It next winds through sleepy farmlands in the control of the Harleston club for a distance of over one and a half miles and is excellent roach and chub fishing with very large tench to be found in the holes. The Bungay Cherry Tree A.C. has two stretches here. Anyone may join the club which controls much local fishing, contact the secretary, Mr. Ian Gosling, 37 St. Mary's Terrace, Bungay (Tel: 01986 892982). Membership costs £30 for adults, £20 senior citizens and disabled and £10 for juniors. A 10 day holiday permit costing £12.50 is also available.

The river passes the Otter Trust and meanders down to Earsham where it divides around a long island and flows through a weir sluice and a mill pool. Way back in the early 1960s a goliath chub of 9½ lb. was found alive one morning in the mill's eel trap and returned to the river. It was probably one of the original stock fish obtained from the River Wissey by the old Water Authority for introduction into the Waveney but was unfortunately not seen again. This is a most interesting area to explore both summer and winter for roach, dace, chub, pike and even shoals of bream between 3 and 7 lb. throughout the network of dykes starting below the mill. These meander across Earsham Common towards Bungay with much of the banks being free or easily accessible to the polite angler who asks first. Carp into double figures are also to be found in this part of the Waveney.

At the end of the Earsham Common three narrow channels flow beneath the old A143 road. The Cherry Tree Club has control of these streamy runs which hold some quality dace, roach and some nice chub. The Waveney then flows beneath the bypass and does a three and a half mile circuit around Bungay Common. There are plenty of nice fish along this Common and if one starts at the Golf Club House and follows the flow from the Suffolk bank, many chub swims are to be found. Day tickets to fish the Common cost £3 and are available from the Caravan Park on the Common (Tel: 01986 892338), who also sell the local Bungay Cherry Tree Club permits. These cost £30 for adults, £20 for senior citizens and disabled, £10 for juniors and cover a wealth of local fishing. Freelined flake, cheese, worms and slugs are killing chub baits here, which should hide a large single hook tied direct to nothing less than a 6 lb. line. These chub run to better than 6 lb. with many in the 3 – 4 lb. class and have in recent years, together with carp to over 20 lb., taken over from roach as the main attraction. In fact one sees few roach on the Common these days unless a long walk to the far end is made where the river deepens. Shoals are not large but individual fish are. Tench are to be expected here also, together with very large bream in holes deepening to 10 feet or more. In the summer of 1992 Malcolm Runacres smashed the five hour match record for the Waveney with 162 lb. of bream including specimens to 8 lb. when pegged behind Earsham Pits half way round Bungay Common. Pike fishing is also good along the Common particularly for the wandering enthusiast who fishes artificial lures or wobbles deadbaits. Numerous double figure pike are found too, with odd fish over 20 lb. At the end of the Common the Waveney flows beneath the bypass and then under Bungay's narrow Town Bridge. Immediately below the bridge there are some cracking roach and chub (free fishing) along the short meadow down to the Falcon Weir. I caught my first ever 2 lb. roach in this very pool way back in 1957. It accepted a grain of stewed wheat, a killing summer bait on the Waveney, and there are still some big roach around for the taking, in addition to good pike and chub. In 1993 Mr. P. Heywood captured the largest chub ever to come from the Waveney on rod and line. It weighed an incredible 8 lb. 2 oz. and confirmed my long held belief that if ever an East Anglian chub was to break the British record it could well come from the Waveney.

The Falcon pool is very deep but shallows off at the tail where the course bends downriver to Wainford Maltings. It is in this next mile of the Waveney that, in addition to good stocks of quality roach, one also finds isolated shoals of those famously large upper Waveney bream. These fish are beautifully coloured with blue black shoulders, bronze-golden flanks and fins of a mauve hue. They are so unlike their tidal, lower river contemporaries, being virtually slimeless and able to fight very hard. The average weight is over 4 lb. with specimens to over 8 lb. I find the most rewarding approach for these super bream is to locate the shoals in summer during daylight, wearing polaroid sunglasses and to form some idea of their feeding pattern and the route the shoal takes. They appear to wander among the weeds during daytime and select a deep hole somewhere along their particular route for the evening feed. A good plan is to pre-bait such a swim or two just before dusk with the intention of fishing when the light has really gone and the bream are less timid. Laying a piece of breadflake or paste on the groundbait carpet is my usual method and I float fish 'lift' style using a luminous tipped float. This is a very effective way of night fishing as one can maintain an interest all night long when there is a float to watch. Bites nearly always are a positive 'flat' or a glide away.

The Fleece Angling Club controls half a mile of the river on both banks immediately upstream from Wainford Mill. Around Wainford Maltings the Cherry Tree Club has some interesting fishing. The first 100 yards on the Suffolk bank (which fishes particularly well in flood time) and several hundred yards of the Norfolk bank is controlled by the Southwold and District F.A.P.S. which has a waiting list. Contact the secretary, Mrs. B. Reid (Tel: 015602 518198). The club also has control of over half a mile of the southern bank starting immediately upstream of Ellingham Mill. As the river slowly bends for two miles to Ellingham it is very deep in parts and contains good sized shoals of big bream with individual specimens topping 8 lb. The roach also average high and there is a strong head of pounders. In addition there are some nice tench, a few perch and one or two really large pike among numerous lesser fish. Eels, of course, pave the bottom as they do throughout the Waveney. The upper Waveney ends at Ellingham where the course splits into three channels just upstream of the mill. These then rejoin a little downstream of the road bridges spanning them, in what is now strictly speaking the tidal reaches though little difference is noted this far upriver as regards flow and colour etc. Some of the fishing here is accessible provided one enquires locally for permission, with the exception of the two mill pools (private). There are some large carp to over 30 lb., roach to over 2 lb., dace, chub, perch,

good tench, pike and, at times, a shoal of good-sized bream makes its way upriver into this area though the average size is not as high as around Wainford.

Upon leaving Ellingham the river bends slowly for three miles through marshland until it reaches Geldeston. Much of this section is accessible to those who obtain permission from local landowners and, in addition to roach and bream, there are numbers of double-figure pike with specimens exceeding 20 lb., plus some very large chub to 6 lb. plus. Cherry Tree Club members have access to some great roach fishing downstream of the bridge on the Suffolk bank and on the north bank at Dairy Farm. The Club controls still more water further downstream at Shipmeadow (southern bank) with access off the A1116 road through Nunnery Farm. Before reaching the river there are nice roach, tench and bream in the large dyke and in the mainstream which averages around 6 feet deep, roach are both prolific and of an excellent stamp, running to well over the pound. There is also a stock of bream and a strong head of pike, some reaching to large proportions. Below the Cherry Tree water on the same 'Suffolk' bank control is in the hands of the Southwold and District F.A.P.S. for several hundred yards, with access via a lane close to White House Farm on the Low Road.

At Geldeston Lock access is unfortunately rather limited. But for sport with both roach and pike during the winter fishing is free along the dyke which starts at Geldeston village and joins the Waveney at Three Rivers. The Cherry Tree Club also control a length of the Norfolk bank at Geldeston down to Three Rivers. On the Suffolk bank there are two miles of free fishing along Barsham Marshes down to Beccles, controlled by the Environment Agency.

On the Norfolk bank a one and a quarter mile length at Gillingham is under the control of the Southwold and District F.A.P.S. which has a waiting list. (Contact the secretary, Mrs. B. Reid on 01502 518198.) Despite the tidal influences in these last few miles before flowing through the town of Beccles, the Waveney retains that special friendliness for which it is perhaps best loved. In parts it runs deep and quite narrow between beds of thick reeds and holds isolated, yet quite large shoals of bream to 4 lb., in addition to a prolific roach population.

Throughout the sheltered first half mile upstream of Beccles town road bridge where boatyards and hotels front the water, winter sport is particularly good – regardless of weather – with quality roach predominating. Below the bridge the quay at Beccles fishes particularly well from October onwards for quality roach and a few bream with float fished casters producing the best results though maggots take fish also, if somewhat smaller. There are also numbers of pike along this stretch with some really big fish among the hordes of jacks. Whether roach or pike fishing the tidal Waveney, fishing from a dinghy produces the very best of results. These may be hired locally from Aston Boats (Tel: 01502 713960). Anglers may also launch their own small craft from the slipway on Beccles Quay, next to the Harbour Master's Office. Depth really increases from Beccles Quay going downriver, depending on the state of the tide, with most swims holding between 8 and 12 feet of water through the middle of the river. Darren Farrington hooked into a surprise 30 lb. wels catfish here whilst pike fishing in 1999 at Beccles. On the southern bank is excellent free fishing as the Waveney winds through Beccles Marshes. The largest pike ever to be caught from the river came from the top of this stretch in 1980 to the rod of Dave Humphries and weighed 30 lb. 1 oz. There is, in fact, a terrific head of pike throughout these tidal reaches fed by massive shoals of roach and dace as the river twists down to the old railway supports. Immediately downstream (on the Norfolk bank) on the left is free mooring for 24 hours at a staithe which leads up to excellent summer stillwater fishing at Aldeby Hall Farm Pits (Tel: 01502 677648) – five small pits well stocked with carp. Next comes Aldeby Staithe and on to Worlingham, where the Environment Agency owns a short but nicely wooded length of the southern bank. There are some really comfortable swims here with depths to 17 feet. Access is from Marsh Lane, off the large roundabout out of Beccles which bypasses Worlingham. Unfortunately most of the Waveney in these lower reaches is simply inaccessible from the bank which is a pity because in addition to providing good sport during early and late sessions in the summer, winter fishing is really marvellous. So organising a boat back at Beccles and motoring downriver is well worthwhile. In addition to good bags of quality roach and dace, plus the odd sizeable bream, I have taken lots of pike up to 25 lb. from between Beccles and Worlingham and usually without seeing a soul all day after the cruisers have been put away from November onwards.

Below Worlingham down to Barnby and on to Burgh St. Peter fishing is of a similar quality all the way, although the flow gets stronger and the water is more coloured comparable to the Lower Yare in the region of Buckenham Ferry and the tactics of ledgering with a substantial amount of lead, in conjunction with plenty of stiff groundbait work well.

Bread is often preferred to worms and maggots, particularly if quality fish are sought. Maggots are a good winter bait though. There are good stocks of bream between 2 and 4 lb. and many roach with a high average size in the 6 – 8 oz. range. Naturally there are hordes of eels and flounders also. Really huge bags of bream, often in excess of a hundredweight, with individual fish topping 5 lb. were once considered only ordinary catches from these lower reaches. However, as elsewhere the Waveney no longer produces such numbers of bream. Today a 50 lb. bag is exceptional. Winding through lonely marshlands the Waveney feeds Oulton Dyke which leads to Oulton Broad (see 'The Broads') from its southern bank. There is excellent sport to be had in this area, particularly in the dyke at night during the summer months. One of the best bream spots in Broadland.

From Oulton Dyke the course passes through wide bends onwards for four miles to Somerleyton, St. Olaves and Haddiscoe where the New Cut flows off from the Norfolk bank, joining the Waveney to the Yare at Reedham Ferry. This straight man-made channel offers two and a half miles of free fishing in deep water which can flow very fast at times. It is spanned by the A143 Yarmouth to Beccles road 300 yards down from its junction with the Waveney, with access from the towpath running parallel along the northern bank from Haddiscoe Bridge. From this point downstream there is just four miles remaining of this wonderful river before it enters the brackish water of Breydon water. These last few miles do harbour fish at times, depending on the prevailing tides and how far the salt penetrates upriver on the flood. However, one would do well to leave this section well alone, for the fishing is always patchy.

Bottom Left: John (Jinx) Davey from Bungay with a superb 24 lb. pike caught on ledgered herring from the tidal Waveney at Burgh St. Peter

History of the Broads Enigma

To tell the story of how Broadland evolved is not as simple as it might seem. Did it originate as we know it today from the deepest areas of valleys, formerly the bed of an enormous estuary fed by the North Sea? Or did peat excavations during the Middle Ages help to create our now threatened playground of reed-fringed fisheries? Historians disagree in the case of the Broads, with many conflicting ideas as to exactly how this water playground originated. For due to gaps in the stratigraphical record, unresolved problems are numerous. In the eyes of some (particularly the older Broadsmen still living who cut reeds or run boats) there will always be differences of opinion despite the efforts of Dr. Joyce Lambert, whose conclusive work in the 1950s favoured that such steep-sided islands of peat left around the margins of most broads could only have been made by the efforts of man removing peat for fuel to burn. Surely the name of 'Barton Turf' is a reminder as to its origin, and there are many other references to 'Turbaries'.

As many of these excavations and the peninsulas they left were found to run in parallel lines and actually follow old parish boundaries, and as no mention of large expanses of open water were recorded before the fifteenth century, the case for man's involvement is almost beyond question. Samuel Woodward suspected there was an 'artificial' link in 1834, but not until the 1950s was scientific evidence amassed in abundance.

It is a fair assumption that most broads are no more than five or six hundred years old, although it has been suggested that digging peat for fuel and thus creating pits or broads (as they later became flooded)

could date back to as early as the twelfth century.

That east Norfolk itself was one gigantic estuary only a thousand years ago and millions of years before that actually part of the seabed, there is little doubt. The geological history of Norfolk runs side by side with data we were all given at school. During the Roman conquest, for instance, the estuary was so vast that strongholds at Burgh and at Caister were built to deter the attacks of invaders by sea who might have sailed all the way inland to Norwich. And their fears were well founded. In 1004 Sweyn sailed a Danish fleet up to Norwich, which he plundered and burnt.

At this time 'fingers' of the estuary went as far north as Horsey, while the mouth of the Yare extended from Caister to Gorleston, a distance of four miles. Sandbanks eventually formed in the mouth over the succeeding years (to become Great Yarmouth), as the inland waters decreased and the estuary narrowed. The banking up of debris in the Yare estuary which created Great Yarmouth arose from the erosion of the cliffs to the north. Over 20 miles of the Norfolk coastline have been subjected to this erosion, with the sediment being deposited southwards by the great tidal currents, and of course it's still going on today. One look at the houses balanced precariously on the edge of the cliffs at Happisburgh and Mundesley tells the story instantly. So even from as recently as the time of Christ, a comparatively short period in historical and geological terms, the entire composition of east Norfolk and Suffolk has been constantly changing with water levels rising and falling, debris being displaced and banked, not to mention man's intervention. Certainly water levels must have been much reduced in the

Middle Ages for peat to have been excavated from some of the broads as we know them today. Archaeological evidence from the Great Yarmouth area does in fact suggest that the sea level, relative to the level of the land, was lower by 13 feet during the thirteenth century.

The Bure broads, for instance, like the Hoveton group, Decoy, Wroxham, South Walsham and Ranworth Broads, plus Rockland Broad on the Yare, although mostly now all badly silted to various levels of between just 2 and 10 feet of fishable water, must have at some time been excavated as deep as 20 feet. However, one wonders how the upper Thurne broads like Hickling, for instance, were formed, because for the most part the bottom is hard and the depth but 3 feet. Was a thin layer of turf taken from this irregular-shaped complex and the diggings allowed to fill up? Or are these upper Thurne broads completely natural? The nearby and now landlocked broads of Filby, Rollesby and Ormesby also pose some interesting questions. Why is such an enormous sheet of interconnected waters, whether formed from old peat workings or simply once part of a deep estuary valley, now so cut off from the tidal influence? Was the Ormesby complex once filled through the tiny Muck Fleet Dyke (to the tidal Bure), then part of the estuary maze which bisected east Norfolk? Or has the land between (once all estuary) simply been back-filled or reclaimed by the silts of time? And what, I hear you ask, of those broads which are completely landlocked, some several miles from tidal water like Alderfen Broad, Mautby Broad, Barnby Broad, and Benacre Broad? Were they all once part of the giant estuary, or were they too merely localised peat workings later to become flooded? It is difficult to imagine broads like Alderfen once part of an estuary. But then, equally, it's hard to picture Norwich once totally beneath the sea. With regard to Alderfen, however, and I quote from a paper by Dr. J. M. Lambert which appeared in the *New Scientist* in 1960:

'even in the twelfth and thirteenth centuries turf was dug from deep pits. "Alderfen pyttes" were so recorded in 1209 and are presumably now represented by Alderfen Broad. Although field evidence shows the basins of the broads must have been dug out by man, neither pollen analysis nor the stratigraphy of peats, muds and clays indicate with any precision when the excavations were made or when and under what conditions they were flooded and abandoned.'

A very intriguing puzzle indeed is the enigma of the Broads. Of course it is pointless wondering how they originated, when – if we are not careful and extensive dredging does not take place within the next couple of decades – new generations of anglers (if there are any) in a couple of hundred years' time, may well be asking the question, did the Broads ever exist? And they might indeed have a point, for since the Broads came to be, vegetation has formed around their margins considerably reducing their areas. Some broads have completely disappeared in just the few hundred years since they were dug, while others have merely 'decades left' before they too silt into extinction.

Unfortunately it's a simple fact that the Broads are physically self-destructing. Those thick around the margins with carr or sallow, and especially alders, fare worse than others, as the debris of leaves and wood from the trees expedites the inevitable and helps hold the silt together. A typical example of this being the small portion left of what was once Womack Broad in Ludham village. Part of today's relatively rapid deterioration lies in the fact that commercial usage of the broads is linked almost entirely to the boating industry.

Since the last war the number of power boats, both hire craft and privately owned, has dramatically escalated, although for the present their numbers have stabilised. Boat bookings over the past few years have even fallen, due no doubt in part to cheaper package holidays abroad. But the damage has already been done insofar as the angler is concerned. Erosion of the river banks is widespread because of power craft, with perhaps a little help from the burrowing of coypu, although these rodents have now been trapped to the point of extinction. During the holiday season the water is kept in a permanent state of turbidity, which apart from cutting out light needed by rooted water plants to exist, and for fish to spawn upon, results in a downriver movement of sediment. The bottom line being that some of the broads are now silting up at the rate of over a centimetre each year.

But it would be wrong to lump all of Broadland's problems on to the boating industry as we anglers tend to. As members of a society which requires an efficient disposal of its sewage, which demands a variety of vegetables available throughout the year, and which uses two gallons of water every time we pull the chain, we are all to blame. One of the biggest problems responsible for high phytoplankton production is the unacceptable levels of phosphorus entering the broads system through our treated sewage effluent. This is being cleared up to some extent by phosphate stripping at the main sewage plant at Stalham which feeds into the River Ant and then Barton Broad. But phosphorus still enters the system from pig farms, and from the surface run-off of herbicides and pesticides, although the highest percentage by far comes from treated effluent.

At this point, and at the risk of sounding contradictory, I must admit to always holding the view that some of the broads now badly silted and seemingly coming rapidly to the end of their lives, have only deteriorated during the last few decades or comparatively recently. But after delving into numerous books, this would appear not to be so. For instance, it would seem that Rockland Broad, now extremely silted and shallow except for the boat channels, was no different at least 100 years ago at the turn of the century. I quote from the book *The Norfolk Broads* by W.A. Dutt (1904).

'Rockland has an advantage over some of the more popular broads in its being unnavigable to the larger kinds of river craft. Its swampy shores helping to retain its primitive aspect.'

Rockland today in 2002 to the penny. Nevertheless, most of the broads really are noticeably on the way out and they can so easily be preserved from extinction. Proof of the pudding is Brundall Broad, off the River Yare near Norwich, once badly silted and overgrown, which has been dredged and restored in depth to its former glory by private enterprise.

It is my own personal view that teams of dredgers in permanent employment for the foreseeable future would be needed to keep Broadland in a reasonable state of repair, considering the pressure it receives from both commercial and natural causes. If it can be done by private enterprise then surely the nation owes these medieval peat diggings continued existence.

There is at the present time much excellent work going on in the hope of restoring certain broads. The University of East Anglia have regular projects testing both fish and plant life, with perhaps the most successful of their work to date being the complete change seen on Alderfen Broad during the past two decades. First, all drainage dykes leading from the surrounding farmland by which surface run-off could enter the broad were blocked up. Then a separate 'outer' channel was dug around the perimeter to contain the amount of herbicides and insecticides rich in nitrogen, phosphorus and potassium. This restriction of the food of green phytoplanktons has brought about quite staggering results, turning pea-green water to clear. In 1982 for the first summer I could remember in over 10 years of tench fishing on Alderfen, the water remained beautifully clear throughout the warmer months with a much restored carpet of bottom-rooted weed, mostly hornwort. In time it is hoped Alderfen's ecology can be restored to how it was back in the 1930s when the Norfolk Naturalists Trust purchased the broad, with the surface then a mass of beautiful white water lilies. As far as the fishing is concerned, however, changing the water from pea-green to crystal-clear has created problems for the angler. Without lilies to shade the surface, fish retreat into the reeds around the margins and into the thickets of hornwort during daylight hours, whereas when the broad was thick pea-green they fed with less caution. But then you can't have everything.

The Norfolk Naturalists Trust started purchasing waters as far back as 1928 with Martham Broad. The Hickling estate was acquired in 1945 and now the Trust has control of 30 nature reserves in Norfolk, one third of which is Broadland – though not necessarily all water. It boasts 10,000 members and is one of the few organisations whose aim is to preserve the bird, animal and fish life of the region. I would like to have said that the Anglian Water Authority complied with its

Nowadays anglers return their pike. This massive haul from Rockland Broad at the turn of the century would of course have been eaten. It portrays how rich Broadland fishing was before commercialisation

statutory obligation of maintaining and promoting fisheries, prior to the birth of the National Rivers Authority in 1989. But it did not. It started by ditching most of its non-tidal holdings in 1982 as a result of economic shake-ups at headquarters at Huntingdon and sold anglers down the river thereafter. Now the N.R.A. has changed to the Environment Agency, who have since given up still more stretches of Broadland river bank where anglers once were able to fish. I wonder what wonderful title the Environment Agency will be changed to in another four years? As it most surely will. Cynical? Yes, of course I am.

Going back in time through the old record books of Broadland is quite fascinating. Yet by and large not everything has changed during the past 100 years – at least not in terms of the tackle and fishing techniques. We have simply become more sophisticated because there are far fewer fish about.

But what of Broadland in its heyday? Was the fishing really as good as we have been led to believe? Well, from talking to some of the old watermen who have cut reeds and rented out boats all their lives, it most certainly was. At the turn of the century fishing was so good that inns and hotels catered especially for anglers, with boats readily available almost everywhere. Which is more than can be said of today's facilities.

I do not, however, think we would fancy the rods then in use, made from greenheart and lancewood, in lengths from 12 to 14 feet. They weighed not ounces, but pounds in those days. Reels were wooden centre-pins, a three inch diameter being most popular, holding 30 yards of line, mainly of plaited silk, while terminal tackle consisted of separate gut casts and hooks tied to even finer gut. Floats were manufactured from bird quills – pelican, goose and crow – with porcupine and Norfolk reed floats also popular. Incidentally, if you have never tried making and using Norfolk 'reed floats' you don't know what you're missing. The materials are even free. As for baits, worms were far more widely used than today, both brandlings and lobs being considered the premier bait for bream, as was a large lump of breadpaste. Gentles, as they were commonly called, were just another bait, and not as many now see them the only way to catch fish. Babbing or bobbing for eels was practised by many marshmen, using a bunch of lobworms threaded on to wool and lowered on the end of a line and pole. Again, this is something today's anglers might like to try their hands at. It's great fun.

Groundbaits were mainly concocted from boiled wheat, rice and barley meal, although even in those days mixes to which just water was added were sometimes available from the tackle dealers. For ledgering the old pierced bullet seemed to be the order of the day, and most anglers used a two hook rig. While in later years I cannot recall being asked for them, up to the end of the 1970s the occasional elderly angler still enquired in my shop for two hook river paternosters with wire booms. Honestly!

It would seem that at the turn of the century, 5 lb. bream were commonplace

Top Right: Norfolk pike specialist Chris Newell finally gets the better of a large double figure fish whilst out afloat on Lily Broad

Bottom Right: Massive Barton Broad, fed by the River Ant. Its accumulation of phosphorus-rich silt was dredged during the 1990s. Called the Clearwater Project 2000, depth now averages 6 feet on the broad

and catches of this prolific Broadland fish were rated in stones rather than pounds – 20 stone hauls between two anglers being nothing out of the ordinary. They were even eaten as, of course, were many of the pike caught. With fish everywhere the need for conservation did not exist.

Fishing was mostly by boat, moored to long stout poles, which in the rivers were always parallel to the flow about a third of the way out. The only river traffic was wherries taking coal to the towns and the mills and returning with grain. For an angler it must have been a wonderful life when you think about it, with quality bream as thick on the ground as roach, and with rudd and perch everywhere, not to mention the pike fishing. It would appear, however, that in terms of overall size (with the exception of those particularly large upper Thurne broads' pike – an entity unto themselves) pike were on average no larger than they are caught today. There were simply a lot more of them because the fodder-fish shoals were so numerous. A popular pursuit was dry fly fishing for rudd on Barton and on Hickling, using thick bodied patterns, such as the Palmers, Coachman, Black Gnat and Governor, etc. A bunch of six to eight maggots cast like a fly was also used with effect. Old Archie Taylor of Rockland Broad, now sadly passed on, always used a maggot tipped fly when he wasn't cutting reeds, accounting for roach and sometimes rudd to over 2 lb. from Rockland at least up to the early 1970s. I can remember him now, putting out on the broad with his old cane fly rod during the worst of weather (while I was piking) to take the odd roach.

The old record books show oddities like a

Left: A visiting angler searches amongst the lilies on Rockland Broad for pike using surface lures

salmon taken from a flooded marsh near Norwich in 1886 (sea trout still run up to the city – but cannot migrate upstream) and going back still further a sturgeon weighing 11 stones was taken from the Waveney above Beccles in 1753. Some of the old angling writers like A.J. Rudd even mentioned the burbot, but not in enough detail for us to form a picture of their distribution. The same writer also mentions that even as early as the turn of the century, common or wild carp were plentiful in parts of Broadland, particularly the River Yare. I wonder what happened to them. And did they originate from the monasteries such as St. Benet's Abbey? The late Bill Cooper recalled the days back in the 1920s and 1930s when there was a holding pen alongside the stagings on Ormesby Broad for anglers to retain their nets of large bream, so holidaymakers could see the catches. Ormesby in fact produced some huge bream in that period. A cased specimen of 12 lb. was displayed in the Eel's Foot Hotel until a few years ago.

But the real heyday of the Broads was the 20 year span of the 1950s and 1960s. As the fishing became more widely known through the angling press, and as anglers in poor fishing areas travelled further afield, the Broads fishing really took off. They came from Coventry, from Sheffield, Birmingham and London in their droves. Catches of bream were fantastic, with weekly catches in excess of 1000 lb. to anglers who fished at night. Although it must be said that the daytime sport was so wonderful no one needed to lose sleep.

The Broads rightly gained the reputation of being the finest fishing in Britain. The Hickling, Heigham Sounds complex was simply fantastic. Wherever you went and no matter how you fished, you caught sparkling roach and rudd, bream of all sizes and mountains of perch, with tench and pike available to those who specialised. After an apprenticeship on the hard-fished canalised River Lea in north London, my first week's holiday at Martham in the late 1950s was a revelation.

The upper Thurne system is still unique and like no other Broadland complex in that the water is all extremely shallow with a high saline content which enters through seepage and through land drainage pumps via the salty marshes. Readings of 10 per cent salt have in fact been recorded in Horsey Mere. And it is in this saline environment that brine shrimps live, a valuable food source readily available to young roach, rudd and bream at every stage of their growth. I am convinced this is why everything grows so fast and so large in these broads, perhaps even the pike, which consequently never have a lack of the right-sized food throughout their lives from 3 oz. to 30 pounders.

Sport was also good on all the other broads, of course, particularly Barton for pike, bream and perch, and not forgetting Oulton Broad for those truly giant perch. All the Bure-fed broads were also crammed with fish, but the fact remained that the upper Thurne complex took the honours because it was outstanding.

To give a date for when the fishing actually first started to decline is impossible. There have been numerous localised setbacks in just these last 100 years, usually as a result of the sea breaking through the defences at Horsey, affecting the Thurne-fed broads – something the sea has been doing for over 200 years. In the late 1700s there were enormous fish kills caused by breaks in the sand hills at Horsey with salt water covering the marshes for several miles inland. Since then, of course, acre by acre all over Broadland, swamps have been turned into rush marshes and marshes into grazing ground by banking up the tidal rivers and pumping water off the land. Steam and wind pump mills were also used to free the marshes of regular rain floods, but today insofar as the fishing is concerned, pumping water off the land is too effective by far. One look at the horrible 'orange' colour of Waxham Cut which runs into Horsey Mere tells the story. The thick suspension of iron oxide sediment simply covers everything and deters rooted plants from growing by cutting out the light they need. Altogether there has been a tremendous decline of aquatic conditions in the Broads since the Second World War. In modern times I suppose more happened to start a downhill trend in the late 1960s than at any other time previously recorded. For starters the alga *Prymnesium* hit the upper Thurne system in 1969, decimating the entire stocks and putting to an end unquestionably the finest fishing in England, just a year after Horsey Mere had produced the record pike of 40 lb. 1 oz. to the rod of Peter Hancock. Incidentally, although *Prymnesium* which releases a powerful toxin to interfere with fishes' gills, struck so disastrously in 1969, it might have been responsible for fish kills as far back as 1911. Other outbreaks have occurred since in 1970, 1973, 1975, 1982, 1984, 1985, 1986, 1987 and throughout the 1990s. In addition to the huge pike, specimen rudd, perch, bream and tench were also prolific in the upper Thurne system and have all perished to varying degrees. Also in the late 1960s and throughout Broadland came both the national roach and perch diseases. Those massive perch of Oulton Broad, from where Sid Baker of Norwich caught the English record, were wiped out, as were perch all over East Anglia. Thankfully perch are now prolific throughout the river systems again. And if roach and perch diseases, plus *Prymnesium* outbreaks were not enough, Broadland has had to combat escalating pressure from angling, from motor boats and from a reduction in areas where fish can spawn, in addition to the previously mentioned unacceptable levels of phosphorus. Small wonder there has been a massive decline. I have heard it said and recently too that taking the Broads as a whole there are not a quarter of the fish present now that there were 40 years ago. And it would take a brave man to argue. Although there are indeed still quite a few signs to be pleased about for the future.

Now that we have entered the second millennium however the biggest threat to Broadland, indeed all low lying land within Norfolk and Suffolk, is global warming. Since the bad floods of 1953 sea levels have in fact risen by up to 6 cm. which means that a catastrophe is there waiting to happen whenever a fierce and prolonged north-westerly gale coincides with strong spring tides. This combination could at any time within the next 50 years create a major disaster to the entire eco system of Broadland as we know it.

How to Fish the Broadland Waterways

While this book is not intended to be instructional, it will no doubt be read by beginners and holiday anglers alike, whose knowledge of basic techniques could be rather limited. So because the Broadland waterways with their strong tidal influences are so very different from the venues most anglers fish, I think some hints on local techniques and end tackles will not go amiss.

To start with it pays to accept that, unlike currants in a well-baked cake, fish are certainly not spread evenly throughout the Broads. Just like people, they prefer to live in locations which suit them and where food is within easy reach. This may sound an over-simplification but, generally speaking, river fish have their food brought along with the current every day, while those inhabiting the large, static even-depth broads, such as Hickling, tend to graze over the bottom, covering very much more ground. Bream shoals, for instance, may roam hundreds of yards in just a few hours, so they need tracking down visually by looking for things like patches of bubbles or fish

actually rolling on the surface. Alternatively, try pre-baiting just before dark with a carpet of mashed-up stale bread, well soaked and stiffened with a cereal groundbait and then plan to fish through the night, or at least until bites cease.

Of course river fish roam too but on a day-to-day basis seldom anything like as far as those living in stillwater. So when after roach or bream in the tidal rivers, any swim is worth persevering with if signs of fish are present, or if fish have been caught from the same spot the day before. During the winter months the roach shoals in particular become very hot-spotted. Enormous concentrations of fish which occupy the lower tidal reaches throughout the summer migrate upriver to evade the salt tides once the really harsh weather has set in. This is why sheltered town areas, such as the Bure at Wroxham and Horning, or Beccles on the Waveney, are crammed with fish from December onwards.

The holiday angler, however, can rest assured that by the time 16 June comes

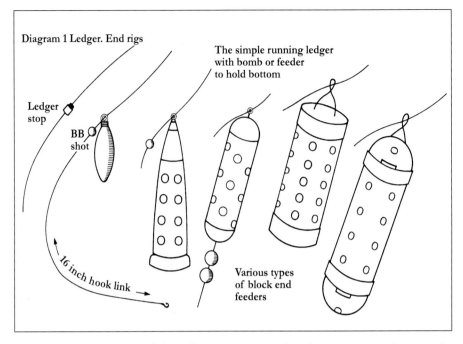

Diagram 1 Ledger. End rigs

The simple running ledger with bomb or feeder to hold bottom

Ledger stop

BB shot

16 inch hook link →

Various types of block end feeders

round again these same fish will once more be spread out throughout the middle to lower reaches where they provide excellent consistent sport during the summer and autumn. Fishing these tidal reaches, where depths can vary anywhere between eight and 20 feet, can pose real problems for those not used to a deep, fast river. And, of course, by far the easiest way of getting the bait down on the bottom right where the fish are is to ledger with a heavy block end swim-feeder, and utilising a sensitive quiver-tip bite indicator. The feeder's secret is that once filled with maggots or casters it delivers the hook bait right next to the loose feed. And so bites come quickly and more regularly. Regular casting is necessary to concentrate a good shoal of roach or bream, so at least a couple of pints of maggots are needed for a session lasting several hours.

Do not cast straight out across the current, but downstream and across. In fact, over the very spot where you intend the feeder to hold bottom. Otherwise most of the maggots will be deposited in a long line across the river as the feeder bumps along before coming to rest. Keep the rod tip as high as possible to minimise water pressure against the line, and watch the quiver-tip carefully. Any sudden jerk, either forwards or backwards, once the feeder has settled properly, should be considered a bite and worth striking. Sometimes it could merely be the feeder repositioning itself in a strong flow. But then a fish may have grabbed the bait and dislodged the feeder, causing the tip to 'jerk' or 'nod' backwards, so strike anyway.

Due to the immense water pressure which can rip a tiny hook from a fish brought upstream too quickly against the flow, stick to sizes 14 and 16, going smaller only if bites are not forthcoming. Tidal river fish are nowhere near so hook conscious or shy biting as their clearwater counterparts, so tackle can be what many would call on the heavy side. A reel line of around 4 lb. test is ideal, with hook lengths from 1½ to 2½ lb. If seeking large bream on size 6 and 8 hooks holding a large lump of breadflake, then stick to the 4 lb. line right through. But be prepared to vary the hook link from a basic 16 inch long down to say 6 inch if bites are really 'twitchy'. Alternatively, do not be afraid to increase the hook link to 4 feet when fish are taking the bait 'on the drop', just before it settles on the bottom. As in Diagram 2.

Swim feeders, or a simple bomb ledger, can run directly on the line as in Diagram 1, being topped with a single BB shot or a ledger stop at the desired distance from the hook. Or better still, make a simple fixed lead paternoster as in Diagram 2 using a size 10 swivel as the junction, or use a four turn water knot for tying hook length to the reel line. Both hook and bomb or feeder links may be altered in seconds without dismantling, and bites are registered in exactly the same way as with a running ledger. The beauty of the 'paternoster' or 'fixed lead' is that you do not need to keep worrying whether it is still running or not, because it does not matter anyway.

So much for presenting the bait on the bottom. Now what about some float-fishing to offer the bait on the move, tumbling just above the bottom, simulating how the current deposits it? The most effective way of trotting at close range is with a stick float (see Diagram 3, Fig. 1). Spread the shot fairly evenly down the line between float and hook, using a smaller shot, either a dust or a no. 6 around 18 – 20

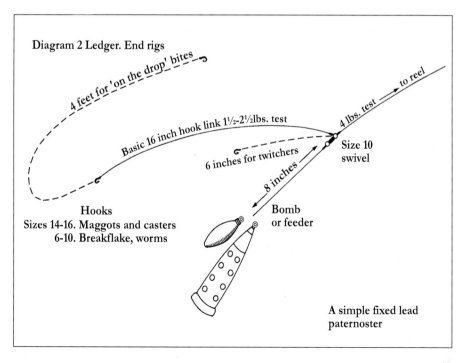

Diagram 2 Ledger. End rigs

4 feet for 'on the drop' bites

Basic 16 inch hook link 1½-2½lbs. test

6 inches for twitchers

8 inches

4 lbs. test to reel

Size 10 swivel

Hooks
Sizes 14-16. Maggots and casters
6-10. Breakflake, worms

Bomb or feeder

A simple fixed lead paternoster

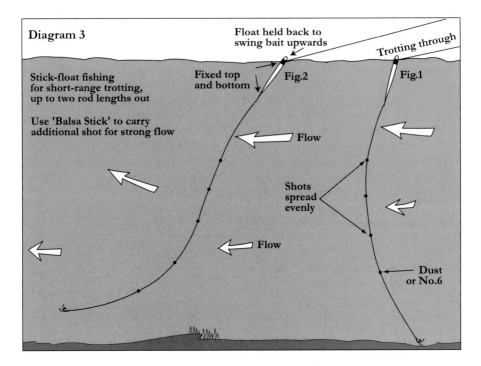

Diagram 3

Stick-float fishing
for short-range trotting,
up to two rod lengths out

Use 'Balsa Stick' to carry
additional shot for strong flow

Float held back to
swing bait upwards

Trotting through

Fixed top
and bottom

Fig.2

Fig.1

Flow

Shots
spread
evenly

Flow

Dust
or No.6

inches from the hook. Plumb the depth carefully and set the float slightly over depth. The real secret of stick float fishing is to actually overshot the float so it is almost sunk. Then as it is pulled along by the current keep it gently in check. Try not to 'over control' or it will drift off course and be presenting the maggots along a different course from where you have thrown in the loose feed. This calls for careful manipulation of the tackle and a delicate touch, but it is a deadly way of catching roach and dace. Every so often hold back a little on the float to make the bait swing enticingly upwards (as in Diagram 3, Fig. 2). Bites can then be expected almost any time as the bait drifts down again, often within a second of the float continuing its trot through. On some days roach will only take a bait which is being slowed down by holding back hard. So

do not be afraid of fishing well over depth and easing the float down really slowly. Where the current is even paced and the water, say less than 8 feet deep, a stick float carrying six no. 4 shot or three no. 1 is adequate. But step up for one holding between 3 and 5 BB where the depth is greater accompanied by a strong flow. If in doubt always choose a float carrying more lead than the flow would indicate rather than less.

For fishing in windy conditions and always at distances say further than two rod lengths, whether on still or running water, the floats to use are straight peacock wagglers, and with a body to hold extra shot if required. These are always fished bottom end only except when laying on), either by locking either side of the bottom ring with a split shot, or with a couple of float bands (see Diagram 4, Fig. 1).

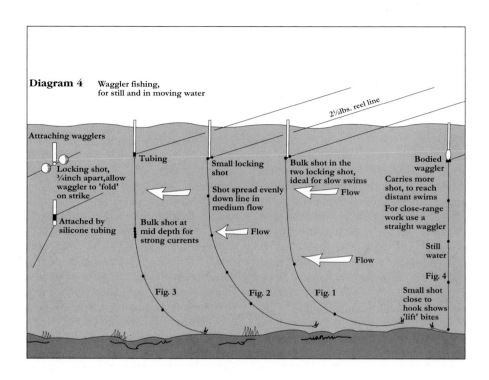

Diagram 4   Waggler fishing,
for still and in moving water

2½lbs. reel line

Attraching wagglers

Locking shot,
¾inch apart, allow
waggler to 'fold'
on strike

Attached by
silicone tubing

Tubing

Bulk shot at
mid depth for
strong currents

Fig. 3

Small locking
shot

Shot spread evenly
down line in
medium flow

Flow

Fig. 2

Bulk shot in the
two locking shot,
ideal for slow swims

Flow

Flow

Fig. 1

Bodied
waggler

Carries more
shot, to reach
distant swims

For close-range
work use a
straight waggler

Still
water

Fig. 4

Small shot
close to
hook shows
'lift' bites

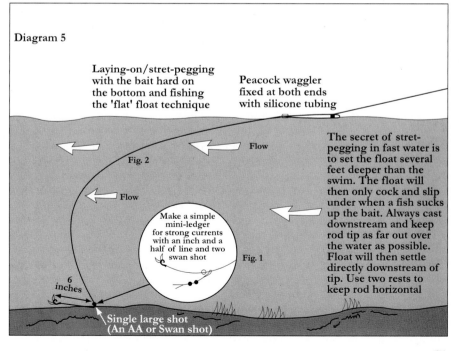

Diagram 5

Laying-on/stret-pegging
with the bait hard on
the bottom and fishing
the 'flat' float technique

Peacock waggler
fixed at both ends
with silicone tubing

Flow

Fig. 2

Flow

Flow

Make a simple
mini-ledger
for strong currents
with an inch and a
half of line and two
swan shot

Fig. 1

6
inches

Single large shot
(An AA or Swan shot)

The secret of stret-
pegging in fast water is
to set the float several
feet deeper than the
swim. The float will
then only cock and slip
under when a fish sucks
up the bait. Always cast
downstream and keep
rod tip as far out over
the water as possible.
Float will then settle
directly downstream of
tip. Use two rests to
keep rod horizontal

In a slow flow concentrate most of the lead in these two locking shot with the minimum spread down the line. Whereas for fishing a medium flow, where you need to get the bait down quickly, keep all the shot spread down the line as with the stick float (see Diagram 4, Fig. 2). In really fast water don't bother with spreading it too evenly. Bulk most of the shot at around mid depth and then graduate down to the hook (see Diagram 4, Fig. 3).

The float should not be checked as with the stick (except when straightening the line) but simply allowed to trot through smoothly at current speed with the bait trundling along well behind. As the float really precedes the bait when waggler fishing be prepared for a long sweep-through strike, to set the hook, particularly if long-trotting or fishing 30 – 40 yards out into a broad. Of course the bait does not always have to be set to fish just above bottom. There will be times during the summer months when the roach and even bream will be well off bottom and will want to take the bait at the level at which they are swimming. So experiment at different depths until bites come. To revert to fishing on the bottom to encourage 'lift' bites (as in Diagram 4, Fig. 4), fix a small shot four inches from the hook and set the float to fish a little over depth. A good general rig for static water on the broads this, and for casting extra distances use a bodied waggler which carries more shot.

For laying the bait hard on the bottom in a river (often called stret-pegging) fix a straight peacock waggler on the line with a band at both ends, just like a stick float, and fix just one large shot, an AA or swan, 6 inches from the hook (see Diagram 5, Fig. 2). If extra shot are required condense them into a mini-ledger (as in Diagram 5, Fig. 1) because shot down the line are not required. The secret of stret-pegging is to fish with the float lying perfectly flat and set at least a couple of feet over depth. In strong currents it will need to be fished 5 or 6 feet over depth or even more. Just consider how the line is curved by the force of the current in Diagram 5, Fig. 2, and you can see why. Always cast downstream and across so the float comes to rest directly down from the rod tip, although the bait might be situated a little further out. Bites are invariably very bold, with the float simply cocking and slipping straight under without any prior warning, other than an occasional 'shake' from the float.

This method of stret-pegging, laying-on, float-ledgering – call it what you will – is a killing method of presenting a static bait. It works on a whole variety of occasions when after river fish, from the roach and bream of the broads to taking specimen roach, bream, chub and barbel from the upper reaches of the Bure, Wensum, Yare and Waveney. What's more, simply by adding a luminous element to the tip of the float, it is a method which can be used after dark to take those extra shy whoppers. From the upper Wensum alone stret-pegging after dark has produced for me double figure barbel, chub to nearly 6 lb. and countless roach over 2 lb. So I have numerous good reasons for recommending it. Try it for yourself and see.

QUICK REFERENCE GUIDE to boat hire and slipways within the tidal Broadland system where anglers can launch their own dinghies.

BROADS

Barton Broad (leading to River Ant)
Slipway opposite the Barton Angler Hotel, launching costs £3 (Tel: 01692 630740).
Slipway at Cox's Boatyard, costs £5 (Tel: 01692 536206).

Great Ormesby (Eels Foot Broad) Broad
No boat launching. Angling dinghies can be hired from The Eels Foot Hotel at £10. Special disabled boat available – free of charge (Tel: 01493 730342). Angling dinghies also available (costing £8) from Mr. Barnes at the broad's southern end via the A1064 road adjacent to Filby Broad (Tel: 01493 368142). Boats can be taken beneath road bridge into Filby Broad.

Hickling Broad (leading to River Thurne)
Slipway at Whispering Reeds Boatyard, costs £7 (Tel: 01692 598314). Whispering Reeds also rent out angling dinghies at £16.50 per day.

Horsey Mere (Waxham Cut)
Dinghy with outboard motor cost £15 from Mr. Matthews at Waxham Cut (Tel: 01692 598630). Winter months only.

Oulton Broad (leading to River Waveney)
Slipway situated at The Water Sports Centre at the rear of Nicholas Everet Park. Launching is free with parking 100 yards away.

Rockland Broad (leading to River Yare)
Slipway is adjacent to the dyke in Rockland St. Mary with key to gate across slipway available from Mr. Saxton (Tel: 01508 538622). Cost for launching is £2.

Little Ormesby (Sportman's) Broad
No boat launching. Angling dinghies are for hire from Paul or Debbie at the Kingfisher Jetty at £10 per day (Tel: 01493 748724). These can be taken beneath the road bridge into Rollesby Broad, Lily, Great Ormesby (Eels Foot) Broad or Filby Broad. Electric outboards are permitted.

South Walsham Broad
Boat hire at £10 per day from Russell Marine Limited (Tel: 01603 270262).

Wroxham Broad (leading to River Bure)
Slipway and car park is adjacent to the Yacht Club at the Broad. A charge of £5 is made to anglers launching their own dinghies (Tel: Yacht Club: 01603 782808).

RIVERS

River Ant – Wayford Bridge
Slipway is adjacent to Urwins Day Boats and anglers may launch their own dinghies free of charge. Anglers' dinghies cost £15 per day from Urwins Day Boats. These are bookable in advance only (Tel: 01692 582071).

River Ant – Stalham Staithe
Slipway at Richardsons Boatyard costs £7.30 (Tel: 01692 581081).

River Bure – Horning
Slipway adjacent to the Swan Public House costs £5 with the key available from Ralph's Newsagent of Lower Street (Tel: 01692 630434). Can only be used 6.30 a.m. – 6.00 p.m.

River Bure - Wroxham
Rowing dinghies cost £10 and aluminium boats with engine cost £28 from Fineway Leisure of Riverside Road (Tel: 01603 782309).

River Bure – Upton
Slipway is situated at the end of Upton Dyke and is for public use. It can accommodate dinghies no longer than 14 feet. Adjacent public car park.

River Chet – Loddon Marina
Slipway costs £5 at Greenway Marine (Tel: 01508 520397).
Slipway costs £4 at Princess Cruisers and angling dinghies cost £10 (Tel: 01508 520353).
Angling dinghies cost £10 from Loddon Boatyard (Tel: 01508 528735).

River Thurne – Martham Ferry
Angling punts cost £25 per day from Thurne Boat Building (Tel: 01493 740303).

River Thurne – Potter Heigham
Slipway at Phoenix Fleet Boatyard costs £6 all year round. 17 foot dinghy for hire at £30 per day including motor (Tel: 01692 670460).

River Waveney – Geldeston
Slipway at Rowan Craft costs £4.50 (Tel: 01508 518208).

River Waveney – Beccles Quay
Slipway adjacent to Yacht Station (Tel: 01502 712225) is free but only from April to November. It is boarded up during the winter months and not usable.

River Waveney – Beccles
Slipway at Aston Boats costs £10 per day. Angling dinghies to hire cost £10 per day (Tel: 01502 713960). Open all year.

River Waveney – Burgh St. Peter
Slipway at the Waveney Inn Public House costs £5 all year round (Tel: 01502 677217).

River Waveney – Burgh Castle Marina
Slipway at the Marina costs £10 usable only between 9.00 a.m. and 6.00 p.m. (Tel: 01493 780331).

River Wensum - Bishopgate Bridge, Riverside Road, Norwich
Customers of the Red Lion Public House may use the slipway free of charge. There is a charity box for non customers (contact Mr. J. Barlow Tel: 01603 620154).

River Wensum – Friars Quay, City Centre
Slipway is behind riverside flats. Launching from this steep slipway is free. Cars and trailers must not be left adjacent to the slipway. Difficult area to park car and trailer.

River Yare – Brundall
Slipway costs £5 and angling dinghies £10 from Fencraft (Tel: 01603 715011). Angling dinghies (rowing) cost £15 and (with engine) £30, from Brundall Angling and Yare Boatique (Tel: 01603 715289).

River Yare – Reedham Ferry
Slipway controlled by Reedham Ferry Inn Public House. Cost for launching £3 (Tel: 01493 700429).

River Yare – Thorpe, Norwich
Slipway costs £5. Rowing boats at £10 or with either electric or petrol engine at £20 from Griffin Marine who also sell tackle and bait (Tel: 01603 433253).

THE BROADS

BARTON BROAD, Norfolk

Barton Broad covers some 150 acres and is fed by the tidal River Ant which furrows down the centre of the broad and is well marked for navigation. The Ant leaves Barton a little south of Pleasure Hill Island, which is navigable on both sides. Through the western gap a broad dyke leads off to the Old Gay Staithe and the Barton Lodge Hotel. There is a £3 charge for non-residents wishing to launch their own boats from the hotel slipway (Tel: 01692 630740). There is also a slipway at Cox's Boatyard costing £5 (Tel: 01692 536206). Further along the dyke, close to Neatishead village, there is excellent fishing particularly on mild days during the winter months. This is because roach and rudd join the bream shoals and often leave the broad itself to avoid the salt tides which may penetrate high up the River Ant. Caster and maggot baits prove most fruitful in this dyke.

Where the Ant enters the broad at the northern end, a dyke leads off to Barton Turf Staithe and Inn. All fishing on the broad is by boat and the visitor should make sure he has mud weights on board, before leaving the slipway. Ironically, at the time of my writing this in March 2002, an angling dinghy cannot be hired at Barton Broad. So anglers must launch their own craft from the two available slipways. Remember also always row slowly and with the least amount of noise when approaching your swim. Avoid clanging things like bait tins and vacuum flasks, etc., on the decking, for these vibrations are the quickest way to ensure poor sport. Lastly try to moor as far away from your intended swim

as casting permits. To alleviate the broad of phosphorus-rich muds dredging was started during the mid 1990s. Called the Clearwater 2000 project this massive dredging operation was carried out by the Broads Authority in conjunction with the Soap and Detergent Industry Association's Environmental Trust, Norfolk Wildlife Trust, the Environment Agency, English Nature and Anglian Water. It was completed in 2001 and included the planting of lilies in addition to removing much of the broad's sediment to a depth of 6 feet.

Bream may be taken from almost anywhere and can be encouraged to feed by offering some light cereal groundbait. Bread and maggots are the most popular hook baits but the bigger bream and tench sometimes show a preference for worms. Watch out for eels though. Laying well on the bottom with float tackle will nearly always sort out the quality fish, while 'bream flats', roach and the occasional rudd are often taken on the drop. It pays to experiment if bites are not forthcoming and even to consider leaving a baited swim should sport not materialise. It will be found that early morning and evening sessions are particularly worthwhile and anglers who actually fish through the night often take huge bream hauls. Most fish run from around 12 oz. to 4 lb., but much larger bream do exist. Tench of reasonable size are taken periodically close to the reed islands or among the patches of surface weed. Winter pike fishing can prove a little inconsistent on the broad proper. Best prospects are in and around Neatishead Dyke and particularly around Cox's Boatyard and

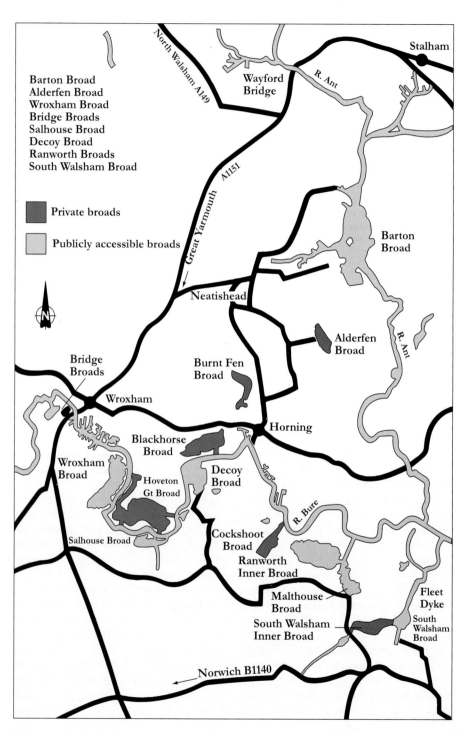

up the River Ant all the way to Wayford Bridge.

Route. To reach Barton Broad from Norwich take the A1151 road to one and a half miles beyond Wroxham and then take the Neatishead road. In Neatishead village keep straight ahead to reach the Barton Lodge Hotel and boats or turn left and follow the signposts to Barton Turf and Staithe.

BRIDGE BROAD (WEST), Wroxham, Norfolk

This two acre irregular shaped western end of Bridge Broad (divided off from the eastern end) and sometimes called Little Bridge Broad is full of nooks and crannies and averages about 4 feet deep. There is a prolific head of roach and hybrids plus some good pike during the winter months. Access is by boat only from the River Bure just a few hundred yards upstream (via the southern bank) of Wroxham Bridge immediately beyond the railway bridge. Fishing dinghies are available in Wroxham from Fineway Leisure (Tel: 01603 782309).

DECOY BROAD, Woodbastwick, Norfolk

This large sheet of water covering over 30 acres is controlled by the Norwich and District Angling Association and is boat fishing for members only. Membership from the secretary, Mr. C. Wigg, 3 Coppice Avenue, Norwich (Tel: 01603 423625) or local tackle dealers. Boats are bookable in advance from the secretary and local tackle shops.

There is a deep area through the centre of the broad and shallow water with large lily beds around the perimeter where the bottom is largely of mud. The colour tends to fluctuate due to the influx of water from the River Bure which feeds the broad. Decoy holds a head of bream in the 1½ – 4

lb. range which are not always easy to track down and a prolific head of roach under the pound. Summer sport with light float tackle can be excellent, providing the broad holds some colour. And there is always a chance of contacting a tench which run to over 4 lb. Other species are eels, a few perch and some cracking pike. Among a fair head of jacks plus fish running into double figures there are one or two real whoppers, best being a 32 pounder in 1982.

Route. Take the B1140 to a distance of about six miles beyond Norwich and turn left at the signpost to Woodbastwick village at Primrose Corner and proceed along road skirting Woodbastwick church. Then turn left at the cottages at the bottom of the hill. Follow sign to Decoy Broad and park in space provided behind cottages.

HICKLING BROAD AND HEIGHAM SOUND, Norfolk

The area of Hickling Broad and Heigham Sound covers some 700 acres. The two are joined together by Whiteslea and boats may navigate between them via Deep Dyke. This entire area is linked with the coloured and tidal waters of the River Thurne so that the further north one travels the clearer the water becomes. The best sport is usually to be had well away from the boat traffic and the never-ending swell it produces in and around the countless reedy bays and inlets. Although after dark the boating channel can really come alive.

Depth other than in the boating channel seldom exceeds 4 feet and there are large patches of weed, not always apparent whenever the broad is coloured by algae bloom. Hickling, largest of all the broads, contains vast quantities of roach from a couple of ounces up to a pound with ever-increasing number of beautiful rudd. There are also a few perch and tench plus some very big pike among hordes of jacks. The bream here grow large, averaging between 4 and 6 lb., and on the right day over 100 lb. catches are not uncommon. One of the largest catches, over 1000 lb. of bream to 7 lb. was made in 1994 by four holiday-makers boat fishing at night during a three day stint. These large bream, which can often prove difficult to track down if the surface is ruffled so that bubbles and the odd rolling fish are not evident, are sometimes scared off by heavy groundbaiting. So it pays to go easy by fishing at a distance and loose feeding with a catapult, unless night fishing, when the shoals usually move over a cereal carpet some time during the hours of darkness. Good areas are along the western shoreline near Catfield Dyke and at the southern end near the mouth of Deep Dyke.

In Deep Dyke itself there is good sport from bream after dark as they move through from Heigham Sound. Regular groundbaiting throughout the night, with breadflake or lobworms on the hook, accounts for large bream catches, including the occasional hybrids in the 2 – 3 lb. range. I have enjoyed some super evenings here, and always around dawn the bream suddenly switch off the feed and the roach come on until the cruisers start ploughing through. The point where Deep Dyke merges with Heigham South is also a good bream and roach area. Fishing near to the actual boat channel between the marker posts and the reed islands can be good at times and when the boat traffic ceases the channel itself fishes well, particularly at night.

Travelling further south towards the bottom of the Sound where it funnels into Candle Dyke, depth is slightly better and some good roach bags are taken all along this reach during the autumn, right the way down, past the old eel set to the junction with the River Thurne.

The huge expanse of Hickling Broad can be seen in the distance with access via deep dyke (foreground) from Heigham Sound

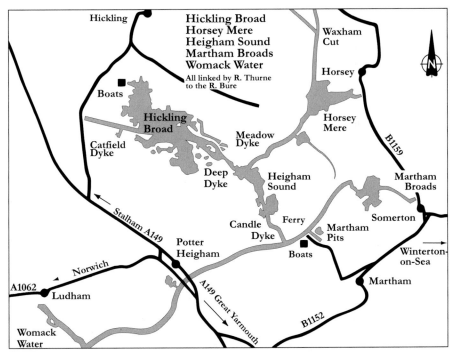

There are good bream bags here for
night hawks, even during the winter
months and, of course, pike fishing is
excellent. In recent years several pike
over 25 lb. have been taken on ledgered
deadbaits in this vicinity but there are
numerous jacks to wade through.

There is a little bank fishing at the start of
Candle Dyke and along parts of Deep
Dyke. But just about everywhere else is
surrounded by marshland thick with
Norfolk reeds. It is in fact the epitome of
how a Norfolk broad should look and
fishing is exclusively by boat. One may
either hire a boat from Martham Ferry
and navigate along the Thurne up
through Candle Dyke into Heigham
South, or obtain one from the northern
end of Hickling and start from there. The
actual distance by boat from the top end
of Hickling to Martham Ferry is the best
part of four miles. It is, therefore,
advisable to put some thought into

planning a fishing trip and hire a boat
well in advance.

Boat Hire.
MARTHAM – Thurne Boat Building
(Tel: 01493 740303) have punts at £25 a
day.
HICKLING – Whispering Reeds
Boatyard (Tel: 01692 598314) have angling
boats available at £16.50 per day.
Route. From Norwich take the A1151 to
just beyond Wroxham and turn on to the
A1062 to Potter Heigham. From there
turn south and cross the Thurne on to the
A149 and take the B1152 at the next
crossroads into Martham. For Hickling
and the boatyards turn north on to the
A149 and follow signposts.

HORSEY MERE, Norfolk
Horsey Mere is a nature reserve of
approximately 100 acres, linked to the
tidal water of the River Thurne via

Meadow Dyke, situated at the top of Heigham Sound. There is also a dyke which is part-source of Horsey and which enters at its northern end known as Waxham Cut. Horsey offers similar fishing to Hickling Broad in that it is generally shallow and may be quite clear at times, with prolific summer weed growth. There is a good stock of roach, rudd, perch and bream with numbers of fish in the 6 – 7 lb. range. A 10½ pounder was taken here by Mr. C. Barker in 1994. But Horsey has always been most renowned for its fine head of specimen pike. The 40 lb. 1 oz. pike caught here on a dead roach in 1967 by Peter Hancock once held the English record prior to the stocks being wiped out by *Prymnesium* in the late 1960s. But sport with large pike is now back to an enjoyable level again and most winters see at least one monster over 30 lb. being caught. The fishing is controlled by Mr. J. Buxton of Horsey Hall and anglers are allowed to boat fish the broad from 16 June to 31 October. There is then a long pause for the conservation of wildfowl until 1 March when the mere reopens to anglers until the end of the season. Pike anglers should note that livebaiting is NOT allowed. There are no boats for hire at Horsey so anyone wishing to boat fish must make the long journey up through Meadow Dyke from either Martham or Hickling.

For Boats contact Whispering Reeds of Hickling (Tel: 01692 598314) or Thurne Boat Building at Martham Ferry (Tel: 01493 740303). Alternatively, a boat with engine is available from Mr. Matthews of Waxham Cut (Tel: 01692 598630). This is in fact the quickest way of getting on to the broad, Waxham Cut being accessible from a lane off the B1159 coast road between Waxham and Horsey. Once on

Horsey Mere a warden will come round to boat anglers. A charge of £2 per rod is made. There is also a small amount of bank fishing from Horsey village staithe (anglers can fish here all winter through) where tickets costing £2 per rod (two rods only) are available from either the Staithe Stores (summer months only) or Mr. D. Applegate of Farm House, Horsey (Tel: 01493 393511).

Route. To reach Horsey Staithe by road take the A47 from Norwich to Acle and then the A1064 and B1152 into West Somerton. Turn north in the village on to the B1159 which leads direct to Horsey. The hall and staithe are close to the road.

LITTLE ORMESBY, ROLLESBY, LILY, GREAT ORMESBY AND FILBY BROADS, Norfolk

Covering over 800 acres these broads form the largest complex of angling waters in the whole of Norfolk. What is more they are not connected to a tidal channel and therefore not overrun by holiday craft. The only boats allowed are a few sailing dinghies and the craft of anglers. In fact, because the banks are marshland and thickly reeded, only boat fishing is possible, although there are several good bankside swims adjacent to the two roads which bisect these broads (see map).

Route. To reach the A149 road separating Little Ormesby Broad from Rollesby Broad take the A1151 from Norwich to

---

Top Right: During a calm morning's pike fishing on Oulton Broad, John's wife Jo puts the bacon on, as the pike are unco-operative

Bottom Right: One of the two entrances from the River Bure onto Wroxham Broad, home of the Norfolk Broads Yacht Club, and great roach and pike fishing

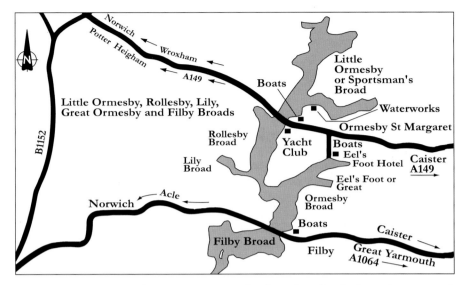

Map showing Little Ormesby, Rollesby, Lily, Great Ormesby and Filby Broads, with locations including Norwich, Potter Heigham, Wroxham, A149, B1152, Little Ormesby or Sportsman's Broad, Waterworks, Boats, Rollesby Broad, Yacht Club, Ormesby St Margaret, Eel's Foot Hotel, Caister A149, Lily Broad, Eel's Foot or Great Ormesby Broad, Acle, Norwich, Boats, Filby Broad, Filby, Caister, Great Yarmouth A1064.

Wroxham and on to Stalham. Carry on along the Stalham by-pass over the River Thurne at Potter Heigham and on to Ormesby St. Margaret. To reach the A1064 road separating Filby Broad from Great Ormesby (Eel's Foot) Broad take the A47 from Norwich passing through Acle and follow signposts to Filby.

LITTLE ORMESBY (SPORTSMAN'S) BROAD

This, the most northerly of these five broads, is completely reed-fringed and fairly deep through the middle section. At the junction of the long eastern arm there is around 9 feet of water close to the water tower, a favourite winter piking area. But the arm itself eventually shallows off to between 3 and 4 feet. There are really big tench, best sought along the reedy margins, and bream

Top Left: An aerial photo showing how the River Thume bisects Martham North (right) and South (left) Broads at Somerton

Bottom Left: Salhouse Broad just off the tidal River Bure, Norfolk

shoals with individual specimens over 8 lb. Pike are numerous and 20 pounders are regularly taken from October onwards. When there is a good blow on go for static or twitched deadbaits. And in cold clear water conditions free swimming or paternostered livebaits sort out the better fish. T. Wilson took a 32 lb. pike here in 1989. To fish this broad boats can be hired from Paul and Debbie of Kingfisher Boat Hire (Tel: 01493 748724). These cost £10 per day and may be taken beneath the road bridge into Rollesby Broad and into the other broads in this system. Anglers may NOT launch their own boats to fish this group of broads. ONLY electric outboard motors are allowed.

ROLLESBY BROAD

This wide reed-fringed sheet of water varies from 3 feet deep in the margins, where specimen tench are to be located, to over 10 feet deep through the middle channel at the road end. Mixed catches of roach, hybrids and bream are taken on light float tackle, baiting with either maggots, casters or breadflake in conjunction with a little cereal groundbait. Pike fishing hots up during October when the temperatures start to fall and among numerous pike running into high double figures there is a good sprinkling of fish between 20 and 25 lb. Fish the reed beds early on and the deeper water once winter has really set in. All methods work well but deadbaits invariably produce the biggies. Once the more common baits such as herring and mackerel have lost their effectiveness give oddities such as eels, lampreys, smelt, sand eels and brown or rainbow trout a try. The pike definitely 'group up' on these broads, probably because shoals of bait fish are somewhere close by, so do not be in too much of a hurry to move when the first pike has been taken.

LILY BROAD

A lovely intimate little broad averaging between just 3 and 5 feet deep. After rowing down Rollesby's eastern shoreline or coming across the bottom end of Great Ormesby (see map) 'Lily' is reached and once inside there is a definite feeling of friendliness. The southern bank is mostly alder-carr and the best areas are through the middle or along the reed lined margins of the northern shore. Good stocks of roach and bream plus a few tench and rudd are to be found here along with a most prolific head of pike running well into the 20 lb. bracket. In the strongest winds calm water can always be found and float fishing with maggots or casters over a carpet of loose feed produces some good mixed catches, especially when the water holds a fair colour.

GREAT ORMESBY (EEL'S FOOT) BROAD

To fish this long 100 acre broad boats may be hired at the northern end from the Eel's Foot Hotel who have boats available at £10 a day, plus a special disabled boat (Tel: 01493 730342), and at the southern end from the café who have boats available at £8 a day (Tel: Mr. Barnes on 01493 368142).

Some huge catches of bream come from this broad with individual specimens topping 10 lb. Favourite areas are at the southern end where it merges with Rollesby, and off Jerusalem Bay, halfway down the eastern shore. Tall reeds grow from the shallows all along the margins and there are numerous little bays and inlets, all worth exploring for tench and bream not to forget the pike which are widespread. Working a livebait or plug along the reeds is an exciting way of catching pike here. But as with all these broads, a static deadbait either hard on or suspended just off bottom catches the whoppers, with perhaps a paternostered livebait running a close second.

FILBY BROAD

This is the most southerly of the complex and, particularly during westerly winds, the most coloured. There is no boatshed on the broad and anglers must row beneath the A1064 road bridge into Filby after hiring craft at the southern end of Great Ormesby from the café (Tel: Mr. Barnes on 01493 368142). Filby is heavily reed-fringed all the way round, with the deepest area about 100 yards directly out from the road bridge. It is a consistently productive area for pike during the winter months and for both roach and bream through the summer. When there is a good colour roach can be readily taken in good bags with fish topping the pound all over the broad. The largest bream, however, which run to over 10 lb. can prove elusive at times. Eels to 6 lb. have been caught here. The best pike fishing is when the broad has a good ripple on it and I personally rate the chances of really big pike turning up when a stiff south-westerly or westerly rips down the entire length. Once again lures and livebaits produce more but deadbaits seem generally to produce the largest pike in these broads. Derek Allen took a 31 lb. specimen here in 1983.

MARTHAM NORTH BROAD,
Somerton, Norfolk

There are two smallish, private broads at Somerton and they lie immediately to the north and the south of the River Thurne which bisects them. Both are owned by the Norfolk Wildlife Trust and are very weedy, gin clear and very shallow. Both are also strictly private to anglers. However during the past decade the N.W.T. has tried an experiment from October through to February by allowing just limited numbers of pike anglers to sample the fabulous pike fishing. There are only two boats allowed each day and

fishing is on Thursday, Friday and Saturday only. Naturally these permits must be booked well in advance by writing to the N.W.T., 22 Thorpe Road, Norwich with a stamped addressed envelope for a permit application form. This should then be sent with the S.A.E. to the Warden, Mr. R. Starling, 1 The Street, Somerton, Norfolk including the fee of £5 and a selection of preferable days from 1 October. To secure a permit, it's a bit of a rigmarole, but the pike fishing on Martham North Broad could prove well worth the effort as fish over 30 lb. have been caught. It must be pointed out, however, that permission to fish by the N.W.T. will only continue so long as anglers abide by the rules by which the permits are granted, which includes no livebaiting and no artificial lures. Only deadbaiting for pike is allowed and the use of two rods only. Anglers must also only tie up to mooring stakes provided and not fish just anywhere in the Broad. At this point in time, however, the broad

My good friend the late Doug Allen from Norwich with one of the many big pike he caught from the Norfolk Broads

is in a recovery period from two consecutive bouts of *Prymnesium* which decimated stocks of all species during 2000 and 2001. It will, given time, return I am certain to its former glory.

Route. To reach Martham Ferry dyke take the A47 from Norwich to Acle and then the A1064 and B1152 into Martham village. Take Staithe Road which leads directly to Dyke and Ferry Boatyards.

OULTON BROAD, Lowestoft, Suffolk

Oulton Broad is a large sheet of water in excess of 100 acres which is connected by a dyke to the tidal River Waveney. It is situated in the suburbs of Lowestoft and, due to this location, has in recent years become a playground for holidaymakers. Much of the broad, especially at weekends, is taken up by pleasure boats, hydroplanes and water skiing enthusiasts. But there is still enough water for the angler and from October onwards he virtually has the entire broad to himself.

For many years Oulton was without question the finest perch fishery in Great Britain. The British record weighed 4 lb. 12 oz. and was caught here in 1962 by Sid Baker of Norwich. However, this glorious era of monster perch ended around 1968 when fishing in general started to deteriorate. Today a 4 lb. perch is as rare from Oulton as it is anywhere but perch are now commonly taken up to a pound plus along with roach of a good average size. Occasionally a tench turns up but in terms of specimen fish from the broad anglers now turn to bream which are taken during the summer months to close on 9 lb., the average size being in the 4 – 6 lb. range. There are also plenty of eels and flounders which devour maggots and worms eagerly. This is possibly a good reason for persevering with either bread or stewed wheat baits. But for anglers seeking a real challenge how about trying to lure one of the many mullet which invade the broad each summer? These super fighting estuary fish often fall to bread paste or maggot baits on light float tackle and individual specimens may reach 5lb. or more.

Pike fishing during the quiet winter months is excellent and towards the end of the season a big one from the broad is not unlikely, the best area being the huge reed-fringed bay along the south-western shore and in the north bay. All over the broad there is a general lack of weed growth and the bottom is largely of firm mud or clay, consequently the water is always well coloured. The depth fluctuates with a two foot drop in tides and there is a depth of between 5 and 9 feet. For mixed catches popular swims are found along the reedy margins of the North Bay, at the top of the eastern end, known locally as 'Dead End' and in the dyke at the western end which connects Oulton to the River Waveney. There is excellent fishing here and all the way up the Waveney. In fact the fishing in this area is possibly better than in the broad itself.

Night fishing for bream in Oulton Dyke can produce good bags during the summer months with individual specimens topping 6 lb. There is a little bank fishing but fishing from a boat is more rewarding. Anglers' dinghies may be launched free of charge from the slipway situated at the Water Sports Centre at the rear of Nicholas Everet Park.

Route. Take the A146 road from Norwich which actually separates Oulton Broad from Lake Lothing in the town of Lowestoft.

RANWORTH (including MALTHOUSE) BROAD, Norfolk

Ranworth is a large 100 acre broad fed by the tidal River Bure. It has both 'inner' and 'outer' sections which are separated by a series of stakes and a chaingate. This is to protect the inner broad which is actually a wildlife reserve and the larger of the two sections. Ranworth 'inner' is fairly shallow all over with no more than 5 feet of water and usually of a good colour. It is boat fishing only. The fishing is controlled by Norwich and District Angling Association and boats are available from the association via local tackle dealers or the secretary, Mr. C. Wigg, 3 Coppice Avenue, Norwich (Tel: 01603 423625).

Fishing is from 16 June to 30 September ONLY when the inner broad offers good mixed bags of roach, bream and hybrids in really peaceful surroundings. For the rest of the season the Inner Broad is closed to anglers. The outer section where the Bure is joined to the broad by a long dyke (also very good fishing) is known as Malthouse Broad. Fishing is free from the staithe and from the dyke and the Bure itself but during the summer months boat traffic spoils serious daytime angling. Early morning and late evenings can produce fair bream and roach to baits presented hard on the bottom over a groundbait carpet. Night fishing is good but winter fishing is a far better proposition on this part of the broad. A big pike is not unlikely.

Route. From Norwich take the B1140 to Panxworth. The Ranworth road is then well signposted and leads alongside the broad by the Maltsters Inn.

ROCKLAND BROAD, Norfolk

Rockland Broad is over 40 acres and is completely surrounded by marshland and fringed with tall reeds of the Norfolk 'house thatching' variety. At the start of the boat dyke at the southern end of the broad, adjacent to the road and the New Inn, Rockland Beck flows in from Poringland (see map), while at the northern end two separate navigable channels called Fleet and Short Dyke lead off Rockland into the tidal River Yare. There is a tidal rise and fall of around 3 feet and occasionally a particularly low

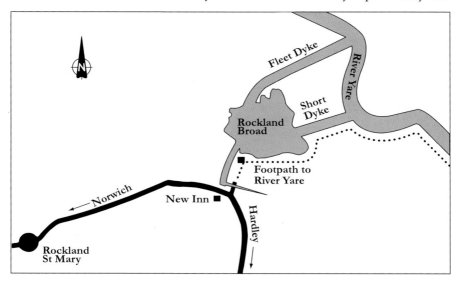

tide may leave boats high and dry. Visitors are therefore warned to be careful of mooring. In any event the best fishing is usually in or around the boat channels in the deeper water.

Being very weedy with huge expanses of water lilies in summer, the broad is a feeding ground for fish that come up from the Yare on the flood tide, like roach and bream. And at this period fishing is often at its best. Good sized bream are widespread with perhaps the chance of a real specimen. So too are roach and one generally takes fish of a high average size. This is found to be the same in both the dykes leading into the Yare and especially in the fast waters of the Yare itself. Tench live in the weed beds and occasionally one or a brace are taken. Although they average on the large size they are never common but the eels at Rockland are and so too are flounders.

Apart from a few rudd and perch, pike are perhaps the favourite quarry of Rockland fishers and one generally needs to wait until the end of September for the weeds to rot and vanish and for the water to clear a little before pike fishing becomes consistent, though working surface plugs during the summer months provide great fun. The average size is quite good and double figure fish are common with the occasional fish in excess of 20 lb. A fish said to weigh 31½ lb. was caught way back in 1912. All methods of pike fishing work well on Rockland though livebaiting has the edge and usually sorts out the better sized fish. Light to medium tackle is recommended especially when spinning around the margins for the countless jacks. Beware of the tough lily roots though.

Apart from a little bank fishing along Short Dyke to which there is a public footpath from the village (see map), Rockland can only be fished from a boat.

There are none locally available but anglers may launch their own craft from the slipway in Rockland Dyke for which a £2 charge is made. Contact Mr. Saxton (Tel: 01508 538622) who provides a key for unlocking the gate across the slipway for the owners, Rockland Poors Trust. Alternatively boats may be hired further upriver at Brundall from Fencraft (Tel: 01603 715011) or Brundall Angling and Yare Boatique (Tel: 01603 715289) and motored downstream into Rockland Broad.

SALHOUSE BROAD, Salhouse, Norfolk

Salhouse Broad lies between Wroxham and Woodbastwick on the southern bank of the River Bure. It has two separate entrance dykes leading into the Bure for the angler to navigate his boat through. Once on the broad there is a small charge which is collected by the warden. There is also some bank fishing for which a charge is also made and unless one arrives by boat from either Wroxham or Horning one must reach the broad by road via the village of Salhouse. However the final stage necessitates a long walk. Depth averages around 5 feet and there is some good general fishing to be had on light float tackle with roach, hybrids and bream plus the odd perch and tench. There is also a reasonable head of pike on Salhouse, including fish of over 20 lb. However, perhaps because of the location which means a fair row from Wroxham, Salhouse Broad is comparatively little fished, especially in the winter.

Deadbaiting or livebait paternosting should pay off well here for there is good colour and the bottom is not too silty with little weed to worry about.

Boats may be hired from Fineway Leisure in Wroxham (Tel: 01603 782309) and motored downstream. Alternatively, anglers may launch their own craft from nearby Wroxham Broad from the slipway adjacent to the Yacht Club (Tel: 01603 782808).

Route. To approach the broad from the road with a view to bank fishing take the A1151 from Norwich, turning right at the signpost to Salhouse village which is just before Wroxham. Alternatively follow route directions for Wroxham Broad if wishing to launch your own craft from the Yacht Club's slipway.

SOUTH WALSHAM BROAD, Norfolk

South Walsham Broad is similar to Ranworth, in as much as it also has an inner and outer section. The inner part, substantially larger than the outer, is private and barred to anglers. The outer section is fairly shallow and fishing is almost entirely from boats. Much of the bankside is privately owned except for the right bank of Fleet Dyke and the village staithe where anglers may bank fish and launch their own boats. Boat hire at £10 per day from Russell Marine Limited (Tel: 01603 270262).

The dyke offers good fishing and is between 4 and 7 feet deep. It joins the broad to the River Bure where the fishing is also good and the depth greater. River traffic after 8 a.m. during the summer months is heavy and the fishing as a result difficult. Night fishing is exceptionally good here, almost anywhere along Fleet Dyke. Species to be expected on the broad are bream, roach and some hybrids and good pike. Winter piking is very good indeed, but the broad is prone to salt tides. Bream are the predominating species and may run up to the 5 – 6 lb. mark with an average weight of between 2 and 3 lb., although there are numerous skimmers to wade through.

Route. Take the B1140 from Norwich, going beyond the town of South Walsham. The first left turn out of town is signposted to the broad and staithe.

SURLINGHAM BROAD, Surlingham, Norfolk

Surlingham Broad lies on the southern bank of the River Yare between Postwick and Strumpshaw and is directly opposite Brundall on the north bank. Over the years it has been grossly reduced by silting and local people talk of its area once being ten times its present 18 acres. However, although on ebb tides much of the broad is just a maze of mud flats, good sized roach and a few bream enter the broad via the two connecting dykes on the flood tide. So angling is certainly a viable proposition. Pike fishing is particularly rewarding.

There has been a little dredging work in recent years at the mouth of the dykes where one enters the broad from the Yare and these spots, especially along the downstream dyke, are exceptionally good for mixed catches. Night fishing can be particularly rewarding but wherever anglers fish on the broad they are requested to bear in mind that the broad is, in fact, a nature reserve. The nearest slipway for boat owners is at Coldham Hall (Tel: 01508 538591) where the landlord can arrange launching facilities, via his slipway shared with the local sailing club. One may also hire boats from Brundall to reach the broad and to fish the tidal Yare. (See 'Quick Reference Guide to boat hire and slipways within tidal Broadland',p.73).

Route. To reach Brundall from Norwich take the A47 road. To reach Surlingham Ferry, take the Rockland St. Mary road from Norwich, turning left at Bramerton to the village of Surlingham.

WOMACK WATER, Ludham, Norfolk

Womack Water is a most attractive narrow fishery of about three-quarters of a mile which leads off the northern bank of the River Thurne, just one and a half miles upstream of Thurne Mouth. It is in fact a lengthy collection of bays, inlets and an island, with what is left of the old Womack Broad at the north-western end close by the public staithe. Boats may tie up here and there is a mooring fee. Bank fishing is free from the staithe and also from the half-mile stretch starting at the County Sailing Club, right down to the junction of the Thurne. There is a slight draw on the water, which is always well coloured and depth varies between three and 5 feet with odd holes around the island and boat dykes.

Sport can be patchy but there are many 'bream flats' present with better sized fish up to the 4 lb. mark. Roach are quite widespread, including the odd big hybrid. Eels, of course, are plentiful as they are all over Broadland. There appears to be a deficiency of pike here though, with just the odd fish running into double figures taken during the winter. Night fishing is good for bream with bread baits for the better fish and maggots or worms for sheer numbers, although meaty baits are prone to attract eels during the summer months. Winter fishing is very good, especially when the Thurne is full of floodwater and some nice roach are taken on light float tackle with maggots or caster proving effective.

Route. To reach Womack Water take the A1151 from Norwich to Wroxham. Then take the B1354 to Ludham village where a well signposted lane leads to the staithe.

WROXHAM BROAD, Norfolk

Fed by the tidal River Bure and the home of the Norfolk Broads Yacht Club, Wroxham Broad covers well over 100 acres of good fishing. The centre of the broad is deepish and generally left well alone from an angling point of view, particularly when the yachts are racing. There is a little bankside fishing close to the moorings of the Yacht club but the visitor would do well to go afloat and explore the countless weedy bays and inlets in the shallow water at either the northern or southern ends of the broad.

Wroxham Broad holds an immense head of quality roach and 20 lb. bags are not uncommon. It fishes well all summer through up until the first hard frosts and among the roach are odd hybrids, perch and bream. In recent years the bream have been difficult to track down but the occasional bag including fish over 4 lb. is taken by anglers who night fish. The broad undoubtedly holds some very large pike as fish between 25 and 30 lb. are taken each winter from the River Bure close to the two entrances. These fish obviously migrate and follow the roach shoals from river to broad and so there is much scope for those willing to specialise.

Boats may be hired in Wroxham and rowed down the Bure into the broad via either of the two connecting dykes. Alternatively there is a £5 charge to boat owners wishing to launch their own craft from the picnic area adjacent to the Yacht Club (Tel: 01603 782808).

Route. To reach the Yacht Club from Norwich take the A1151 turning right just before Wroxham following the signpost to Broad House and on to the Club. To reach the Wroxham boatyards carry along the A1151 into Wroxham centre.

STILLWATERS

When I first penned *Where to Fish in Norfolk and Suffolk* way back in 1973 I wrote that *'Much of the finest fishing exists in the unlimited acres of ponds, gravel pits, lakes and meres, all isolated from boats, pollution and water abstraction, not only of today but particularly for the future.'* Since that time 30 years have elapsed and in addition to my hair turning from dark brown to silvery grey, the balance has indeed swung away from river fishing and changed no less dramatically. We cannot prevent the sands, or more appropriately the silts, of time from slowly strangling our waterways – unfortunately.

To maintain a stabilised situation with present fish stocks in our rivers is, I feel, the very best we can hope for. Indeed, there are even some actual improvements, such as the proliferation of good sized chub and barbel – even carp throughout the upper reaches of the rivers Yare, Bure, Waveney and Wensum, albeit at the expense of the roach, though cormorants have much to answer for in this department. And the sooner we have a combined government, M.A.F.F. and an Environment Agency admission which recognises that this predatory sea bird needs to be put on the vermin list the better. Personally I would first and foremost sooner be long-trotting a fast river for roach than enjoying any other kind of fishing. But then again I would rather enjoy the fruits of a well stocked carp lake or pit than have access to no fishing at all. And this swing away from rivers to the excitement and quality of stillwater fishing currently available is proved by the fact that there is now a choice of no less than 380 different waters in this chapter compared to 289 in 1995, 190 in 1989 and just 37 way back in 1973.

Many of these lakes and meres are situated in public parks, private estates or adjacent to country mansions where fishing is available only on the strength that anglers will respect other people's property. Similarly, many of the gravel pits are club or syndicate controlled, with day tickets available to all anglers. It is therefore essential and up to each individual to respect the fishing of others, be it a tiny pond or a secluded lake, by adhering to the country code of leaving no litter and in general leaving the bankside as it was found. Lastly in an effort to make the whereabouts of accessible fishing available to all, should any reader know of day ticket or club waters not mentioned in this chapter perhaps he or she would be kind enough to contact me.

John Wilson
Great Witchingham 2002

Correspondence please to:
Barnwell's Timescape Publishing Ltd
Tel: 01692 503057.

CLOSE SEASON LAWS

Anglers should note that in 1995 the close season laws applying to stillwater fisheries, i.e., ponds, pits, lakes, reservoirs etc., were changed. Personally I think the worse thing we ever did was abolishing the old close season. But that's life. Of course the statutory close season for all RIVER systems, including the Norfolk and Suffolk Broads, ending on 14 March and starting again on 16 June still stands. Thank goodness. However, during this period fishing is now allowed on stillwaters provided the owner of that fishery concerned decides to waive the close season rules, as the then N.R.A, now the Environment Agency, has done.

Many fishery owners are, however, retaining the statutory close season in order to give their waters and accompanying wildlife a rest. So always check by asking the fishery owner, manager or bailiff of the water you intend fishing about close season rules, or lack of them, before starting off. Do not automatically assume that close season fishing is allowed. Many fisheries are now open all year round, and where this is so I have mentioned the fact.

STILLWATERS — DAY TICKET

ALDEBY HALL FARM PITS, Aldeby, Suffolk

Secluded and most interesting collection of five small pits offering a variety of species including rudd, crucian carp, tench, bream and a strong head of king carp reaching to 30 lb. Ideal fishing for youngsters with wooden stagings in all swims, some of which cater especially for disabled anglers. Depths vary between 2 and 8 feet and the water is always well coloured. There are adjacent car parking and toilet facilities. For additional information telephone 01502 677648. Day tickets are available from the bailiff who calls round. These cost £5 for adults and £3 for juniors, senior citizens and disabled anglers. A special £75 season permit is also available. Caravan site only one mile away at Toft Monks.

Route. Take the A146 from Norwich to just before Beccles, turning on to the A143 at a large roundabout. One mile further on turn right to Aldeby and one mile further on again look for a track on the right going through the farm. Proceed down the track (actually an old railway track) and half a mile further on the pits are on the left, bordered by woodlands. They are well signposted.

ALTON WATER RESERVOIR, Holbrook, Suffolk

This 350 acre water is really unique. It is the only reservoir within the counties of Norfolk and Suffolk and the first developed coarse fishing reservoir in Great Britain. It was started in 1972 as a water storage project covering the Ipswich area. But Alton has materialised into very much more because, due to its size, other facilities have been catered for such as sub-aqua, sailing and nature reserves, etc. The Alton Water Users Panel advises the owners, Anglian Water, on a range of activities. Certain locations around the perimeter for instance have been designated for particular interests. It was opened for fishing in 1981. Almost everywhere there is a depth of between 8 and 12 feet, just three to four rod lengths out, though this fluctuates. Due to various reasons (dare I say cormorants?) the roach population here has certainly declined in recent years, although restocking has been done to compensate. The bream now average 5 lb. plus and of these there are huge shoals, but with little in the way of young fish coming through. So really fishing here is a 'specimen or nothing' situation. In terms of predators there are perch to be caught along with the occasional large pike and eel.

Access to the reservoir is from the B1080 road at Holbrook which is the main entrance and from Lemon's Hill Bridge at Tattingstone. Anglers must use the car parks provided at all times and note that tickets are not sold on the bank. These must be arranged in advance. Day tickets cost £2.50 (concessionary at £1.25) from the visitor centre and Holbrook Post Office and a few local tackle shops.

Route. To reach Alton take the B1080 or the A137 from Ipswich with access via Tattingstone and Holbrook respectively.

ATTLEBOROUGH FISH FARM LAKES, Besthorpe, Norfolk

The fishery comprises three man-made lakes and two canals. The 'first' is a well established kidney-shaped ex clay pit of around three-quarters of an acre with two islands. The water is always well coloured and depths vary between 4 and 10 feet. There are just nine prepared swims and the lake contains a head of carp into double figures plus tench, perch, roach, crucian carp and koi carp variants.

The 'second' lake is oblong-shaped and around half an acre with depths to 8 feet. There are 15 pegs and stocks are the same as the first lake, but much smaller fish. The 'third' lake is also oblong-shaped with three small islands and covers two acres, with depths between 6 and 10 feet. Its silver fish stock includes roach, rudd, bream, perch and tench.

The two canals are around 100 yards long and built specifically for pole fishing. They contain carp to 12 lb. Fishing is from 9 a.m. until 5.30 p.m. Day tickets cost £4 available from the farm shop on site.

Route. Take A11 from Norwich, turning left at Attleborough, signposted towards the town, then first left down Mill Lane. At the T-junction turn left into Silver Street and continue over bridge. Then turn left and around half a mile further on fishery entrance gates are on the right with adjacent parking and farm shop complex.

BALLANS PIT, Lyng, Norfolk

This tiny pit of around a quarter of an acre shelves to around 6 feet deep and contains roach, skimmer bream, perch to 2 lb. and carp to 8 lb. It is an ideal youngster's float water. Day tickets are £2.50 available on the bank and issued through Lyng and District A.C. who control the fishing.

Route. From Norwich take the A1067 Fakenham Road to one and a half miles past Lenwade and then take left turn to Lyng. Proceed over bridge spanning River Wensum adjacent to the mill and follow road around right bend. Take third lane on the left up Cadders Hill and 400 yards further on turn right on to bridle path. The pit is then 200 yards along path on the left.

BARHAM PIT, near Claydon, Suffolk

This four acre gravel pit has a small island and depths vary from 7 to 12 feet. The pit contains a strong head of roach, rudd, tench and bream plus a big head of carp to over 20 lb. A water which is popular with both match anglers and specimen hunters alike. Day tickets cost £4 dawn until dusk (£7 for a 24 hour ticket) and must be obtained in advance from Breakaway Tackle of Ipswich (Tel: 01473 741393). Youngsters under 16 must be accompanied by an adult.

Route. From Ipswich take the A14 and branch on to the Claydon Road (old Norwich Road). Turn left at Pest House Lane which leads directly to a large complex. The pit is then directly in front of you as you enter the complex.

BARFORD LAKES, Barford, Norfolk

This fishery comprises four man-made lakes each with depths fluctuating between 5 and 14 feet. The 'pleasure lake' is key-hole shaped around two acres and holds perch, roach, bream, rudd, tench, crucian carp and a good stock of king carp running into double figures plus ghost koi. Day tickets at £6 are available from the office prior to fishing. Toilet and disabled anglers' swims. No night fishing. There is a small shop stocking cold drinks, snacks, tackle sundries and limited bait.

The other two lakes are oblong and square in shape, hold 30 and 16 peg swims and are one and a half acres and three-quarters of an acre respectively with depths to 12 feet. These are only available for matches. The stocks include roach, perch, rudd and tench plus a prolific head of small carp. Match bookings at £5 per peg in advance only from Sarah Thomson (Tel: 01603 759624). There is also a starter lake less than the size of a tennis court, containing roach, rudd, crucian carp and small king carp. Day ticket reductions for beginners.

Route. From Norwich take the B1108 Watton Road into Barford and turn right opposite the Cock Public House. Proceed to T-junction and then turn right and go through village. Half a mile further on look for fishery signposts at entrance lane on the right.

BARTLES LODGE LAKES, Elsing, Norfolk

Set in beautifully landscaped countryside, these two spring-fed man-made lakes of around one acre apiece have tree clad islands and a variation in depths between 2 and 8 feet. There is a prolific head of roach, rudd and small tench plus koi, ghost koi and king carp running into high double figures. This is real bran tub fishing where simple techniques and baits are encouraged. Boilies are banned. Night fishing is allowed by residents only. An adjacent stable block has been converted into farmhouse accommodation for up to 16 anglers. Children under 15 are not allowed to fish unless accompanied by an adult. Day tickets cost £5 available from the bailiff who calls round. For additional information Tel: 01362 637177.

Route. From Norwich take the A1067 Fakenham Road and turn left opposite Bawdeswell Garden Centre towards Elsing. Cross over bridge spanning the River Wensum and turn right to the village. The lake is then next to the Mermaid Inn (excellent food) opposite Elsing church.

BLAXHALL DECOY, nr Snape Maltings, Suffolk

A two acre oblong-shaped man-made lake averaging 3 to 5 feet deep, nicely reeded around the perimeter with two small islands in the middle. Species include crucian carp to 1½ lb. plus common and mirror carp into double figures. There are also some nice roach over the pound, skimmer bream, rudd and a prolific head of tench averaging 3 – 4 lb. Owned by the Woodbridge and District A.C. which has an open membership. Contact the secretary, Geoff Abbot (Tel: 01394 383898) or local tackle dealers who sell club membership cards costing £30 yearly. Day tickets cost £5 from Saxmundham Angling Centre (Tel: 01728 603443) and Stuart Clay Traps in Melton (Tel: 01394 385567) which must be purchased in advance.

Route. From Saxmundham take the A12 to just before Farnham and turn left on to the A1094 heading towards Snape and Aldeburgh. After three-quarters of a mile the road goes beneath a railway line and then over a river. Half a mile past the river bridge look on the left for a track with signpost leading to Woodbridge and District Fishery. An adjacent car park.

BLICKLING LAKE, Aylsham, Norfolk

Blickling is a long, wide, very open water of over 20 acres set in the grounds of Blickling Hall, now owned by the National Trust. It is shallow and weedy at the Hall end with an average depth through the middle of around 6 feet all the way up the lake to the dam end where depth increases to over 10 feet in the middle. The most popular spot is naturally off the dam wall where a thick spinney shelters anglers from northerly winds. The lake holds a good head of roach to over the pound plus the odd perch and crucian carp. But the bream are what most anglers come to Blickling Hall for. In addition to huge shoals of skimmers from a few ounces upwards there are really strong shoals of fish between 5 and 8 lb. 100 lb. catches being quite common. The occasional bream over 10 lb. is also taken. There are also some nice tench to over 8 lb., and mirror carp to nearly 30 lb. Pike fishing here is excellent both for numbers and for big fish to over 20 lb., best being 34½ lb. taken in 2000. Pike fishing is not allowed until 1 October. NO NIGHT FISHING. Wheelchair anglers are well catered for at Blickling with two special stagings and over 100 yards of level banking along the dam wall.

Day tickets cost £5 (£3 for juniors and senior citizens) from the bailiff who calls round. Contact Mr. Cooper on 01263 734181 for additional information.

Route. Take A140 from Norwich to one mile beyond Aylsham. Go through the town (ignore bypass) and take the road on left to Blickling, immediately before Ingworth road bridge. After a short distance bear right when road divides and keep straight ahead for half a mile. This leads directly to the northern end of the lake and car park.

BLUE WATERS (SWAN LAKE), Woolpit, Suffolk

This picturesque flooded brick pit of some two acres shelves down to over 20 feet in places and the water is nearly always extremely clear. Species include roach, rudd, perch to over 3 lb. and pike, plus a nice head of bream to 7 lb. Day tickets cost £3 from the bailiff who calls round to anglers. Fishing is controlled by Mr. Baker (Tel: 01359 240293) for additional information.

Route. Take the A14 Stowmarket Road from Bury St. Edmunds and take the right turn off to Woolpit. Just before Woolpit village turn left and proceed down to a 'No Through Road' (old Stowmarket Road). The lake is then 600 yards further along on the right, hidden behind laurel hedging.

BODHAM POND, Bodham, Norfolk

An old marl pit of around half an acre with steep banks. It is deep one end and can be extremely weedy at times. Holds a good head of crucian carp and the occasional wildie, plus tench and rudd. Open all year round. Day tickets cost £1.50 (£1 juniors) from the post office within Bodham Village Stores, open 8.30 a.m. until 5.30 p.m. (Tel: 01263 588209 for additional information).

Route. From Norwich take the B1149 to Holt turning on to the A148 to Bodham. In the village turn right and then sharp right again down to a T-junction. Directly opposite is a lane with the pond situated 200 yards along on the left.

BOOTON CLAY PIT, Booton, Norfolk

A triangle-shaped beautifully wooded old pit of about four acres. The water is usually well coloured and for the most part quite deep with long peninsulas of reeds topping the shallow bars. It holds a prolific stock of tench between 3 and 5 lb. plus roach, rudd, pike and bream, including one or two whoppers. There is a prolific head of mirror carp running into double figures plus one or two exceptionally large specimens. Carp over 30 lb. have been caught in seasons past. A 24 lb. pike was taken in 2002. Day tickets cost £5 (£10 for a 24 hour ticket) from the bailiff who calls round. The fishery is controlled by Cawston Angling Club (Tel: secretary, Mr. Steven Brownsel, on 01263 732263).

Route. From Norwich take the Reepham Road and just before Reepham village turn right to Haveringland and Buxton. Keep straight ahead for a distance of about one and a half miles and the pit is on the left hand side of the road hidden by a hedge of tall trees. Not the easiest of spots to find in daylight, let alone in the dark.

BOUGHTON POND, West Norfolk

A shallow pond of around one and a half acres, surrounded by grassland. It is weedy and usually nicely coloured, containing a mixed stock with roach predominating. Ideal for the younger angler. FREE FISHING.

Route. From Norwich take the A47 branching on the A1122 Downham Road, about five miles past Swaffham, look on the left for a road to Barton Bendish. Go through the village, following signs to Boughton. The pond is then in the middle of Boughton village on the left close to the road.

BREAKAWAY PITS, Melton, Suffolk

There are two fabulous pits here. The smaller is around three acres with even banked swims and caters for both pleasure and match fishermen. There is a most prolific mixed stock of roach, rudd, crucian carp, bream, tench and mirror carp. Great pole fishing.

The larger pit is very much a specialist's water and covers over seven acres with a long reed covered island skirting the northern bank. Depths vary between 6 and 12 feet and stocks include a phenomenal head of bream between 7 and 13 lb. It is arguably the most prolific fishery for double figure bream in East Anglia. My brother David and I caught specimens to over 10 lb. when I featured Breakaway Pits in my television series *Go Fishing* in 2002, along with tench over 6 lb. and several carp into double figures. There is, in fact, an excellent head of carp to nearly 30 lb., plus some sizeable roach, chub, rudd and a few huge pike. The tench have been taken to over 9 lb. The fishery is controlled by Breakaway Tackle in Ipswich (Tel: 01473 741393) who issue day tickets. These cost £4 for one rod or £5 for two rods, or £7 for a 24 hour ticket (big lake only). Day tickets are also available closer to the fishery from Stuart Clay Traps in Melton (Tel: 01394 385567) and there is also a ticket machine at the fishery.

Route. From Ipswich take the A12 to Woodbridge turning off at Bentwaters roundabout on to the A1152. Go through Melton and over the level crossing. Entrance to the fishery car park is then on the left immediately past Wilford Bridge Public House.

BRIDGE FARM FISHERIES, Litcham, Norfolk

Two lakes of around one acre apiece. Both have two islands and depths shelve between 4 and 10 feet. One is irregular in shape and tree lined with rushes around the perimeter and patches of lilies. The other is kidney-shaped. The first lake includes mirror and ghost carp into double figures plus tench to 5 lb., roach, rudd, golden rudd and golden orfe. The second lake has a prolific stock of carp into high double figures plus some sizeable golden orfe to 6 lb. No keep nets. Unhooking mats are compulsory, as are barbless hooks. Day tickets cost £5 on the bank from the owner who calls round. For additional information Tel: 01328 701699. Toilet facilities on site and meals are available on request. Open all year round dawn until dusk – NO NIGHT FISHING.

Route. From Dereham take the A47 towards Swaffham. Turn off to Beeston and go through village past the Ploughshare Public House, following signs for Litcham. Bridge Farm Fishery is then on the corner of Watery Lane and Dereham Road, and is well signposted.

BRIDGE FISHERY LAKE, Lenwade, Norfolk

This five acre well established lake has a long spit in the middle almost splitting it into two halves. The banks are nicely wooded and reed lined with a choice of both shallow and deep swims in depths ranging from 6 to over 20 feet. Species include perch, roach and pike plus a good head of tench between 3 and 5 lb. A good head of bream in the 5 – 6 lb. range is also present (fish the deeper swims) plus carp to over 20 lb. Day tickets (for two rods) cost £5 from dawn until dusk or from dusk until dawn and are available from the pub, fishery lodge or bailiff who calls. A limited amount of yearly permits costing £60 are also available. Cost of day tickets includes adjacent fishing on a fast and shallow 600 yard stretch of the River Wensum, famous for its chub, roach and barbel (see River Wensum) and on a 12 peg 'fun pond' ideal for youngsters. For

In the foreground are the three Common Lakes in Lenwade. In the distance are two lakes called Catch 22 Fishery – famous for big carp. All are day ticket fisheries

additional information Tel: the Bridge Public House on 01603 872248 who specialise in anglers' accommodation.

Route. From Norwich take the A1067 Fakenham Road into Lenwade and turn right immediately over the bridge spanning the River Wensum which takes you straight into the pub car park.

BROOKE PIT, Norfolk

A most unusually situated, deeply wooded steep-sided old gravel pit of around two acres which is very deep in places under the control of the East Anglian Piscatorial Society. There are secluded swims cut into the banking affording wind shielded fishing over lily pads for roach, perch, bream to 5 lb., some sizeable crucian carp, big pike and a good head of tench to over 4 lb. Livebaiting for pike is not allowed. Day tickets £3.50 from the bailiff who will call round. No-one is allowed under 18. Additional information from Mr. N. Hunt (Tel: 01508 493687).

Route. From Norwich take the A146 and then the B1332 Bungay Road. One mile past Poringland look on the right for the Dove Public House and the pit is then at the bottom of the hill on the right through gravel workings with adjacent parking.

BROOME PITS, near Bungay, Suffolk

These four irregular-shaped tree lined gravel pits vary in size from one to four acres and are generally quite deep. Almost throughout, apart from the two small pits, a depth of 10 feet or more can be found just a rod length out. They provide excellent sport on the float for a variety of species with roach predominating and there is a super stock of mirror carp, best in recent years being a 26 lb. whopper. There are also crucian carp to 2 lb. and bream to 8 lb. Pike grow large in these pits, the best to date being a 27 pounder.

Livebaiting is not allowed. Bungay Cherry Tree Club controls the waters and has a policy project for stocking. A leaflet about the pits has in fact been produced by the club and this is available to members. Anyone may join for £30 per season through the secretary, Mr. Ian Gosling, 37 St. Mary's Terrace, Bungay (Tel: 01986 892982) and local tackle shops. The club has numerous other waters, both running and still, within the area. Anyone wishing to arrange matches should contact the secretary, Ian Gosling. Day tickets cost £2.50 (two rods) and £2 for juniors from the bailiff at the pits who calls round to anglers. Only club members may night fish.

Route. Take the B1332 from Norwich to the large bypass roundabout just before Bungay. Turn left and the pits are then on the left, hidden behind hedging one mile further on in Broome village.

BUCKINGHAM PITS, Mundford, Norfolk

There are two pits here, both of around an acre apiece and both shelving down to 12 feet deep. They hold tench averaging around the 3½ lb. mark, plus bream in all sizes, with eels, roach and some perch up to a pound. There is a prolific head of king carp up to the 20 lb. mark. These are Mundford A.C. waters and day tickets, which cost £5, must be obtained in advance from Barry Walker and Sons Garage, Ickworth (Tel: 01842 878759). Season permits cost £15, husband and wife £20, senior citizens £10 and juniors £7.50.

Route. From Norwich take the A47 to Swaffham. Then take the A1065 to Mundford. About one mile from Mundford in Ickburgh village turn left at the white cottage, and the pits are one and a half miles further on, one each side of the road just before the road goes across the River Wissey.

BURE VALLEY LAKES, nr Aylsham, Norfolk

This well managed, long established gravel pit fishery comprises of two beautiful lakes skirted by the charming and diminutive reaches of the Upper River Bure, full of wild brown trout (see 'Trout Fishing – Syndicate waters').

'Mike's Lake' is irregularly-shaped covering two acres, with depths varying from 3 to 12 feet and the banks are nicely reeded. It is renowned for specimen sized roach to over 2 lb., tench to 6 lb., and ghost carp running into double figures. The occasional rudd over 2 lb. is also taken.

'Home Lake' is an oblong-shaped water of four acres with depths fluctuating between 6 and 22 feet. The banks are heavily bordered by bushes, trees and tall reedbeds and the water is invariably on the clear side. The lake contains a strong head of both common and mirror carp averaging over 20 lb., with several into the 30s, lake record being a 33 lb. mirror caught by the manager, Geoff Cooper, in 2001. Other species include some extremely large roach, possibly to 3 lb. and a few perch.

There is a well stocked tackle and bait shop and coffee room where day tickets can be purchased before fishing (Tel: 01263 587666). Breakfasts and suppers are available to those choosing to fish over night. Day tickets cost £5 for Mike's Lake (£2.50 for juniors and £4 senior citizens). Day tickets for Home Lake cost £7.50 and £12.50 for a 24 hour ticket. Holiday accommodation available on site.

Route. From Norwich take the A140 to Aylsham and proceed into the town (ignoring bypass) turning left on to the B1354 Saxthorpe Road. Entrance to the fishery is then on the right and well signposted around four miles out of Aylsham.

BURES LAKE, Bures, Suffolk

This well matured beautifully wooded gravel pit of four and a half acres contains a super head of specimen tench between 4 and 6 lb. In the past the lake has produced tench in excess of 8 lb. There is a handful of bream to 9 lb., a few perch plus just a few wily old carp to 25 lb. Depth varies between 4 and 6 feet and the water is sometimes very clear with a weed growth that can be prolific one season, yet sparse the next. NO NIGHT FISHING. Day tickets cost £3 per rod (juniors £1.50 per rod) from Sudbury Angling Centre (Tel: 01787 312118). Controlled by the London Anglers Association and for clubs affiliated. There is also an associate membership for which anyone may apply costing £36 yearly, £19 for juniors, senior citizens and disabled, £53 for a husband and wife ticket. Apply by sending a stamped addressed envelope to the London Anglers Association, Isaac Walton House, 2A Hervey Park Road, London, E17 6LJ (Tel: 0208 520 7477).

Route. From Colchester take the B1508 into the village of Bures and proceed over the bridge spanning the River Stour. Then turn right immediately past the church and proceed along the Nayland Road, passing the mill; 500 yards further on the L.A.A. sign and entrance gate can be seen on the right with the lake adjacent to the northern bank of the Stour.

BUSS CREEK, Southwold, Suffolk

Buss Creek was in fact named after the boats which, in medieval times, carried herring to Southwold, and was given to the town council to mark its charter. Now this spring-fed, completely dammed one and a quarter mile channel provides coarse fishing and is a tribute to members of the Southwold and District F.A.P.S. who re-established it as a fishery by clearing the overgrown bed and banks. Thirty plus swims are available on Reydon bank only. There are two disabled swims. NO NIGHT FISHING. One rod only. It contains both bream and tench to over 7 lb., plus rudd, roach, perch and chub. Day tickets £4 (£1.50 juniors). These should be booked in advance from Purdys Newsagents, High Street, Southwold (Tel: 01502 724250).

Route. From Southwold take the A1095. Access is available on foot from the road bridge spanning Buss Creek – or proceed to the society's car park area serving Reydon Pits and enter by the footpath at Gordon Bridge (west) end.

CAMELOT LAKE, Wortwell, Suffolk

This beautifully landscaped man-made fishery, which can be seen beside the A143 Wortwell bypass between Homersfield and Harleston, is an irregular-shaped ex gravel workings of around two and a half acres with one small island and an interesting assortment of swims affording depths of between 8 and 15 feet close in beyond the marginal shelf. Species include roach, specimen perch to 4 lb., plus bream, eels, tench and carp to over 30 lb. Lakeside facilities include timber framed seating, bar and barbecue, electricity points, water, etc. In fact everything for the organised family day out. Day tickets cost £4.50, £12 for 24 hours – open all year round. Additional information from Phil on 01986 788208.

Route. From Norwich take the B1332 road to Bungay and turn right at the first roundabout on to the bypass which goes straight alongside the lake just beyond Homersfield.

CANOE PIT, Lenwade, Norfolk

This irregular-shaped gravel pit of one and a half acres is nicely wooded all around with depths shelving to 10 feet. It contains roach, perch and both carp and pike running into double figures. It is controlled by the Lyng and District A.C. who issue £5 day tickets on the bank.

Route. From Norwich take the A1067 Fakenham Road to Lenwade. At the crossroads immediately before the road bridge over the River Wensum turn right; 500 yards further on turn left into the Marriots Way car park. The pit is then just 20 yards away opposite the car park adjacent to the River Wensum.

CATCH 22 FISHING CENTRE, Lyng Easthaugh, Norfolk

This prolific two lake carp fishery is simply jam packed full of hard fighting common, leather and mirror carp, and open all year round except February. The big lake covers around 20 acres with a good average depth and contains specimens to nearly 40 lb. Over one-third of the lake's carp stock are in excess of 20 lb. Other species include bream to 14 lb. plus, tench to 10 lb. plus, pike to over 35 lb. and some specimen sized roach and rudd. I featured this fabulous fishery in Series 10 of my *Go Fishing* television programmes in 1996 and I honestly lost count of the double figure carp up to 20 lb. that I caught in the day's fishing. Day tickets cost £15 (two rods) or £20 for a 24 hour ticket, from the fishery reception which also sells bait and a full range of tackle. Additional information from the manager, Mr. David Wilby (tel/fax: 01603 872948). No. 2 lake covers four and a half acres with depths to 12 feet and is a season/syndicate carp fishery stocked with specimens to 37 lb. Yearly permits cost £300.

Route. The fishery is around 11 miles west of Norwich, off the A1067 Fakenham Road. Proceed to Lenwade

Terry Houseago (left) and John show a nice brace of carp from the famous Catch 22 Fishery at Lyng Easthaugh, 11 miles west of Norwich

and turn left at the crossroads just before Lenwade road bridge spanning the River Wensum. Take the first right turn 500 years further on and the entrance is then half a mile down the lane, just past Walnut Tree Farm via a gravel track leading to the fishery car park.

CHAPEL ROAD LAKE, Roughton, Norfolk

This one and a half acre long and narrow irregular-shaped man-made lake has two small islands and is heavily reeded along the margins. Depths vary from 3 to 8 feet and the water is always well coloured. Species include roach, rudd, perch and tench plus a most prolific head of carp of between 5 and 15 lb. with the possibility of a 20 pounder. Fishing is from dawn until dusk and day tickets cost £4 from the bailiff who calls round. Night fishing is only by prior arrangement (Tel: 01263 761369).

Route. From Norwich take the A140

Cromer Road to Roughton and turn left just past the garage on to the B1436 Felbrigg Road. Entrance to the fishery is then just 200 yards along on the left beside the Old Forge.

CHISWICK PIT, Stow, Norfolk

Typical well coloured farm pond, averaging around 5 feet deep and nicely tree lined. It holds a prolific stock of rudd, a few tench, plus common and mirror carp into double figures. Dawn until dusk only. NO NIGHT FISHING. Day tickets cost £4 and must be obtained in advance from Stow Estates Office in Stow Bardolph village (Tel: 01366 382162). Only three tickets issued for each day. Boilies not allowed.

Route. From Norwich take the A47 branching on to the A1122 Downham Road to Stradsett. Then turn right on to the A34 towards King's Lynn. In Shouldham Thorpe turn left and one mile further on turn left down a farm track, the pit is then 300 yards further on, on the left opposite the farmhouse.

CHURCH FARM FISHERY, Burgh Castle, Norfolk

A widened reed-fringed dyke covering around three-quarters of an acre with depths to 8 feet. Contains roach, rudd, tench and perch. A good float water for youngsters and the family. Day tickets cost £3 from adjacent Church Farm Restaurant (Tel: 01493 780251).

Route. From Great Yarmouth take A143 to the White Horse roundabout and follow signs to Burgh Castle. After two miles turn right at cross roads signposted to the village. Church Farm is then situated at the end of the road.

COBBLEACRE PARK LAKES, Hevingham, Norfolk

This interesting complex of four man-made gravel and clay pits offers a variety of species. In the largest three and a half acre lake which is oval in shape, depth varies from 4 to 16 feet and there are two islands. There is a prolific stock of ghost koi and mirror carp to over 25 lb. plus tench, crucian carp and roach.

The second lake is oblong in shape with three islands and around one and a half acres, the depths varying from 4 to 10 feet. Species present are crucian carp, bream, roach, rudd, tench and carp to 20 lb.

The third lake is just quarter of an acre, averaging around 4 feet deep and L-shaped. It holds roach, rudd, crucian carp, tench and bream. The fourth lake is oblong in shape of around an acre with two islands and depths to 8 feet. Holds roach, rudd, tench, ide, bream, crucian carp and some huge perch. There is an anglers' car park with adjacent shower and toilet facilities and the bailiff will call round to anglers. Day tickets cost £6 (including two rods) or £15 for a 24 hour

session. Evening tickets cost £4 and there is a season permit at £150. For additional information Tel: 01603 754305 or mobile 07765 547871.

Route. From Norwich take the B1149 Holt Road passing through Horsford and three-quarters of a mile past Shorthorn crossroads turn right alongside the woodyard down Brick Kiln Road. Entrance to the lakes is then on the right three-quarters of a mile past Bailey's Barn.

COMMON LAKES, Lenwade, Norfolk

Situated on Lenwade Common these fisheries are controlled by the Great Witchingham Fuel Allotment Charity and comprise three gravel pits varying between two and five acres, plus a three-quarter mile length of the River Wensum famous for its roach, chub and pike fishing (see 'River Wensum'). The pits are stocked with a variety of species including roach, rudd, tench between 4 and 7 lb. perch, bream, pike to over 20 lb., plus mirror carp to 30 lb., specimen crucian carp and grass carp over 20 lb. Philip Spinks caught a 27 lb. 10 oz. grass carp here in 2001. Depths fluctuate between 5 and 28 feet and there is an interesting choice of swims. For carp, bream and pike the first lake on the left at the bottom of the lane is recommended. For tench, carp and crucian carp choose the first lake on the right at the bottom of the lane. A 10 lb. 1 oz. tench was caught here in 2001. Day permits cost £5 (£1 senior citizens and juniors) available from the bailiff who calls round; 24 hour permits for those wishing to night fish cost £10. Season permits cost £60 also from the bailiff; £15 for a concessionary permit. Lakes open 1 May and close 14 March.

Route. From Norwich take the A1067 Fakenham Road into Lenwade and then take the first left turn immediately past the village bakery and butchers' shop down common lane. This leads directly to the fishery and adjacent car park.

COSTESSEY (Nos. 1, 2 and 3) LAKES, Costessey, Norfolk

Owned by Anglian Water these three lakes are known locally as the Greenhouse Pit, the Ski Lake (water skiing still takes place) and the Carp Lake respectively.

No. 1 Lake, the Greenhouse Pit, covers around three acres with depths to 10 feet. It contains quality sized bream and tench, some big perch, roach, pike and carp into double figures. Fishing is along the entrance side bank only.

No. 2, the Ski Lake, covers some 15 acres and is nicely wooded around the perimeter with depths varying between 8 and 20 feet. The water is usually well coloured and stocks include a terrific head of roach to over the pound, plus large shoals of bream and many specimens into double figures. The best of 13 lb. 2 oz. was caught by local specialist Des Williams, in 2000. The tench average between 4 and 6 lb. but specimens to over 9 lb. are taken. There are also perch, eels and a fair head of pike including a good sprinkling of doubles plus the occasional 20 pounder. There is also a modest head of carp from 15 to over 30 lb. Level swims are provided adjacent to the car park for wheelchair anglers. A good winter water.

No. 3 known as the Carp Lake covers almost six acres and averages over 10 feet deep with extremely secluded swims cut in around the heavily wooded perimeter. This lake is well known for specimen tench and fish in excess of 8 lb. have been taken. Other species include roach, perch, eels, pike and carp to over 40 lb. A monster of 40¼ lb. was caught in 2001 by James Deacon. A big zander is also not unlikely. These lakes are open all year round.

Day tickets are available only from nearby Taverham Mills Fishery Lodge. These cost £6 per day, £12 for a 24 hour session. A limited amount of season permits are also available from the Fishing Lodge. (For additional information Tel: 01603 861014.) (See also 'Taverham Mills Lake'.)

Route. From Norwich take the A47 Dereham Road and 2 miles from the City turn right down Longwater Lane by the Roundwell Public House. At the bottom of the hill turn left at a T-junction and half a mile further on take the right fork. The three lakes are then situated on the right with the main entrance gate some 400 yards further on. Alternatively take the A1067 Fakenham Road from Norwich into Taverham and turn left at the crossroads down Sandy Lane. At the bottom of the hill go straight ahead at the crossroads and proceed over the bridge spanning the River Wensum. The Lakes are then the first three on the left with an entrance gate 300 yards further on. Tickets are obtained from Taverham Mills Fishery Lodge, the entrance being immediately on the right over the crossroads at Sandy Lane.

CROSS DROVE FISHERY, Hockwold, Norfolk

This irregular-shaped man-made lake covering seven acres has five islands and depth fluctuates between 4 and 6 feet. There are 85 permanent pegs and species include ruffe, perch to over 3 lb., roach, rudd, bream to 6 lb., zander into double figures and a prolific head of mirror and common carp up to 20 lb. A surprise in the form of Wels catfish also exists. A 33 lb. specimen was taken by Jim Murray in 2000. NO NIGHT FISHING. OPEN ALL YEAR ROUND. Day tickets cost £5 from the bailiff who calls round. Additional information from Rob Morter (Tel: 01842 828102).

Route. From Thetford take the Brandon Road and follow signs to Hockwold. Go through Hockwold village to crossroads with the B1112 and turn left heading towards Lakenheath. Once over bridge spanning the Cut Off Channel, take first right turning and the fishery is one mile further along on the right with adjacent parking.

DECOY FARM FISHERY, Ormesby, Norfolk

A narrow and long lake of around two acres with a prolific mixed stock including roach, rudd, perch, crucian carp and bream. There is also a strong head of specimen tench to 6 lb. plus, together with carp running into double figures. An ideal family fishery where youngsters easily catch small fish on the float. Day tickets cost £3 (£1.50 for an evening ticket) and are available from the Farm Office or from the bailiff who calls round. NO NIGHT FISHING. (Tel: 01493 730301 for additional information.)

Route. From Norwich take the A47 Great Yarmouth Road and go over Acle Bridge. Then turn left on to the Caister Road and on to Fleggburgh Kings Arms Public House. Turn left and proceed to Rollesby. At T-junction with the A149 turn right and after crossing the linking bridge between Ormesby and Rollesby Broads take the first left turn following signs for Decoy Farm Lake which leads directly to the fishery.

DENTS OF HILGAY, Hilgay, Norfolk

An interesting collection of five clay pit fisheries bordered by reeds and trees close to the River Wissey. The largest covers around six acres with depths to 5

feet, and is primarily a pleasure anglers' fishery containing a prolific and mixed stock of tench averaging 3 to 4 lb. (occasional specimens to 6 lb. plus), roach, crucian carp, perch and king carp averaging high double figures up to 30 lb. Adjacent to this lake is a half acre pond containing roach, carp and even a few barbel. Situated 400 yards away but part of the same complex are three other lakes of three and a half acres, three acres and one and a half acres respectively. Depths vary between five and ten feet in each, with central islands. Stocking is predominantly king carp to over 20 lb., plus barbel to 2 lb., chub to 4 lb., roach to 2 lb. and tench over 5 lb. This is a member of 'Premier Fisheries'.

Day tickets cost £5 available from the bailiff who calls round or the farm shop adjacent to the anglers' car park. Fishing is from dawn until dusk only. There is a 'barbless hook only' rule in force. Match bookings are available through Dents of Hilgay Farm Shop (Tel: 01366 385661).

Route. From Downham Market take the A10 towards Ely, passing over bridges spanning the Cut Off Channel and River Wissey. The lakes and farm shop are then 200 yards on the right past the next left bend. Parking is between shop and lakes only.

DOCKING VILLAGE POND, Docking, Norfolk

A most prolific fishery of around an acre with depths varying between three and four feet. Being an old marl pit the water is always well coloured and holds a strong head of crucians and wild, common carp up to 8 lb. There are also roach and some tench. Day tickets cost £4 for adults (£1 for senior citizens and juniors) and are only issued on the same day. Just 12 tickets are available on a first come, first served basis from the Post Office Stores in Station Road (Tel: 01485 518220). Fishing is from 7.30 a.m. until 11.00 p.m. only Monday to Saturday. No Sunday tickets.

Route. Take the A1067 from Norwich going through Fakenham and all the way through to Docking.

DUNHAM CARP AND TENCH LAKES, Little Dunham, Norfolk

A unique and extremely interesting series of five, inter-connected long and narrow lakes, which are actually part of an old railway line system that has been flooded and dammed. The banks are nicely overgrown and depths vary between 3 and 8 feet and there are extensive beds of dwarf pond lily. The lakes are well stocked with a variety of species including king carp to 25 lb., plus the odd very much larger specimen, with roach, rudd, tench to 6 lb. and crucian carp to over 2 lb., all of which can be taken on the float at close range. Fishing is from 6.30 a.m. to 8.00 p.m. only and day tickets cost £4 from the bailiff who calls round. A limited number of season permits are also available at £55. No groundbait allowed, barbless hooks only. (For additional information Tel: 01760 725286 – mobile 07860 323285.)

Route. From Norwich take the A47 King's Lynn road and just before the service station at Necton turn right following the sign to Little Dunham. Proceed straight ahead for one and a half miles to Dunham museum on the left and immediately opposite look on the right (just before old railway bridge) for signs at fishery entrance and to car parks.

EDWARDS PIT, Belton, nr Great Yarmouth, Norfolk

Two small, shallow, weedy ponds holding roach, perch, tench and carp into double figures. Day tickets cost £4 from the bailiff who calls round.

Route. From Norwich take the A146 to Hales and look out on the left for the B1136 to Haddiscoe. In Haddiscoe turn left on to the A143 and four miles further on at dual carriageway turn left on to Belton and Burgh Castle road. Take first on right along Butt Lane and the ponds are then 200 yards on right down a narrow farm track.

THE EVERGLADES, Denver, Norfolk

Two reed-lined ponds of half an acre and one acre in size respectively. Plus an old moat with a centre island, all set in wooded parkland. Depths in the moat go to 4 feet and the two ponds shelve from 2 to 6 feet. Stocks include roach, perch, bream, tench, barbel and carp just into double figures. Three really well stocked fisheries, ideal for youngsters and the family day out. Open all year round, dawn until dusk. Day tickets cost £4 at the fishery. Additional information from Mr. Riches (Tel: 01366 383291).

Route. Take the A10 from King's Lynn and 12 miles from the town look for 'To the Windmill' sign on the right. Turn right and the Everglades Fishery is then 50 yards along on the left.

FELBRIGG LAKE, North Norfolk

A beautiful estate lake of around four acres, dammed at one end and fed by a brook at the other. Depth varies from 2 to 5 feet and during the summer months the weed can sometimes be very thick. There is a most prolific stock of tench averaging 4 – 5 lb. plus eels, pike (including the odd double) and plenty of rudd including fish to over 2 lb. Day tickets cost £5 and must be obtained in advance from the Estates Office at Felbrigg Hall during office hours (or by post) (Tel: 01263 837444).

John nets a nice tench from Felbrigg in North Norfolk. Shoals of quality rudd accompany the tench here

Route. Take the A140 Cromer Road from Norwich to Roughton and turn left on to the Felbrigg Road which leads to the estate entrance gate (on left) three miles further on.

FELMINGHAM MILL LAKES, nr Aylsham, Norfolk

There are three attractive one acre, stream-fed lakes here varying between 3 and 10 feet in depth. Stocks include roach, perch, crucian carp, tench to 6 lb. and mirror carp running to over 20 lb. Touring caravanners are welcomed here (25 spaces) with toilet and shower block facilities adjacent to the lakes. Day tickets cost £4 with juniors and senior citizens at £2.50. These must be obtained prior to fishing from Mr. Moore at the Mill House adjacent to the water (Tel: 01263 735106). Ticket includes fishing in the tiny mill stream which holds roach, dace, pike, trout and even the odd grayling. Nice winter trotting especially for dace.

Route. From Norwich go to Aylsham on the A140 and take bypass towards Cromer. Then take fourth turning on the right, the B1145 to Felmingham. One mile before the village take left turn down to the mill. It is well signposted.

FELTHORPE LAKES, Felthorpe, Norfolk

This man-made fun fishery comprises of three lakes varying in size from one to two and a half acres with a variation in depth of between 3 and 7 feet. They contain a prolific head of ghost koi and mirror carp up to 30 lb. plus tench, perch and roach. The smaller lake (match lake) also contains gold fish and smaller carp varieties. Day tickets cost £5 from David, the bailiff (Tel: 07769 704808) who calls round to anglers. Open all year through.
Route. Take the B1149 Holt Road from Norwich passing through Horsford. Beyond the crossroads take the next right turn past the kennels down Brick Kiln

Road, and the entrance to the fishery is then on the right, 100 yards further on adjacent to conifer woods.

FIELD FARM FISHERIES, Wrentham, Suffolk

A collection of smallish man-made ponds with depths varying between 4 and 8 feet providing great fun fishing on the float. Stocks include roach, perch, rudd, crucian carp, tench and a good mixture of king carp variants including ghosties running into high double figures. Open all year round. Day tickets cost £5 and £3 for juniors, from the bailiff who calls round. (For additional information Tel: 01502 675273.)

Route. From Lowestoft take the A12 towards Ipswich and take first road on the right after passing through Wrentham; 200 hundred yards along on the left is a signpost to the fishery with adjacent parking.

THE FLOODPARK, Haverhill, Suffolk

An oblong-shaped two acre lake created as a flood plain defence reservoir for the town of Haverhill. Depths vary from 3 to 5 feet and there is a tree covered central island. Species include gudgeon, roach, chub, rudd, perch, skimmer bream, tench to 6 lb. and an interesting stock of specimen carp reaching to 30 lb. Open all year round. Day tickets cost £5 adult, £3 juniors and must be purchased in advance from Haverhill Angling Centre (Tel: 01440 705011).

Route. From Haverhill Town Centre head towards Cambridge on the Withersfield Road. The lake is then directly opposite Sainsbury's supermarket on the right of the road, with car parking through iron gates.

FRITTON LAKE, Suffolk

This 175 acre lake is part of the huge Fritton Country Park complex where in addition to fishing, sports such as golf, boating etc., may also be enjoyed. There is also a falconry centre. By far the largest lake in Suffolk, Fritton is actually thought to be a broad dug for its peat during the Middle Ages. These were the conclusions of Dr. J. Lambert whose studies of the Broads during the 1950s brought scientific evidence to the subject (See 'History of the Broads Enigma'). Depth varies between 8 and 12 feet and the water is usually well coloured. Bank fishing is restricted to the north-western end close to the entrance where numerous swims have been cut in between thick reed beds – in all about 1000 yards of bank fishing. Boats have access to much of the lake. These cost £5 per day. There are huge shoals of bream in Fritton averaging around 6 – 10 lb.: not always easy to track down, but when they are, 100 lb. plus catches are nothing out of the ordinary. Roach are widespread with plenty over the pound and float fishing two rod lengths out with either maggots or casters produces some nice bags, plus the odd bream and perch. There are also a few wily carp and a good head of pike which go to over 20 lb. A really super family-cum-fishing venue.

Day tickets cost £5.60 (£3.90 juniors) from the main gate and this includes entrance to the beautiful gardens and amusements. These are available from 10.00 a.m. and the park closes at 5.30 p.m. NO NIGHT FISHING. Fishing is all year round and those wishing to fish from dawn until dusk can do so by telephoning first. There are also some super holiday cottages for rent set in very secluded parts of the estate. (For more information contact the Manager on 01493 488288.)

Route. Take the A146 from Norwich and turn on to the B1136 at Hales towards Haddiscoe. Continue over the bridge spanning the River Waveney at St. Olaves and Fritton Lake is then on the right a little further on.

GIMMINGHAM LAKES, nr Cromer, Norfolk

Three man-made reed lined spring-fed lakes with a reputation for producing specimen mirror and common carp over 30 lb., plus tench, rudd, roach, perch and bream. The largest lake has two islands, varies from 4 to 15 feet in depth and is around three and a half acres. The two smaller lakes are narrow and long, about one and a half acres each and vary in depth from 5 to 8 feet. Day permits costs £3 from the owner who calls round to anglers. Season permits are also available. Good car parking and toilet facilities adjacent to the lakes. (Tel: 01263 720432 for additional information.)

Route. From Norwich take the B1150 road going through Coltishall and into North Walsham. From North Walsham proceed on the Mundesley Road for one mile bearing left through the village of Trunch. Then go straight ahead into Gimmingham village and the old mill and turn left following signs for fishery.

GLEMSFORD LAKES, nr Sudbury, Suffolk

These three irregular shaped ex gravel workings have in fact been made a 'Triple S' site (a site of special scientific interest) by the Countryside Commission. They are well matured, nicely interspersed with islands and surrounded by deep woodlands in the Suffolk Stour valley. NO NIGHT FISHING.

No. 1 lake lies along the Stour's southern bank and is the largest at around 18 acres. The water is always well coloured and holds a prolific head of roach, rudd, bream to 8 lb., plus tench averaging 4 – 5 lb. There are also pike and zander into double figures.

No. 2 lake is around four acres and exceptionally shallow. Though it contains roach, rudd and tench fishing is virtually impossible due to the exceptionally heavy weed growth.

No. 3 lake is the smallest at three acres with depths varying from 4 to 12 feet. It holds roach, rudd, pike and zander plus a strong head of tench to over 4 lb. Bags of up to 10 tench at a sitting are commonplace. Day tickets cost £3 per rod (Juniors £1.50 per rod) from Sudbury Angling Centre (Tel: 01787 312118). Controlled by the London Anglers Association and for clubs affiliated. There is also an associate membership for which anyone may apply costing £36 yearly (£19 for juniors, senior citizens and disabled – £53 for a husband and wife ticket). Apply by sending a stamped addressed envelope to the London Anglers Association, Isaac Walton House, 2A Hervey Park Road, London, E17 6LJ (Tel: 0208 520 7477).

Route. From Sudbury take the A134 road to Long Melford and then the A1092 to Cavendish. The lakes are then situated on the left, almost opposite the Glemsford Road, immediately after crossing the River Glem. This entrance is for No. 1 lake only. For No. 2 and No. 3 lakes take the first left turn past the entrance to No. 1 lake and 50 yards along go over a level crossing. The L.A.A. gate and signpost is then immediately on the left before crossing the River Stour.

GLEN MERE LAKES, nr Cromer, Norfolk

There are two man-made lakes here set in woodland. One is around half an acre with a centre island and depths to 4 feet, the second is oblong also with an island, around three-quarters of an acre in size with depths to 5 feet. The smaller lake contains roach, rudd, crucian carp and king carp running into high double figures. Day tickets cost £4 available on the bank from the owner, Mr. S. Barratt (Tel: 01263 761303 for additional information). The larger lake is available on a season ticket only costing £70 (waiting list in force) and contains a similar stock of fish.

Route. From Norwich take the A140 road to Cromer. Go well beyond Aylsham on the bypass and look for Alby Garage on the right. Half a mile on look for monument on the left and turn left. Proceed over Hanworth Common and over crossroads. Go over second cattle grid on the road to Susted and 100 yards further on the fishery signpost can be seen on the right. The two lakes are situated through the woods.

GOLDEN PONDS, nr Hickling, Norfolk

A fun fishery ideal for youngsters and beginners alike, comprising of two small man-made lakes of between half to three-quarters of an acre each where disabled anglers are well catered for. The stock includes chub, tench, roach, rudd and carp into double figures. Open all year round. Day tickets cost £5 from the owner who calls round. (For additional information Tel: 01692 581016.)

Route. From Norwich take the A1151 passing through Wroxham and on to Stalham. Beyond Stalham turn off on the left opposite Sutton Staithe Hotel and proceed to T-junction. Turn right at junction and then take third turning on left to the next T-junction. Then turn right and ponds are 400 yards along on the left and well signposted. Adjacent car park.

GREAT MASSINGHAM VILLAGE POND, Norfolk

A typical village pond – shallow, coloured and containing a most prolific stock of wild carp. Fishing is free to parishioners and pupils of Great Massingham Primary School, who should apply to the local Parish Council. To all outsiders there are 10 tickets issued each day costing £3 from the Village Store and Post Office adjacent to the church. The store opens from 8.00 a.m. until 5.30 p.m. Tel: 01485 520272. NO NIGHT FISHING or ground baiting.

Route. From Norwich take the A1067 Fakenham Road and turn on to the B1145 at Bawdeswell. Go through Brisley and Litcham and six miles further on look out on the right for the sign to Great Massingham. The pond is then bang in the middle of the village.

GREENS PITS, Belton, nr Great Yarmouth, Norfolk

Two irregular-shaped gravel pits of around two acres in all with depths to 12 feet. Good stock of roach and tench plus pike, bream and carp into double figures with specimens approaching 30 lb. Day tickets cost £5 from the bailiff who calls round. Season permits are also available.

Route. From Norwich take the A146 to Hales and look out on the left for the B1136 to Haddiscoe. In Haddiscoe turn left on to the A143 and four miles further on at dual carriageway turn left on to the Belton and Burgh Castle Road. Take first on right along Butt Lane and after one mile look for the sign to the fishery on the left.

GUNTHORPE HALL LAKE, Melton Constable, Norfolk

Typical Norfolk estate lake of around three acres set in deep woodland. Depths vary between 2 and 12 feet. Deepest water around dam end. Species include roach, crucian carp, rudd, perch, pike in plenty, tench and common carp into double figures. Day tickets cost £5 from the Hall. Only five issued per day by prior booking only (Tel: 01263 861373). No Sunday fishing. NO NIGHT FISHING – dawn until dusk only.

Route. Take the A1067 Fakenham Road from Norwich to Guist and turn right on to the B1110 road. Proceed to Melton Constable and turn left at the crossroads on to the B1354. Take next right turn and go into Gunthorpe village, taking second turn on left (just before church) down to the lake and Hall.

GUNTON PARK LAKE, Norfolk

This is an almost square-shaped estate lake of around 12 acres, often referred to by its old name of Sawmills Lake. Depth varies between 2 and 5 feet and the water is always well coloured, holding a prolific head of bream between 4 and 7 lb. There is also a strong head of roach to over the pound, plus one or two hybrids. Other species include perch and a growing head of carp to over 20 lb. Also present are pike into high double figures plus the odd very much larger specimen. A good float water for mixed catches with comfortable banks and an ideal family venue. Keep nets not allowed until 1 September and there is NO NIGHT FISHING. Open all year round. Day tickets cost £4.50 and are available from ticket machine in car park. For additional information and match bookings contact Mr. Richardson (Tel: 01263 761433).

Route. Take the A140 road from Norwich to about five miles beyond Aylsham and look on the left for the Alby craft centre. Then look out on the right for a signpost to Suffield. Turn right and at the bottom of the hill bear right, proceeding past archway gate on the left and take next entrance on the left which leads to the anglers' car park and lake.

A visiting angler looks justifiably pleased with a big double figure ghost koi carp from Heacham Park Lake. Great day ticket action

HALL FARM LAKE, Burgh Hall, Norfolk

An L-shaped man-made lake of around two acres. Behind the two small islands there are extensive weed beds. Stocks include roach, rudd, tench, crucian carp to 1½ lb. plus a strong head of common and mirror carp running into double figures with individual specimens topping 25 lb. Depths vary from 6 to over 12 feet. Open all year round. Day tickets cost £3 with juniors and senior citizens at £2, from the bailiff who calls round. (For additional information Tel: 01493 781521.)

Route. From Great Yarmouth go over Breydon Water bridge towards Gorleston and turn right at next roundabout. Proceed through chicane up to small roundabout and turn right. Carry on down road to T-junction and turn left. Then look for left turn to fishery entrance, some 300 yards further on just before the Cherry Tree Caravan Park which is on the right.

HAVERINGLAND LAKE, Norfolk

This wide and long stream-fed estate lake which covers some 14 acres is for the most part quite shallow with around 5 feet of water at the dam end. It contains roach, perch, some nice tench and large shoals of bream in the 5 – 7 lb. class. Also present is a good stock of pike with specimens to 20 lb. plus. Day permits cost £5 and must be booked over the telephone in advance from the office (Tel: 01603 871302). Season tickets costing £45 are also available. Campers wishing to pitch their own tents and touring caravaners are also welcome. Static holiday homes also available for hire. Open all year round.

Route. From Norwich take the B1149 Holt Road and after several miles take turn on the left to Eastgate. At the Ratcatchers Pub and restaurant turn left. After half a mile turn left through Haveringland Hall Lodge gates, and follow concrete road for half a mile to reception.

HAYLINGS POND, Leiston, Suffolk

A half acre, shallow pond containing roach, perch, tench and mirror carp. An ideal youngster's water. Easy float fishing. Day tickets cost £2 from Saxmundham Angling Centre (Tel: 01728 603443); yearly permits cost £7.50, £4 juniors. Controlled by the Leiston Youth Club.

Route. From Saxmundham take the B1119 road into Leiston. Then turn right at T-junction and follow road into Haylings Road. Then turn left into Haylings Grove where the pond is situated on the recreation ground with adjacent parking.

HEACHAM PARK FISHERY, Heacham, Norfolk

A 100 year old, four acre estate lake with a centre island, fed by the tiny River Hitch. Depths vary from 3 to 5 feet and there are patches of lilies. Stocks include bream to over 7 lb. and a most prolific head of king carp and ghost carp (Koi crosses) averaging double figures and reaching to over 25 lb. I caught two of these beautiful fish during the filming of my TV series, *Go Fishing*, here in 1998. They fight incredibly hard. Unhooking mats are mandatory. Day tickets cost £5 (£12 for a two rod, 24 hour ticket) and should be booked in advance from the bailiff, Mr. Jim Agate (Tel: (mobile) 07788 937338).

Route. Turn off the A149 King's Lynn to Hunstanton Road opposite the Lavender Centre, into Heacham village. Then take the first right turn and fishery entrance is 60 yards along on the left.

HEVINGHAM LAKES, Hevingham, Norfolk

There are three smallish man-made lakes at Hevingham, all nicely mature and reeded, situated quite close together. Depth varies between 3 and 9 feet and they are always well coloured. The carp fishing is really excellent for mirrors, leathers and commons and there is a strong head between 3 and 10 lb., plus some nice doubles and odd fish over 20 lb. There are also crucians, roach, rudd, tench and bream to 5 lb. Anglers wishing to stay overnight may, for a small charge, pitch their own tents and there are caravans to let on site for anglers. Toilet and shower facilities are available to all. Touring caravans are also welcome and there is a holiday farmhouse to let. Night fishing is allowed only by those who stay on site. Day tickets cost £3 per rod and these must be purchased at the bungalow at the entrance from Mr. C. J. Matthewson (Tel: 01603 754368).

Route. Take the Holt Road, the B1149, from Norwich, turning right at the second (ignore the first) signpost to Hevingham, some six miles out of the city. The fishery entrance is then on the left about one mile further on and well signposted.

HIGHFIELD FISHERY, Thorpe Abbots, nr Diss, Norfolk

This man-made well established fishery complex which is well coloured and dotted with patches of lilies, suits both the pleasure fisherman and the match angler alike and comprises of three lakes. The smallest (ideal for youngsters) is sausage-shaped, averages between 5 and 6 feet deep and is around three-quarters of an acre. The second lake is one and three quarter acres in size with a tree clad island and is most irregular in shape with

an average depth of between 6 and 7 feet. The third lake covers around two and a half acres with depths to 7 feet and an island at one end. All three lakes contain a varied stock of roach, rudd, chub, perch, crucian carp, bream, tench and king carp with specimen carp running to over 30 lb. in the largest lake. There are also ghost carp running into double figures. Day tickets cost £4 (£2.50 juniors and senior citizens) (dawn until dusk) from the bailiff who calls round. Night fishing is only by prior arrangement. (For additional information Tel: Mr. Ken Avery on 01986 874869.) There is a special discount for block bookings to the secretaries of angling clubs.

Route. From Harleston take the A143 road towards Scole, passing through Needham and Brockdish. One mile past Brockdish take right turn following signpost to Thorpe Abbots. Fishery entrance is then on the left 400 yards further on and well signposted with an adjacent car park via dirt track road.

HINDERCLAY LAKES, Hinderclay, Norfolk

The fishery comprises of four picturesque man-made lakes with depths varying between 2 and 7 feet. Stocks include roach, rudd, bream, perch, tench to 6 lb., crucian carp to over 2½ lb., plus king, ghost and koi carp running into double figures, the fishery record being a mirror of 28¾ lb. No night fishing. Open all year dawn until dusk. Day tickets cost £4.50 from the bailiff who calls round. No keep nets and no boilies. (Tel: Mr. Stuart Platt on 01379 890110.) Eventually the complex will be enlarged to seven lakes.

Route. From Norwich take the A140 road to Scole and then the A143 Bury road through Wortham Village. One mile further on turn right towards

Rickinghall and proceed through village. Look for signpost on right just before the church, leading to Hinderclay. One mile further on look for concrete pad on right with double gates and sign for the fishery.

HOLTON GRAVEL PIT, nr Halesworth, Suffolk

This two acre pit is nicely reeded around the perimeter and averages about 8 feet deep. The water is usually quite clear and there is a stock of small crucians and tench plus some roach, rudd, and bream with some common and mirror carp up to 30 lb. A real mixed bag fun fishery controlled by the Woodbridge and District A.C. Membership costs £30 yearly from the secretary, Geoff Abbott (Tel: 01394 383898). Day tickets cost £5 and must be purchased in advance from Anglian Photographics in Halesworth (Tel: 01986 873333) or Stuart Clay Traps in Melton (Tel: 01394 385567).

Route. Take the A146 then the B1322 from Norwich into Bungay. Then take the A144 into Halesworth and turn left on to the B1123 into Holton. The pit is then on the left in the middle of the village.

INGHAM POND, nr Bury St Edmunds, Suffolk

Attractive little pond, surrounded by sunken trees, holding roach, perch and crucian carp. FREE FISHING.

Route. From Bury St. Edmunds take the A134 road to Thetford and the pond is on the right, 300 yards past Ingham village crossroads.

JADES FISHERY, Bridgham, Norfolk

This oblong-shaped reservoir covers eight acres with depths varying from 4 to 30 feet. Species include roach, rudd, tench, crucian carp, bream, perch and a prolific head of carp into the mid twenties. Day tickets cost £5 and must be obtained prior to fishing from Mrs J Laurie (Tel: 01842 755485).

Route. From Norwich take A11 to the first roundabout on the Thetford by-pass (signposted Watton). Turn left towards Thetford town and one mile on turn left to Bridgham immediately before Tesco's supermarket. Proceed into Bridgham and take left turn into Timber Hill. Proceed for a further mile and a half and look on left for double gate and high banks of reservoir fishery. Adjacent car parking.

LAKESIDE FISHERIES, East Bilney, Norfolk

There are four lakes here, set in wooded surroundings, offering excellent sport with rudd, golden orfe, grass carp, perch, tench, golden tench, roach, bream, trout and carp to over 20 lb. All are irregular in shape with depths to around 9 feet and three lakes have central islands. The largest has two islands and is three and a half acres. The others average around an acre. Excellent car parking, toilet and shop facilities on site plus meals available. Day tickets cost £6 (which includes the use of two rods) from the lakeside office. Gates open at 7.00 a.m. until dusk. Night fishing by appointment only and costs £10. (Tel: 01362 861015.) Open all year round, seven days a week.

Route. From Norwich take the A47 turning off into Dereham. Proceed through one-way system in town and take the B1146 towards Fakenham. After three miles turn down beside the Corner Nursery which is on the left. After a further two and a half miles look for a Renault garage and 600 yards further on turn left down lane just before road bridge which leads to the fishery and car park.

LAKESIDE FISHERY, Denver, Norfolk
A one and a half acre reed-lined lake with two islands and oval in shape. Depth shelves from 4 to 12 feet and stocks include roach, bream, rudd, perch, tench to 6 lb., plus some barbel and a good head of king carp running into double figures plus specimens to close on 30 lb. Open all year round, dawn until dusk. Day permits are £4 and available on site. Additional information from Mr. Riches (Tel: 01366 383291) which includes accommodation in adjacent caravans.
Route. Take the A10 from King's Lynn and 12 miles from town look for 'To the Windmill' sign on the right. Turn right and the fishery is opposite the windmill on the right hand side of the road.

LAKESIDE – ONEHOUSE, nr.
Stowmarket, Suffolk
A two acre man-made lake, oval in shape, adjacent to the River Rat. Contains a strong head of carp to over 20 lb. and wels catfish to over 40 lb., plus crucian carp, bream and roach. Day tickets cost £3 on the bank from Mrs. Lee who calls round (Tel: 01449 613770).
Route. From Stowmarket take the B1115 towards Great Finborough and three-quarters of a mile out of Stowmarket turn right into Lower Road. The lake is then on the left opposite the Shepherd and Dog Public House.

LETHERINGSETT LAKE,
Letheringsett, Norfolk
An attractive three acre dammed lake with a centre island varying in depth between 3 and 9 feet. Holds a good head of roach, plus tench, crucian carp to 2 lb., perch, eels, pike and carp to 20 lb. Fishing is from dawn until dusk only. Day tickets cost £6 from the Kings Head Public House in Letheringsett (Tel: 01263 712691) and should be obtained before fishing. A bailiff calls round.
Route. Take the B1149 from Norwich into Holt turning left on to the B1156 into Letheringsett. At first crossroads turn right and the lake is situated 400 yards along on the left behind a bank of trees.

LOAM PONDS, Sutton, nr
Woodbridge, Suffolk
Two connected man-made ponds in the shape of a pair of water wings, with depths varying between 6 and 18 feet, covering in all about two acres. Species include bream into double figures, carp to 30 lb., plus roach, rudd, perch, and some large tench. A real specialist's water, controlled by Woodbridge and District A.C., who issue day tickets through local tackle dealers, though anyone may join the club. Contract the secretary, Geoff Abbott (Tel: 01394 383898). Day tickets cost £5 and must be purchased in advance from Stuart Clay Traps in Melton, near Woodbridge (Tel: 01394 385567).
Route. From Melton take the B1083 into Sutton and follow signpost to Sutton Hoo Farms with fishery signpost on the left.

LOCH NEATON FISHERY, Watton,
Norfolk
A shallow one acre lake controlled and well maintained by the Loch Neaton

Top Right: This picturesque part of the Suffolk Stour in Sudbury beside The Mill Hotel, is controlled by the Sudbury and District A.A.

Bottom Right: Bailiff Denis Gooch (left) and John's brother Dave Wilson display the stamp of bream for which the Breakaway Pits have become famous

Management Trust. The lake varies between 2 and 6 feet and is heavily stocked with a variety of species including tench to 4 lb., plus roach, rudd, perch, bream and carp to over 20 lb. A closed season is in force from 14 March to 16 June. Limited day tickets available at £5 adults, £2 juniors. These must be purchased in advance from Rudling DIY, High Street, Watton (Tel: 01953 881760), or Tony Smith, the bailiff who calls round (Tel: (mobile) 07718 005538). Limited membership tickets costing £25 yearly (adults) or £5 (juniors). Handicapped and disabled anglers qualify for free membership. There are in fact two custom-built concrete platforms for the disabled alongside the fishery car park. No keep nets to be used. No carp to be retained. Season ticket holders only may night fish.

Route. From Norwich take the B1108 into Watton and turn right on to the A1075; 400 yards further on turn left into Watton Sports Centre and follow track down to five bar gate and car park.

LYNFORD LAKE, Mundford, Norfolk

This long irregular shaped, five acre nicely secluded water, varies in depth between 2 and 4 feet and contains a strong head of tench between 4 and 5 lb. Also present are specimen sized roach and rudd, the water is invariably quite clear and weedy. A Mundford Angling Club Fishery, with day permits available from Barry Walker and Sons Garage in Ickburgh (Tel: 01842 878759).

Route. From Norwich take A47 to Swaffham and then the A1065 to Mundford roundabout. Then take the A134 West Toft Road and lookout on

Left: Des Williams caught this 20 lb. plus fully scaled mirror carp from Costessey Lakes near Norwich.

the left for track number 23 (Forrestry Roads). The lake is down the track at a dead end.

MARSH FARM LAKES, nr Saxmundham, Suffolk

Complex of three spring–fed clearwater lakes, man-made from peat marshes. The largest lake is an irregular shape of around three acres, averaging 6 feet deep and is nicely reed lined with a good stock of carp to over 25 lb. Lake No. 2 is also irregularly shaped and around one acre in size with reed lined banks and an overall depth of 6 feet, containing roach, rudd, perch, tench to 6 lb. and bream to 7 lb. Lake No. 3 is really a small pond, designed specifically for youngsters. The shallow water contains roach, rudd, carp and tench. Ideal float fishing. Day tickets cost £5 for the use of one rod only or £6 for two rods and must be obtained prior to fishing from the farm shop close to the lake's car park. Touring caravans are welcome here but space must be booked in advance (Tel: Mr. Bloomfield on 01728 602168).

Route. From Ipswich take A12 towards Lowestoft and turn right on to the A1094 Aldeburgh Road. One mile further on take left turn to Sternfield, half a mile further on turn left again following signposts to Marsh Farm Lakes.

MARTHAM PITS, Martham Ferry, Norfolk

These super tench fisheries are adjacent to the tidal River Thurne which provides free alternative fishing to the visiting angler. They are an interesting complex of small pits controlled by the Martham and District A.C., being heavily reed-fringed and usually very weedy. Depth fluctuates between 4 and

10 feet and the water is quite clear. There is a terrific head of tench in the 2½ – 5 lb. range, plus one or two whoppers, with the odd bream to 3 lb. plus. Other species are roach, crucian carp, rudd, eels and pike. There is also a strong head of carp into double figures. Good during the early part of the season, especially to those fishing early or late. Day tickets (24 hours using two rods) cost £3.50 in advance from the petrol station in Martham (Tel: 01493 748888). A weekly ticket costing £12 is also available. Special senior citizens yearly permit costs £15. For additional information call the Martham Club secretary, Mr. K. Poole on 01493 748307.

Route. Take the Yarmouth Road from Norwich to Acle. Then take the A1064 and B1152 into Martham. In the village take left turn down Staithe Road which leads to the swing-bridge ferry. Just before the ferry fork right, keeping to the right of the dyke, which leads into the River Thurne and the pits are 100 yards further on.

MIDDLE HARLING LAKE, nr Thetford, Norfolk

The fishery comprises of a lake, a pond and, at the time of writing, a match canal is under construction. The lake is rectangle in shape with an island and affords good mixed fishing for roach, perch, bream, crucian carp and mirror carp to over 20 lb. The small, purpose built pond is full of silver fish and crucian carp, being ideally suited to youngsters and beginners. When completed the canal presently being excavated will measure 400 yards long by 12 yards in width, being geared specifically for pole anglers and stocked to suit. Day tickets cost £4 and must be obtained prior to fishing from the adjacent cottage (Tel: 01953 718205 for additional information).

Route. From Thetford take the A1066 Diss road and after four miles take left fork to East Harling. After three miles turn left towards West Harling. The fishery is then on the left opposite a sharp right hand bend and well signposted.

NARBOROUGH TROUT AND COARSE LAKES, Narborough, Norfolk

Two one-acre, well stocked lakes, containing carp into double figures, plus tench, roach, perch, bream and chub. Depths vary from 6 to over 10 feet with deep water close in over the marginal reeds. Meadow Lake is very much a specimen fish water, while Millers Lake caters for the general pleasure angler. Day tickets available from the adjacent fisheries lodge (see also Narborough Trout and Coarse Lakes in 'Trout Fishing Day Ticket – Stillwaters') cost £6. For more information Tel: 01760 338005. Lakes open 9.00 a.m. – 8.00 p.m. only (closes earlier in the winter). There is a toilet facility and a well stocked tackle and bait shop with coffee and snacks also. Open all year round.

Route. Take the A47 Dereham road from Norwich following signpost into the village of Narborough. The fishery entrance gate is then on the right and well signposted.

NATURES HAVEN FISHING LAKES, Swannington, Norfolk

A three lake man-made fishery situated in mature woodlands. 'The Match Lake' covers around an acre average 5 feet deep and is oblong-shaped with a large central island. It has 33 pegs. Species include all silver fish plus tench, crucian, common and mirror carp. 'Dad 'n' Lads Lake' is doughnut-shaped with a central island and covers half an acre. Depth averages 5 feet. It is heavily stocked with small to medium sized specimens of all the previously mentioned species and is great fun fishing. A learning pool no less. 'Derek's Lake' is an oblong-shaped water of around half an acre varying in depth between 3 and 6 feet containing carp into double figures. There is a snack bar and toilet facilities on site and the lakes are open from dawn until dusk. Day tickets cost £5 (£3.50 for senior citizens and juniors) from the bailiff who calls round. Youngsters under 14 must be accompanied by an adult. For additional information and match bookings Tel: 01603 260303 or mobile 07979 646374.

Route. Take the A1067 Fakenham Road from Norwich and turn off at Attlebridge following sign for Swannington. At the staggered crossroads go straight across and follow road into village. After Swannington church take the next right and the fishery is situated half a mile further along on the right and signposted with adjacent parking.

NEEDHAM LAKE, Needham Market, Suffolk

This seven acre lake is a mere stone's throw away from the railway station at Needham Market. Depths vary between 6 and 20 feet and the banks are of an open aspect. Stocks include roach and rudd, plus tench to over 9 lb., perch, pike, bream to over 9 lb., mirror and crucian carp. This is a multi-use water with facilities for canoeing and miniature power boats etc. The fishery includes a half mile beat of the adjacent River Gipping which backs on to the lake's north bank. Controlled by the Gipping Valley Angling Club who run the lake for the Mid Suffolk District Council. Day tickets cost £3.50, yearly January – December tickets cost £26, juniors £11 and concessionary at £13 all from Bosmere Tackle, Needham Market (Tel: 01449 721808) and entitle members to fish three other pits, plus

three stretches of river.

Route. From Ipswich take the A14 and then the B1078 going to Needham Market. The lake is then on the right, sandwiched between the river and the railway line just over the river bridge.

NORTHFIELD LAKES (formerly Holmans Pits), Southery, Norfolk

Two well established oval-shaped clay pits each around one and a half acres. Depths vary between 2 and 7 feet and species include roach, rudd, tench and bream plus carp to over 20 lb., and large pike. Open 16 June until middle of September. Day tickets cost £3 in advance from Mrs. Langley (Tel: 01366 377551 for additional information). Fishing is dawn until dusk only. Night fishing only by prior arrangement.

Route. From Downham Market take the A10 towards Ely for around five miles and turn left into Southery on the B1386. Entrance to the lakes is then via the second farm turning on the left past the potato store, and well signposted.

NORTON FISHERIES, Norton, nr Bury St. Edmunds, Suffolk

This is a beautifully landscaped two-lake fishery. The smaller lake is oblong-shaped and around an acre in size with depths ranging from 5 to 12 feet and there is a small central island. Stocks include roach, rudd, perch, chub, bream, tench and carp. A good float water. The larger lake is irregular in shape and covers some three acres with two islands. Contains common, mirror and ghost carp averaging double figures with specimens to 30 lb. Other species include tench to 4 lb. and roach. Day tickets cost £10 from the owner, Mr. A. Sanders, who calls round. There is a £100 yearly ticket also available (Tel: 01359 241664 or mobile 0771 1133416 for more information).

Route. From Stowmarket take the A14 heading towards Bury St. Edmunds. Turn off on to the A1088 at Woolpit heading towards Norton. As you come into Norton turn left into Heath Road. The fishery is then on the right with access down bridle path.

PENTNEY LAKES – WILLOW CROFT FISHERIES, nr. Narborough, Norfolk

An enormous eight lake complex interspersed with tree clad islands and bars totalling some 160 acres of exciting coarse fishing, set in 300 acres of mature woodland. Ideal for both the specialist angler and pleasure angler alike. The banks are in places nicely overgrown with bushes, trees, reeds and sedges and there is an enormous variation in depth from 3 to 17 feet, providing a diverse choice of swims. Species stocked into each lake vary considerably and these include roach, perch, tench into double figures, bream to over 12 lb., plus pike, carp and wels catfish to over 30 lb. In some lakes there is a prolific head of carp. Day tickets cost £5 (for two rods) and a 24 hour ticket is £10. Summer season permits cost £100 and winter permits (excellent pike fishing) are £60. The lakes are open all year round and the fishery is open from 8.00 a.m. until 6.00 p.m., except for 24 hour ticket and season permit holders. Day tickets and season permits available from Mr. J. Block, the bailiff, at the Log Cabin (Tel: 01760 338668 for additional information). Caravans for hire on adjacent site (Tel: 01760 338668).

Route. Take A47 from Norwich to East Winch and look out on the left for the Carpenter's Arms Public House. Directly opposite on the left is a by-road. Proceed down this by-road for around two and a half miles and the entrance gate to the fishery is on the left.

THE PUDDLE, Mundesley, Norfolk

A one acre pond, oblong in shape, well wooded around the margins. Depths vary between 2 and 5 feet and there are extensive lily beds. Contains roach, rudd, perch, bream, tench to 5lb., plus a good stock of carp into double figures. A good pole water. Day tickets cost £3.50 from the adjacent caravan site office (Tel: 01263 720665). Season tickets cost £15. Open from March until the end of October.

Route. From Cromer head towards Mundesley on the B1159 coast road. In Mundesley turn right into Church Road. After 400 yards turn right into links road. Go to the top of the road and turn left following signs to golf club. Caravan site is then on the left.

RAILWAY LAKE, North Elmham, Norfolk

A wooded pretty lake of about an acre with depths varying between 2 and 11 feet. It is usually well coloured and holds tench, jumbo-sized crucian carp, roach, rudd, perch and bream to 6 lb., plus a small stock of specimen mirror carp. Controlled by the Fakenham Angling Club, membership is open only to those living within a 10 mile radius of Fakenham and available from Dave's Tackle Shop of Millers Walk, Fakenham (Tel: 01328 862543). There is a first year entry fee of £3 plus £15 (£7.50 senior citizens and juniors) per season thereafter which covers sport on additional stillwater fishing plus some excellent trout and coarse fishing on the River Wensum. Visitors, however, can purchase a day ticket costing £5 from Dave's shop to fish any of the club's waters.

Route. Take the A1067 Fakenham Road from Norwich to Bawdeswell and turn left on the B1145. Just past Billingford village the road goes over the River Wensum then look out on the left for the

Railway Tavern Public House. Just before the pub access to the lake is through a gate and over a cattle grid, then across a meadow to the far left hand corner.

RAILWAY PIT, nr Attleborough, Norfolk

A tiny shallow, weedy pond of around a quarter of an acre, containing small tench, roach, perch, pike and mirror carp. FREE FISHING.

Route. From Norwich take the A11 and three miles beyond Attleborough turn left at Old Buckenham crossroads. Proceed across the railway line and the pit is immediately on the left surrounded by trees.

RECTORY FARM FISHERY, Hingham, Norfolk

There are two man-made lakes here, both of around an acre apiece bordered by bushes and trees. The one in front of the farmhouse varies between 2 and 4 feet deep, whereas the lake behind the house fluctuates in depth from 4 to 12 feet. Both contain roach, rudd, tench, bream, plus common and mirror carp to high double figures. Great fun fishing on the float. Fishing is from dawn until dusk only with day tickets costing £4 (£3 for juniors) from the owner who calls round. The fishery opens on 1 March and closes at the end of October. (Tel: 01953 851509 for additional information.)

Route. Proceed towards Watton from Hingham on the B1108 road and the fishery is situated on the left just outside Hingham directly opposite a turning on the right signposted to Shipdham and Cranworth.

REEPHAM FISHERIES, Reepham, Norfolk

This L-shaped lake of around three acres was once a trout fishery. Now it provides excellent fun fishing on both float and ledger for carp into double figures, plus rudd, tench and crucian carp, in depths ranging from 3 to 12 feet. There is also a stock of the unusually coloured metallic carp, known as ghost koi, which have been caught to 26 lb. Keep nets are not allowed and the carp must only be retained in the landing net for a few minutes prior to photography. Day tickets cost £6 (£4 juniors and senior citizens and disabled) from the owner who calls round. Open 1 February until end of November. Fishing is from dawn until dusk with night fishing ONLY through prior arrangement. (For additional information Tel: 01603 870829.) There is also now a half an acre 'Father and Son' lake built especially for teaching, well stocked with all the previously mentioned species.

Route. Take the Reepham Road from Norwich and the fishery is on the left just before Reepham.

REYDON NO. 1 PIT (SHERWOOD WATER), Southwold, Suffolk

A reed-fringed gravel pit of around three acres which is over 20 feet deep in parts. Stocks include roach and rudd, plus some specimen tench in the 5 – 8 lb. range and a few perch. There are also carp up to 20 lb. One rod only to be used and there is NO NIGHT FISHING. Fishing is not allowed before 9.00 a.m. and there is no day ticket fishing on Sundays. A limited number of day tickets are available from Purdys Newsagents, High Street, Southwold (Tel: 01502 724250). Environment Agency rod licences must be shown in newsagents to secure a day ticket. There are two disabled swims with adjacent car park. Day tickets cost £4 and must be purchased in advance. The fishery is run by the Southwold and District Freshwater Angling Preservation

Society. For additional information regarding the club's other waters contact the Membership Secretary, Mrs. B . Reid of 24 Royal Avenue, Lowestoft (Tel: 01502 518198).

Route. From Southwold take the A1095 and after going over a bridge spanning Buss Creek look for Lakeside Park development on the left. The estate road leads to the car parking area behind the pit.

RICHARDSON'S PIT, Stalham, Norfolk

A tiny well coloured pond quite weedy and averaging about 7 feet deep. Holds some roach, eels, tench and a few carp into double figures. Fun fishing on the float. Day tickets must be obtained in advance from Richardson's Boatyard directly opposite on the other side of the by-pass (Tel: 01692 581081 for additional information).

Route. Take the A1151 from Norwich passing through Wroxham and on to Stalham. Just through the village on the by-pass Richardson's Boatyard can be seen on the right with the pit directly opposite on the left.

RINGLAND LAKES, Ringland, Norfolk

A beautifully matured complex of four old gravel workings set adjacent to the River Wensum at the foot of Ringland Hills. A quarter mile of the Wensum is, in fact, included with the fishery containing dace, chub, roach and pike. The lakes hold a variety of coarse fish with roach, bream and tench predominating. In the largest lake, called Days Water (first along the track on the left) there is also a modest stock of large carp running from double figures to over 30 lb., plus a small head of bream in the 5 – 10 lb. bracket, and jumbo-sized tench. Good perch, big crucians, rudd and specimen tench to over 6 lb. are spread throughout the other lakes, some of which are mostly overgrown, consisting of peninsulas, bays and islands all interconnected. There is also a good head of pike, including some nice doubles. Ideal for both pleasure trips and for the specialist angler. Open all year round.

Day tickets, dawn until dusk, cost £4 (juniors, senior citizens and disabled anglers £2) and must be purchased in advance. No night fishing. Season permits to N.A.C.A. members only costing £26 (passport type photo required) are also available and allows the holder to fish at night. These RMC Angling tickets under the control of N.A.C.A. are available from Tom Boulton's Tackle Shop in Norwich (Tel: 01603 426834). Further information from head bailiff, Russell Francis (Tel: 01603 870885).

Route. From Norwich take the old A47 Dereham Road and two miles from the city turn right down Longwater Lane by the Roundwell Public House. At the bottom of the hill turn left at a T-junction and half a mile further on keep left at fork. One mile further on, after passing close to the River Wensum, look on right for a narrow track leading to the fishery.

RIVERSIDE ONEHOUSE, nr Stowmarket, Suffolk

A small (half an acre) man-made lake containing a prolific stock of carp to over 20 lb. Day tickets cost £3 from Mr. Lee who calls round.

Route. From Stowmarket take B1115 towards Great Finborough. Half a mile out of Stowmarket turn left into Wash Lane. The lake is then on the left just before the ford.

RUSHBROOK FARM LAKE, Kettlebaston, Suffolk

An extremely well established oblong-shaped lake of around seven acres with depths varying between 3 and 10 feet. It contains a good head of quality rudd up to 2 lb., bream to 6 lb., and a prolific stock of tench to 4½ lb. Also present are perch and carp running into mid double figures plus the odd 20 pounder. NO NIGHT FISHING. Day tickets cost £6 and are only available in advance from Sudbury Angling Centre, Sudbury (Tel: 01787 312118) and Haverhill Angling Centre (01440 705011).

Route. From Stowmarket take the B1115 road into Hitcham and turn right following the signs for Kettlebaston. Once in the village of Kettlebaston turn right at the telephone box down a dirt track. This leads (after a fair drive) eventually to car parking in an open field adjacent to the lake which is at the top of the hill.

RUSTON REACHES, East Ruston, North Walsham, Norfolk

Two one and a half acre man-made lakes each of which have been most thoughtfully created with bends and islands rather like part of a river system. The banks are reed lined and there is a variation of depths between 4 and 8 feet. One lake is a real mixed fishery with perch, rudd, roach, tench, bream and pike. The second lake contains a stock of common, mirror carp and ghosties running into high double figures, plus the odd specimen over 20 lb. Day tickets cost £5 from the fishery manager's adjacent property, Ruston House. Fishing is dawn until dusk all year round. Additional information from the owner (Tel: 01692 583311). Adjacent lakeside cottages for rent.

Route. From Norwich take the A1151

road passing through Wroxham and almost to Stalham. Then turn left (following signs for Bacton and Happisburgh) into Stepping Stone Lane. Turn left at the next T-junction and then take first left following winding lanes into East Ruston. The fishery entrance is then on the left via an open field (with 'Fishing' signpost) with a line of cottages on both sides.

SCOULTON MERE, nr Hingham, Norfolk

This delightful, extremely secluded estate lake covers a sprawling 20 acres which for the most part averages just 3 feet deep. Only a third of its perimeter is actually open for fishing and this is controlled by the N.C.C. Staff Angling Club. The water is invariably quite clear with patches of marginal lilies and the stock comprises of rudd, roach, perch, pike (including the odd whopper over 20 lb.) plus a few wily old large carp and a strong head of tench averaging over 4 lb. Specimens to over 7 lb. have been caught in recent years. Day permits cost £3 (£2 juniors) from the bailiff who calls round or from the N.C.C. Staff A.C. bailiff, Mr. J. Baker, 28 New Road, Hethersett, Norwich (Tel: 01603 811003).

Route. Take the B1108 road from Norwich to just beyond the village of Hingham. Scoulton Mere is then on the right, well screened by woods, two miles along. Turn right into lane by sign saying Village Hall. Fishery entrance is a few hundred yards further on the right with parking inside gate.

SELBRIGG LAKE, nr Holt, Norfolk

A lovely well established, reed and tree lined four acre lake, which can prove rather weedy in summer. Selbrigg holds a prolific stock of roach, rudd, perch, pike and tench averaging 4 lb. There are one or two really large perch and eels here but both are difficult to track down. Day tickets cost £2 (£1 juniors and senior citizens) from Mr. Wright's farm close to the lake (Tel: 01263 712366). Open all year round.

Route. From Norwich take the B1149 road into Holt and turn right on to the by-pass. Take first right turn around 400 yards further on and then after two miles take the first left turn. The lake is then one mile further on, on the right.

SHALLOW BROOK LAKES, Bridge Farm, Costessey, Norwich

A four lake fishery, split on each side of the road adjacent to the tiny River Tud where along a short stretch fishing is included for dace, roach and chub. 'Meadow Lake' covers around three acres and is oblong in shape with depths between 2 and 12 feet. The stock includes tench to 5 lb., crucian carp, roach, rudd and carp into double figures. 'Horseshoe Lake' covers an acre with 20 pegs. Available for matches only and contains tench, silver fish and small to medium sized carp. Depths average 6 feet. The 'Carp Lake' covers two and a half acres with a central island and fluctuates in depth from 3 to 12 feet. It contains a strong head of double figure carp with the odd specimen over 20 lb. Other species include tench to 8 lb., specimen sized crucians, plus roach and rudd. A 4 lb. crucian carp was caught here by Len Freeman in 1999.

No. 4 lake (across the road), better known as 'Snipe Lake', averages around 12 feet and offers mixed fishing for roach, rudd, perch, chub, bream and tench in around one and half acres of water. Day tickets cost £5 from the bailiff who calls round. £80 season permits are also available as are £3 half day tickets. For more information

contact Martin Green on 01603 747677, or Robin O'Brien on 01603 744680.

Route. Take the A47 Dereham Road from Norwich into New Costessey. Turn right at the traffic lights down Norwich Road and half a mile further on the lakes are on the right and the left immediately past bridge over River Tud. Main entrance is on the left.

SOVEREIGN LAKE, Narborough, Norfolk

This well established irregular-shaped old gravel workings is studded with islands and varies in depth between 2 and 6 feet. During construction of the Narborough by-pass it was cut in half so that it can now be seen on both sides of the A47 King's Lynn to Norwich Road. Stocks include roach, bream, tench, rudd, perch, pike and carp into double figures. Day tickets cost £3 and should be purchased from Mr. John Baron at the adjacent bungalow prior to fishing (Tel: 01760 337288 for additional information), or from Kev's Tackle Shop in Norwich Road, Swaffham (Tel: 01760 720188).

Route. From Norwich take A47 and look out for the lake on both sides of the Narborough by-pass. Take the third sign on the left for 'Narborough' which provides access to the fishery bungalow.

STARFIELD PIT, Long Melford, Suffolk

A mature six acre pit of a most irregular shape, interspersed with islands and varying in depth between 2 and 10 feet with odd weed patches and holding a mixed stock. There is a head of bream in most size ranges plus tench averaging around the 4 lb. mark. The pike run into double figures and there is a good stock of mirror carp to over 20 lb. Day tickets cost £5 and must be obtained in advance from the secretary of the Long Melford and District A.A.,

Mr. N. Mealham, 6 Springfield Terrace, East Street, Sudbury (Tel: 01787 377139). Club membership costs £35 which in addition to the pit covers super fishing throughout the Stour Valley with numerous pieces on the river from Clare down to Long Melford. Renowned for its excellent dace and roach fishing. Members of the Bury St. Edmunds A.A. also have access to this pit.

Route. Take the A134 from Sudbury to Rodbridge Corner and turn left on to the Foxearth Road. Half a mile on carry straight ahead at a very sharp left turn, passing through Liston towards the chemical factory. Keep left of the factory and go down a track on the right in Liston Garden. Starfield Pit is then at the bottom of the track on the right, adjacent to the L.A.A. pits.

STATION PIT, Bungay, Suffolk

This tiny pit is situated near the disused railway station at Bungay Common and is ideal for youngsters. It is shallow and the fishing relatively easy. Light float fishing is recommended. There are plenty of small roach, dace and eels. But a surprise may be in store in the way of big perch which are known to inhabit the pit. Specimens are caught from time to time up to the 3 lb. mark. There are some nice crucian carp too. Day tickets cost £3 (which also includes over three miles of fishing on the nearby River Waveney which skirts Bungay Common) and are available in advance only from the adjacent Outney Meadow Caravan Park reception which opens at 9.00 a.m. NO NIGHT FISHING. Touring caravaners and campers are welcome at the park who rent out boats and canoes on the river. Anglers who stay at the park can also fish a 100 yard stretch of the river frontage. For additional information Tel: Mr. Hancy on 01986

The 'Station Pit' on Bungay Common. Renowned for its large perch and crucian carp

892338. The Station Pit is actually under the control of the Suffolk County A.A. whose members, plus those of the local Cherry Tree A.C., can fish on their club cards.

Route. From Norwich take the A146 then the B1332 to Bungay. Turn right at the by-pass roundabout towards Homersfield and proceed to the next roundabout. Then look on the right for the entrance to Bungay Common (just off roundabout). The pit can then be clearly seen only 150 yards away adjacent to the caravan park.

STONHAM BARNS FISHERY, nr Needham Market, Suffolk

A one and a half acre irregular-shaped man-made lake with three islands, where depth varies between 3 and 7 feet. Contains roach, rudd, bream, tench, perch and crucian carp, plus common and mirror carp running into double figures. No night fishing. Open all year for both pleasure and match fishing (Tel: mobile 07747 614203). Toilet facilities on site and coffee shop where snacks are available. Day tickets cost £5 from the bailiff who calls round. There is an adjacent caravan site.

Route. From Ipswich take the A14 then the A140 heading towards Norwich. In Little Stonham, turn right and follow signposts to Stonham Barns and Birds of Prey Centre.

SUFFOLK WATER PARK FISHERIES, nr Ipswich, Suffolk

This extremely modern, recently developed man-made gravel pit fishery amounts to over 80 acres of water set in 150 acres, split up into six very different lakes.

Lake No. 1 is called 'The Big Fish Lake' and horseshoe in shape with three distinct bays, covering 25 acres. Depths vary between 3 and 14 feet and species include pike to over 30 lb., and carp to nearly 40 lb., plus roach, rudd, tench and bream. Lake No. 2 – 'The Match Lake' – is specifically tailored to competition fishing with 65 permanent pegs. It is round in shape and covers 14 acres. The stock includes small to medium sized carp, plus roach, rudd, bream and tench. Lake No. 3 called 'Long Acre' is a stock lake (no fishing). Lake No. 4 – 'The Traditional Lake' – covers five acres and is stocked with silver species including roach, rudd, tench, bream and perch. Lake No. 5 is in fact a 'Canal' and a mixed fishery with depths averaging 7 feet. Built purposefully for pole fishing it contains a mixed stock of silver fish and carp. Lake No. 6 called 'The Teaching Pool' is around one-third of an acre holding carp and silver species.

Day tickets start at £6 for one rod throughout the complex except for the 'Big Fish Lake' where a £7 ticket covers two rods. A 24 hour (two rod) ticket costs £11. There is a resident angling coach on site, Vince Morgan, and a café which delivers meals to anglers at their swims. Telephone the office on 01473 832327 for additional information and match bookings.

Route. Exit the A14 from Ipswich at the Claydon – Great Blakenham junction and follow the B1113 road to Bramford. The fishery is then on the left and well signposted.

SWALE PIT, Waldringfield, Suffolk

A three acre, irregular-shaped gravel pit varying in depth from 4 to over 15 feet. Well stocked with carp of all sizes from mere ounces up to double figure specimens, plus rudd, roach, bream and tench. Water levels here tend to fluctuate. Day tickets are bookable in advance from Markhams Tackle Shop in Woodbridge

Road, Ipswich who issue 10 tickets per day (Tel: 01473 727841). Fishing is from Monday through Saturday only. No Sunday fishing.

Route. From Ipswich take the A14 towards Felixstowe, turning left towards Waldringfield at the roundabout. One and a half miles further on look on the left for Wilding and Smiths gravel workings where the pit is situated. Until 5.30 p.m. cars can be parked next to the pit, otherwise they must be left at the top of the lane.

SWANGEY LAKES, nr Attleborough, Norfolk

The fishery consists of three gravel pits. No. 1 is around seven acres with depths from 3 to 17 feet and contains a prominent island, offering a wide selection of different swims. The main stock is of carp including commons, mirrors and leathers to over 30 lb., plus crucian carp and tench to specimen proportions. Other species include perch, rudd, roach and bream with a chance encounter of wels catfish over 40 lb. The largest ever weighed 42½ lb., and was taken in 2001. No. 2 lake covers two and a half acres and is long and narrow with one small (approachable) island. Stocks here include a prolific head of carp between 5 and 20 lb., plus crucian carp to 2 lb., and tench to over 5 lb. No. 3 lake (also known as the 'Pike Lake') covers a sprawling 10 acres with a number of islands and depths to 18 feet. This is a mixed fishery containing all those previously mentioned species including pike but excluding catfish. Renowned for its specimen pike. Michael Wilkins caught a 38 lb. pike here in 1999. Day tickets cost £6 (£2.50 juniors) available at the Lakes from the bailiff who calls round. A special 24 hour night fishing ticket is also available at £10 (£5 juniors). Further enquiries Tel: Ray on 01953 452907.

Route. From Norwich take the A11 and along the Attleborough bypass take turn on right to West Carr. Follow road to T-junction and then turn left when road forks, and 100 yards further on turn right. Go over ford and turn sharp left into fishery.

SWANTON MORLEY FISHERIES, Norfolk

Controlled by the Dereham and District A.C., this superb fishery comprises over 30 acres of gravel workings, split into two small and three large pits. Depth fluctuates between 3 and over 20 feet and can vary within just a few feet, especially around the many bars and peninsulas. There is a super stock of roach, including specimens to over 2 lb., an ever-increasing head of bream to over 12 lb., and a fine head of tench between 4 and 7 lb. There are also perch, including the odd whopper, a few crucian and common carp, plus a prolific head of pike. Specimens over 25 lb. are taken most winters and there is a healthy stock of doubles among the hordes of jacks. Deadbaits usually sort out the quality pike. Night fishing is for members only. Anyone can join Dereham and District A.C. by contacting the secretary, Mr. David Appleby (Tel: 01362 637591) after 7.00 p.m.

Running behind the pits and included with the fishery is a super three-quarter mile length of the River Wensum which contains some good roach, dace, chub and pike, plus the odd barbel. No night fishing. Day tickets cost £5 (£2.50 juniors and senior citizens) from the bailiff who calls round and are from dawn until dusk only. Season permits are also available costing £30 (£15 for juniors, ladies, senior citizens and disabled). All these tickets are also available from Myhill's Tackle Shop in Dereham (Tel: 01362 692975 for additional information).

Route. Take the A1067 Fakenham Road from Norwich to Bawdeswell and then the B1147 to Swanton Morley. Go over the Wensum and turn sharp right. The pits are then about 400 yards along on the right with adjacent car parking. Cars can in fact be driven all around the fishery to within easy reach of most swims.

TANNERY LAKE, Worthing, Norfolk

This attractive secluded man-made fishery comprises of a one acre lake plus an interesting reach of the Blackwater Stream well known for its specimen dace, roach, trout and chub The lake is fed from the stream and averages over 10 feet deep with a prolific stock of roach, good perch, and tench to 4 lb. NO NIGHT FISHING. A good pole water for roach approaching specimen proportions. Day tickets cost £3 from the owner who calls round to anglers. For additional information telephone Mr. Eve on 01362 668202. Season permits available costing £35.

Route. Take the A1067 Fakenham Road from Norwich and in Bawdeswell branch on to the B1145 going through Billingford village. Proceed over the bridge spanning the River Wensum and take the next left turn Go over the bridge across the little River Blackwater and the lake is immediately on the right with adjacent car parking beside a huge chestnut tree.

TASWOOD LAKES, Flordon, Norfolk

A collection of seven tree-lined, well maintained lakes which vary in size from one to four and a half acres plus a half mile stretch of the adjacent River Tas best known for its dace and roach fishing. Depths vary from around 5 to 16 feet deep. Most lakes contain a mixture of roach, rudd, bream, tench, perch, crucian carp, and pike but are best known for the prolific stock of king carp, the fishery record being a 32 lb. 6 oz. specimen caught by Jason Low in 2001. There are carp of all strains here including commons to 32 lb., some ghost koi to 25 lb., and the exotic grass carp to over 20 lb. In the two new, recently excavated lakes there are specimen crucian carp, tench and bream only,

Toilet facilities are on site and anglers are asked to note that there is no entry to the fishery during the hours of darkness and that night fishing is by prior arrangement only. Day tickets are available from the adjacent bungalow from 7.00 a.m. and must be booked in advance. Night tickets, 24 hour tickets and long stay tickets are also available. Contact Mr. Ellis (Tel: 01508 470919). Yearly membership tickets are also available on application. There is a tackle and bait shop on site which also sells food.

Route. From Norwich take the A140 to Newton Flotman and take the right fork to Flordon. One and a half miles further on turn left to Tasburgh. The lakes are then a further 200 yards on the left.

TAVERHAM MILLS LAKE, Taverham, Norfolk

Owned by Anglian Water, this beautiful irregular-shaped, well established ex gravel workings covers some 20 acres. Depths vary between 2 and 12 feet and there are extensive beds of lilies, mostly the dwarf pond lily, providing numerous float fishing swims close in. There is a prolific stock of double figure carp plus odd specimens to 30 lb., and an even larger head of tench in the 4 – 10 lb. bracket. Albert Bunn took a 10 lb. 2 oz. tench here in 1999. Other species include roach, rudd, perch, pike (including the odd whopper) and a small stock of bream running between 6 and 12¼ lb. Unhooking mats are essential items of tackle here on the gravel based banks. Day tickets must be purchased prior to fishing from the lodge adjacent to the anglers' car park. There is a £6 day ticket which covers fishing from an hour before dawn to an hour after dusk and a 24 hours ticket for £12. Fishing on the lake goes from 1 March to 30 November. Special angling accommodation next to the lodge is also available for both overnight and holiday purposes. Tel: 01603 861014 for additional information about Taverham Mills Lake Fishery which includes a superb part of the River Wensum. A limited amount of day tickets for the 'river only' are issued from the lodge each year (see 'River Wensum'). Anglers staying in the holiday accommodation however can also purchase permits for the River Wensum.

Route. From Norwich take the A1067 Fakenham Road into Drayton and take the left fork along Taverham Road immediately past the large garage on the left. Proceed for one mile and at the first crossroads in Taverham village the fishery entrance can be seen on the left.

THE CIDER LAKES, Ilketshall St. Lawrence, Suffolk

Two man-made lakes of quarter of an acre and half an acre respectively. Depths vary between 3 and 7 feet. Stocks are similar in both lakes and include all types of carp, commons, mirrors, leathers and ghosties, running into high double figures. Day tickets (only 18 issued each day) cost £4 per rod from the owner who calls round. Open 7.30 a.m. until dusk, all year round. No night fishing. Only youngsters over 14. No boilies. For additional information Tel: 01986 781353.

Route. From Beccles take A145 towards the A12, and take first right (just out of Beccles) past level crossing. Proceed through to Ringsfield crossroads and go straight across towards Ilketshall St. Andrews. Follow road to Ilketshall St.

The beautiful Taverham Mills Lake, owned by Anglian Water and situated just six miles west of Norwich. Great tench and carp fishing

Lawrence and turn left past church on to the A144. After half a mile fishery signpost is on the left.

THORPENESS MERE, Suffolk

This 50 acre sheet of water dotted with numerous islands, is considered more of a boating lake than a fishery. But despite its lack of depth (the lake is just 1 to 2 ½ feet deep) it does contain some nice fish, including a good stock of roach to over the pound, some rudd, eels and carp into high double figures. Fishing is free but from a short 100 yards length of the northern bank only. NO NIGHT FISHING. The rest of the perimeter is restricted and barred to angling. There are over 100 boats to hire on the Mere which provides an ideal family-cum-fishing day out. For additional information contact Mr. C. Block at the boathouse (Tel: 01728 453771) or Mr. G. Ogilvie (Tel: 01728 832523).

Route. From Norwich take the A146 then the B1332 going through Bungay and on to the Halesworth A144 road. Go through Halesworth on the A144 and branch on to the A12 (T) going to Yoxford. Then take the B1122 to just beyond Leiston and turn left on to the B1353 which leads directly to Thorpeness and the Mere.

TURF HOLE POND, Potter Heigham, Norfolk

This is a pond of around three-quarters of an acre with depths varying between 4 and 8 feet. Stocks include roach, perch, rudd, bream, tench, carp and the occasional specimen-sized pike. No night fishing. Day tickets cost £3 (only 15 issued each day) in advance from Red Roof Farm, Ludham Road, Potter Heigham (Tel: 01692 670604) or from the office inside the fishery gates. B & B is available at the farm.

Route. Take the A147 from Norwich to Acle, turning left on to the A1064 towards Potter Heigham. Continue over River Thurne past the ambulance station on the left hand side. The farm yard can be found on the right hand side of the road at Station Road junction. Pull into the farm yard from the A149, then continue along the track for 500 yards.

WALNUT FARM FISHERIES, Attleborough, Norfolk

A modern man-made fishery comprising of a three-quarter acre lake and 350 yard long canal. The lake has two islands and depths fluctuate between 4 and 8 feet. Stocks include golden orfe, perch, and carp to over 20 lb. Note, cereal groundbait is not allowed. Barbless hooks only. Species in the canal which averages 6 feet deep are roach, rudd, crucian carp, bream and tench. Day tickets cost £4 from J.M.P. Tackle, Unit 26, Haverscroft Industrial Estate, New Road, Attleborough, NR17 1YE. Open 9.00 a.m. – 6.00 p.m. (Tel: 01953 455282).

Route. Take A11 from Norwich, turning left at Attleborough signposted towards town, then the first left down Mill Lane. At the T-junction turn left into Silver Street. Half a mile further on turn left opposite shop called 'Unit One', following signpost to fishery.

WAVENEY VALLEY LAKES, Wortwell, Norfolk

This complex is without question the best stocked group of carp fisheries available on day ticket in East Anglia. Huge numbers of 20 and 30 lb. plus specimens exist here, the largest on record being a 38¼ lb. beauty taken by Terry Doyle in 1996. There are in fact 10 lakes ranging in size from two to five acres, affording a variety of swims in a well wooded setting. Depths vary between 3 and 16 feet and the water is usually well coloured in most of the lakes with a good covering of marginal reeds and sedges. Although these lakes contain predominantly carp there are quality tench, bream into double figures, plus roach, perch and pike all reaching to specimen proportions. Two lakes, Marsh Lake and Yew Tree Lake, have been purposefully stocked with wels catfish. These average double figures with a healthy sprinkling of 20 and 30 pounders. Largest on record caught here weighed over 50 lb.

Day tickets are available on the bank from the bailiff who calls round. These cost £10 (three rods) for 12 hours, £20 for 24 hours or £100 for a weekly ticket (Tel: 01986 788676 for additional information). The shop stocks tackle, a good variety of carp baits and general holiday provisions. Anglers wishing to rent one of the luxury lakeside caravans should book well in advance and there are five-star showers and toilet facilities on site for all visitors. Touring caravaners are also welcome and anglers may pitch their own bivvies. No dogs allowed. Open all year round.

Route. From Norwich take the A140 road turning left to Pulham Market. Continue along the B1134 into Harleston and then take the road into Wortwell village. The lakes are well signposted and in the centre of Wortwell on the right.

WELMORE LAKE, Salters Lode, Norfolk

This one and a half acre man-made lake averages around 7 feet deep and contains an interesting stock of specimen fish including both bream and tench to over 5 lb. and carp to 20 lb. Also present are roach, rudd and pike. An ideal venue for the specialist angler.

Fishing is from dawn until dusk only and day tickets which cost £4 must be purchased in advance from Mr. Bob Riches of 15 Sandy Lane, Denver (Tel: 01366 383291).

Route. From Downham Market take the B1122 Wisbech road and just through the village of Salters Lode take the first left turn and go over two bridges, following track to Welmore Lake Sluice. The lake is then well signposted with adjacent car parking.

WEYBREAD FISHERY, Mill Lane, Weybread, Suffolk

Formerly 'Weybread Trout Fishery', this lovely square-shaped lake has been extended to around two and a half acres and varies in depth from 3 to 12 feet with an island accessible by a bridge. The banks are extremely well established with extensive beds of reed, rush and sedge and in addition to big roach (2 lb. specimens are common), crucian carp, tench, specimen chub, perch and mirror carp, bream are very much a target species here because they can be regularly taken off the top. Yes! These bream come up and suck in floaters like mixer biscuits from the surface at what really is an amazing fishery. I featured Weybread Pit in my 2002 series of *Go Fishing* for Anglia TV and it is the only location I have ever expected to catch bream off the top in over 50 years of fishing. Quite unique sport. Anyone can book a day ticket to enjoy this prolific man-made stillwater. Telephone the owner, Denis Gartell on 01379 588141.

Route. From Norwich take the A140 Ipswich Road turning off on to the B1134 through Pulham Market and on to Harleston. In Harleston take the B1116 road to Weybread. In Weybread village take the first left past the garage. The fishery is then around 200 yards down

Mill Lane on the left, adjacent to thatched cottage.

WEYBREAD GRAVEL PITS, nr Harleston, Norfolk

The Harleston and District A.C. control this super complex of six nicely matured ex gravel workings. Two are for members only (anyone can join) and four are available to all on day tickets. No night fishing on day tickets. Depths vary considerably from 3 to over 30 feet and the banks are easily accessible with good adjacent parking. There is a superb stock of mirror carp in the middle pit with numerous doubles and specimens to over 20 lb., plus roach, perch, tench, bream, pike and sizeable crucians spread throughout the complex. The largest pit, aptly called the 'Ocean Pit', is an immense sheet of water and at 100 acres plus is easily the largest gravel pit in Norfolk. It holds a fine head of specimen bream, quality roach, plus tench, pike to over 25 lb., and a small stock of wily but large carp.

Day tickets cost £4 (per rod), £7 (two rods) and £2 for juniors and senior citizens (per rod). These are available and should be purchased in advance from Waveney Angling of London Road, Harleston (Tel: 01379 854886). Weekly tickets cost £16 per rod and £8 (juniors) respectively. The Harleston and District A.C. offers two types of fishing. To join the club costs £21 and entitles members to fish several miles of the River Waveney, in addition to the two club pits (not available on day tickets). Then for an extra £22 per rod (£13 juniors) members also have access to the four day-ticket pits – and only members may night-fish these waters. Additional information from Sue at Waveney Angling.

Route. Take the A140 from Norwich turning left at Pulham Market on to the B1134 Harleston road. Then take the Weybread Road and after crossing the River Waveney at Shotford Bridge the pits will be seen to the right and left of the road half a mile out of Harleston.

WILLSMORE WATER, Fakenham, Norfolk

An irregular shaped man-made lake of about one and a half acres, averaging around 5 feet deep. It contains a nice stock of mirror carp to 25 lb., commons to 20 lb., roach, perch, bream to 8 lb. and tench to over 7 lb. Controlled by the Fakenham Angling Club, membership is open only to those living within a 10 mile radius of Fakenham and available from Dave's Tackle Shop of Millers Walk, Fakenham (Tel: 01328 862543). There is a first year entry fee of £3 plus £15 per season thereafter (£7.50 senior citizens and juniors) which covers additional stillwater fishing plus some excellent trout and coarse fishing on the River Wensum. Visitors, however, can purchase a day ticket costing £5 from Dave's shop to fish any of the club's water.

Route. From Norwich take the A1067 into the town of Fakenham and branch on to the old road which runs parallel to the by-pass going over the River Wensum at what used to be Goggs Mill. The lake access is then via Hayes Lane, off Sandy Lane with adjacent parking.

WINDMILL PONDS, Denver, Norfolk

Two half acre ponds both oval in shape and reed-lined with depths to 6 feet. They contain roach, bream, tench, perch,

Top Right: Dan Leary with his massive 39½ lb. pike caught on deadbait from The Kingfisher Fishing Club Lakes at Lyng

Bottom Right: The galaxy of seven specimen fish packed waters known as Bawburgh Lakes, just off the A47 bypass near Norwich

128

some barbel and king carp to 20 lb. Good fun fishing on the float. Open all year round, dawn until dusk. Day tickets cost £4 at the water. For additional information Tel: Mr. Riches on 01366 383291.

Route. Take the A10 from King's Lynn and 12 miles from the town look for 'To the Windmill' sign on the right. Turn right and the ponds are adjacent to the windmill on the left hand side of the road.

WOODLAKES, Stowbridge, Norfolk

There are over 20 acres of water at Woodlakes, comprising two large (10 and 12 acres respectively) and three small lakes, all set in picturesque wooded countryside adjacent to Woodlakes Log Cabin, Caravan and Camping Park. All the lakes are well coloured and average between 6 and 15 feet. They are well stocked with roach and rudd plus tench and plenty of bream in the 3 – 10 lb. range with a prolific head of carp running to close on 30 lb. Double figure fish are most plentiful. For mixed bags float fishing along the margins with maggots or breadflake is recommended. And for the carp high protein pastes or boilies. An ideal family spot where the specialist can also catch tench, bream and carp of specimen proportions.

Touring caravans are welcome and anglers may, for a small charge, pitch their own tents away from the lakes. No bivvies to be erected. Day permits are available from the reception kiosk or if

Top Left: A 12 lb. 5 oz bream caught distance ledgering by John from the Three Bridges Farm Lakes syndicate fishery at Elsing in Norfolk

Bottom Left: Paul Dawson displays a 21 lb. grass carp caught on floating biscuit from lakeside in Lenwade

closed from the adjacent warden's log cabin. Fishing for up to 12 hours costs £7. Anglers who pay to camp or stay in the log cabins or in their own caravans enjoy reduced fishing rates. There is a shop on site for tackle and bait where flasks are filled and fresh sandwiches made to order. For additional information telephone 01553 810414.

Route. Take the A10 from King's Lynn turning right in Stow Bardolph and proceed towards Stow Bridge; 500 yards before the bridge carry straight ahead at a sharp left turn and Woodlakes can then be seen on the right just 200 yards further on.

WOODRISING CARP LAKE, Cranworth, Norfolk

A two acre man-made lake with three islands and shaped rather like a figure of eight. Depths vary from 4 to 10 feet and the water is always well coloured. There is a prolific stock of both common and mirror carp running into double figures plus the odd specimen over 20 lb., with tench and roach. Day tickets cost £3.50 (£2.50 for juniors), all night permits cost £4 from the bailiff who calls round to anglers. Season permits costing £60 are also available. For additional information call Mr. David Bunning at Jubilee Farm, Cranworth (Tel: 01362 820702). Caravan and camp site nearby for anglers intending a lengthy stay. Lake opens on 28 May and closes 23 December.

Route. Take the B1108 Watton road from Norwich to Hingham. Just beyond the village look out on right for the road to Shipden. Follow Cranworth sign, and Jubilee Farm is in the village on the right. The lake is then a short distance away with adjacent car park.

STILLWATERS — MEMBERS ONLY

ABBEY HEATH LAKE, Thetford, Norfolk

A three acre nicely matured gravel pit fishery varying in depth from 6 to 15 feet, situated beside the Little Ouse within eyesight of the A11 Thetford by-pass. It contains a super head of specimen fish including carp to 25 lb., pike to 28 lb., tench to 6 lb., plus roach, rudd, perch and bream. MEMBERS ONLY WATER of the Bury St. Edmunds Angling Association. Yearly membership costs £38, £15 for juniors, from general manager, John Easdown (Tel: 01284 753602). Membership includes fishing in five other 'members only' lakes and on the Little Ouse.

Route. From Thetford take the B1107 Brandon road to the A11 by-pass roundabout. Head towards Norwich on the A11 and entrance to the fishery is immediately past the road bridge spanning the Little Ouse on the left.

ALDERSON LAKE, Needham Market, Suffolk

Named with deep respect after the General Manager of the Gipping Angling Preservation Society, Mr. George Alderson, who has done so very much for angling in this area, the fishery comprises of two gravel pits which are actually owned by the Society. The largest around seven acres is nicely reeded around the perimeter and has two islands. Depth varies between 6 and 16 feet and the stock includes a good head of roach and rudd to over the pound, plus numbers of specimen bream and tench which have both been caught over 10 lb. Specimen pike are also taken here and the lake has produced fish to 27 lb. in recent years. The smaller lake is about an acre and is extremely well stocked with tench, crucian carp, roach, rudd and pike, providing excellent fishing for the younger angler. MEMBERS ONLY WATER of G.A.P.S. Apply to George Alderson, 37 Heatherhayes, Ipswich, IP2 9SL (Tel: 01473 602828). Yearly membership costs £43 with reduced rates for senior citizens, ladies and juniors, and covers a wealth of local fishing on other pits and over 10 miles of the River Gipping.

Route. From Ipswich take the A14 and then the B1078 going to Needham Market. Entrance to the fishery is down the sharp left turn over the bridge spanning the River Gipping directly opposite Bosmere Mill.

BARHAM PIT, nr Claydon, Suffolk

This huge, irregular-shaped pit can be seen on the left of the track when travelling by train from Norwich to London. It covers a sprawling 20 acres with beautiful willow clad islands and peninsulas. There is a prolific stock of both roach and bream plus some nice tench, perch, and carp to over 30 lb. The pike run to over 20 lb. MEMBERS ONLY WATER of the Gipping Angling Preservation Society with yearly membership through Mr. George Alderson, 37 Heatherhayes, Ipswich, IP2 9SL (Tel: 01473 602828). Membership costs £43 and there are reduced rates for juniors, students and senior citizens. The Society controls several other super stillwaters plus over 10 miles of the River Gipping.

Route. From Ipswich take the A14 then branch on to the Claydon road (old

Norwich Road). Turn left at Pest House Lane which then leads directly to the pits.

BARROW LAKE, Barrow, Suffolk

A one acre man-made lake surrounded by reeds. Depths vary from 3 to 14 feet and species include roach, rudd, crucian carp and tench. Pegs 3 and 5 are earmarked for use by disabled anglers only. Toilet and kitchen facility block on site. MEMBERS ONLY WATER of the Bury St. Edmunds Angling Association. Yearly membership costs £38, £15 for juniors, from General Manager, John Easdown (Tel: 01284 753602) or from 'Baitmait' tackle shop in Hardwick Industrial Estate, Bury St. Edmunds (Tel: 01284 750889). Membership includes fishing on five other 'members only' lakes and on the Little Ouse.

Route. From Bury St. Edmunds take the Barrow Road and take the first turning right (Sharpes Hill) as the village is approached. Stay on that road until a T-junction, then turn left down the hill towards Barrow church. A combination locked gate leading to the fishery is at the bottom of the hill on the right.

BAWBURGH LAKES, south west of Norwich, Norfolk

The full potential of this superb complex of seven ex gravel pits, covering 80 acres of water, has yet to be discovered. The current British bream record taken here from Lodge Lake weighing 18 lb. 8 oz. by Kerry Walker in 2001, gives a good idea of the quality of fishing on offer. Controlled by the Norfolk Anglers Conservation Association (N.A.C.A.) of which I am proud to be president, formed by concerned local anglers way back in 1986. Anyone may join at £10 yearly. A MEMBERS ONLY rule applies to fish the four main lakes and a three-quarter mile length of the charming

Upper River Yare which bisects the fishery (see 'Norfolk Rivers'). A full yearly permit costs £160 with Spring, Season and Winter (pike fishing) tickets also available.

Note: Non members can fish only the three smaller lakes on a day ticket basis for £6 (£5 to members). These contain roach, rudd, perch, tench, bream and pike. Membership cards, full permits, and day tickets are available from most Norwich tackle dealers or N.A.C.A. secretary, Malcolm Hitching (Tel: 01263 732752).

Bawburgh Lake covers over 15 acres and is heart-shaped with one large and two smaller tree covered islands. Depths shelve to 14 feet and stocks include a good head of carp into the mid 20s plus odd specimens to over 30 lb., plus pike to

These two tench of 11 lb. 2 oz and 9 lb. 6 oz caught by Chris Turnbull, are just two of the several monsters he has caught from Bawburgh Lakes

131

28 lb., strong shoals of double figure bream to 13 lb., and a super head of monster tench. Martin Burgess took an 11 lb. 5 oz. beauty here in 1998.

Lodge Farm Lake at 29 acres is the largest and a most irregular shape containing four islands. Depths average over 10 feet and shelve to 16 feet. Pike have been caught here to over 30 lb., and there is a good head of carp running to over 30 lb. There are also small numbers of tench and monster bream. In addition to the British record of 18 lb. 8 oz. caught by Kerry Walker here in 2001, one of 18 lb. 15 oz. (possibly the same fish) was caught but not claimed.

Colney Lake also covers 20 acres and is rectangle in shape with depths to 26 feet, though it averages 8 – 16 feet. Contains a head of carp to over 20 lb. Best caught to date being the 37½ pounder to Ken Norton. There are also bream to over 16 lb., tench into double figures, plus big perch and pike to over 20 lb.

Colney No. 2 Lake. Covers just five acres with depths to 6 feet and can weed up heavily. It holds carp to over 20 lb., plus some nice tench and pike.

Route. From Norwich take the old A47 towards Dereham and, still within the City outskirts, turn left at Bowthorpe roundabout. Proceed to the traffic lights and turn right going around edge of housing estate. Go across mini roundabout and take next right turn into New Road. Go along this narrow road which runs parallel with the River Yare until the fishery entrance gate (well signposted) can be seen on the left. There are various parking areas within the fishery complex.

BEDINGHAM LAKE, nr Ditchingham, Norfolk

A well established, tree-lined oblong-shaped four acre ex gravel working with depths varying between 2 and 22 feet and extensive lily beds around the perimeter. Stocks include both perch and crucian carp to over 3 lb., some very large eels, quality tench plus roach and rudd to over 2 lb. Main attraction at Bedingham Lake however is the prolific head of king carp which are in fact the original stock fish first introduced back in the 1970s. Specimens run to well in excess of 30 lb. and there is an excellent head of 20 pounders. The fishery closes for the months of April and May only. MEMBERS ONLY WATER with applications in writing to Mr. J. Hickleton, 12 St. Matthews Avenue, Banham Road, Beccles, Suffolk, NR34 9PS.

Route. From Norwich take the B1332 Bungay road to Woodton and the lake is situated on the right visible from the road.

BILLINGFORD PIT, Norfolk

This boomerang-shaped little pit of around an acre lies secluded in a hollow, heavily clad in undergrowth of gorse and trees all the way round. Swims have been cut into the steep banking, offering depths varying between 6 and 12 feet under the rod tip, though water levels do fluctuate periodically. It can prove rather weedy in the summer but is excellent tench fishing with specimens to 4 lb. plus, along with lots of small roach and perch. There are also one or two large carp and a few pike. A really big perch is not unlikely. MEMBERS ONLY WATER of the Dereham and District A.C. Membership costs £30 yearly (£15 for senior citizens, ladies, juniors and disabled anglers) from the membership secretary, Mr. D. Appleby, 6 Rump Close, Swanton Morley, Norfolk (Tel: 01362 637591). Membership cards are also available from Myhill's Tackle

Shop of Church Street, Dereham (Tel: 01362 692975).

Route. Take the A1067 from Norwich to Bawdeswell then turn left to Billingford, taking the first left turn in the village to Swanton Morley. Proceed for about 100 yards to the first bend and on the right is a narrow dirt road leading down to the pit and fishery car park.

BIRCHAM PIT, Bircham, Norfolk

Also known as 'The Moor' this small man-made lake contains roach, bream, perch, good rudd, tench, a few carp and enormous gudgeon. Fun fishing on the float. No ground baiting and strict 'No Litter' rules are enforced. MEMBERS ONLY WATER of the Docking A.C. and open only to local anglers who should contact the Chairman, Mr. Rob Parnell on 01485 518315.

Route. Take A1067 from Norwich going through Fakenham towards Docking. Take left fork to Great Bircham and in village turn right on to the B1153 road to Docking. Bircham Pit is then a short distance further on the right opposite Moor Farm.

BOSMERE LAKE, Needham Market, Suffolk

This five acre oval mere was in fact the subject of a study by Cambridge University a few years ago which dated its existence back 10,000 years to the Ice Age. Moving on to the turn of this century when barges last used the adjacent River Gipping to carry coal upstream from Ipswich to all the mills, the mere was used as a turn around and as a reminder there is still evidence of the entrance dyke, now overgrown, from the river. When the Eastern Union Railway started up in 1849 the days of carrying goods by barge were numbered and the old dyke silted up, leaving the mere

isolated. But so much for history. Today the mere varies in depth between 4 and 18 feet and is nicely wooded around the margins, with patches of lilies dotting the surface. It holds predominantly bream to over 5 lb., plus roach, tench, pike and numerous eels, some very large, plus carp to over 30 lb. A really secluded mixed fishery. MEMBERS ONLY WATER of Fishery Management Services Limited. Season permits cost £75 from Mr. Vic Green of Viscount Tackle, Ipswich (Tel: 01473 728179). There is a waiting list in force.

Route. From Ipswich take the A45 and then the B1078 going to Needham Market. The lake is then on the left immediately before the road crosses the River Gipping.

BRADMOOR LAKES, Narborough, Norfolk

Two beautifully matured gravel pits set in the wooded outskirts of Bradmoor Plantation. Both are around four acres and hold a prolific stock of fish, with several species running into specimen size. The old record crucian carp of 5 lb. 10½ oz. was in fact caught here by Graham Halls in 1976 and during the 1980s and 1990s numerous bream into double figures were taken. There are good numbers of roach and rudd, plus tench over 5 lb. and an enormous head of mirror carp up to nearly 30 lb. MEMBERS ONLY WATER of the Swaffham Angling Club. Membership costs £28 yearly (£16 for juniors, senior citizens and disabled anglers) from Kev's Tackle Shop of Norwich Road in Swaffham (Tel: 01760 720188).

Route. From Norwich take the A47 towards King's Lynn. The lakes are then situated on the right of the Narborough by-pass.

CAUSEWAY LAKE, Great Blackenham, Suffolk

This seven acre lake is unique in that it actually has the River Gipping flowing in one end and out the other. Depths vary between 5 and 17 feet and the water is usually well coloured by the river. Bream are the predominant species with good stocks of all sizes, including fish to 7 lb. Bream bags of 100 lb. are nothing out of the ordinary here. There are also some tench, specimen roach and chub which filter through from the river. Perch have been taken to over 3 lb., and a good pike is always on the cards. MEMBERS ONLY WATER of the Gipping Angling Preservation Society with yearly membership through Mr. George Alderson, 37 Heatherhayes, Ipswich, IP2 9SL (Tel: 01473 602828). Membership costs £43 and there are reduced rates for juniors, students and senior citizens. The Society controls several other super stillwaters plus over 10 miles of the River Gipping.

Route. From Ipswich take the old A14 road going through Claydon on the B1113. Half a mile through Great Blackenham turn right down a private road and proceed over the railway bridge. The lake is then on the other side of the River Gipping.

CHARSFIELD RESERVOIRS, nr Wickham Market, Suffolk

Two farm irrigation reservoirs of one and a quarter acres and two acres respectively. Both are tree-lined and depths in the small lake vary from 3 to 10 feet and in the larger between 4 and 16 feet. Levels can naturally fluctuate here. The smaller lake contains crucian carp, roach, rudd, perch, tench and a prolific head of king carp including ghosties running to 20 lb. The larger lake has tench, roach, rudd, perch, bream, carp

into double figures, and a small number of golden orfe to 3 lb. Fishing is dawn until dusk. MEMBERS ONLY WATER of the Framlingham and District A.C. Membership yearly tickets cost £26, juniors, disabled and senior citizens £13. Available from Saxmundham Angling Centre (Tel: 01728 603443), Stuart Clay Traps Limited in Melton (Tel: 01394 385567) and Markhams Tackle in Ipswich (Tel: 01473 727841).

Route. From Ipswich take A12 and turn left to Wickham Market. After half a mile then take the first right turn on to the B1075 heading towards Clopton. Two and a half miles on watch out for 'Priors Roses' on the left and turn down lane immediately opposite on the right. After 600 yards at T-junction turn left and the lakes are then 600 yards on the right.

DISS MERE, Diss, Norfolk

Situated right in the middle of Diss with adjacent parking and shopping facilities, this almost round mere of some four acres shelves down to 20 feet in places with a variety of swims around two-thirds of the perimeter (the other one-third is private frontage) varying between 3 and 10 feet just a rod length out. It holds a prolific head of roach, rudd and especially crucian carp which run to over 2 lb., but average around 12 oz. There are also some eels, small bream, tench to 4 lb., and a strong head of mirror and common carp to close on 20 lb. MEMBERS ONLY WATER of the Diss A.C. with yearly tickets costing £18 from P.M.Pegg Angling Supplies in Diss (Tel: 01379 640430). A two rod permit for night fishing is available on written application to the secretary, Peter Taylor, 'Kerensa', High Street, Thorndon, Eye, Suffolk, IP23 7LX.

Route. Take the A140 road from Norwich and branch off at Scole on to the A1066 to Diss. The mere lies bang in the centre of Diss opposite Waveney Fish Farm.

DITCHINGHAM PIT, Bungay, Suffolk
This attractive three acre pit lies alongside the River Waveney at the back of Bungay Common and is bordered by shrubs and willows. Depth varies between 3 and 7 feet and the water is usually well coloured. Species include a nice stock of carp averaging double figures, with specimens to nearly 30 lb., plus a good head of crucians over the pound. There are also roach, perch, big eels and some tench up to 5 lb. MEMBERS ONLY WATER of the Bungay Cherry Tree A.C. Membership costs £30 (£20 for senior citizens, and disabled – £10 juniors) from the secretary, Mr. Ian Gosling, 37 St. Mary's Terrace, Bungay (Tel: 01986 892982). Membership includes a wealth of other local fishing controlled by the club.
Route. Take the B1332 from Norwich to the large roundabout just before Bungay. Go completely round roundabout to be facing Norwich again and take the first lane on the left beside a bungalow. This leads to the car park and pit.

EYE PONDS, Eye, Suffolk
A collection of oblong-shaped man-made ponds (11 in total) varying in size from a tennis court to half a football pitch. Depths vary from 4 to 9 feet and stocks include roach, rudd, perch, bream, tench and carp into double figures. Great fun fishing on the float. MEMBERS ONLY WATERS of the Diss and District A.C. Anyone can join via P.M. Pegg Angling Supplies (Tel: 01379 640430). Season permits cost £18 which includes the local Diss Mere (see 'Stillwaters – Members only') and fishing on the River Waveney.
Route. From Eye take B1077 road toward Debenham. On exiting Eye just past the end of speed limit sign there are four ponds immediately on the left with small parking area in front of entrance gate. The other seven (on the right) are accessible via a short track opposite the entrance to those on the left.

FOSTERS END PITS, Blackborough End, Norfolk
Three tiny pits plus the main pit of around eight acres. Depths in the big pit vary considerably from 3 to over 25 feet. It holds some hefty crucians and rudd plus both carp and pike into double figures. Pike well in excess of 20 lb. are in fact taken every winter. Also present are bream to over 10 lb., and a good stock of specimen tench. MEMBERS ONLY WATER of the King's Lynn A.A. Club – membership cards cost £28 (£14 for senior citizens and £5 for juniors) from all local tackle shops and from the secretary, Mr. M. Grief, 67 Peckover Way, South Wootton, King's Lynn, PE30 3UE (Tel: 01553 671545).
Route. From Norwich take the A47 King's Lynn road to East Winch. In the village turn left down a track just before the church and the pits are then one mile ahead on the left.

HADDISCOE LAKE, Haddiscoe, Suffolk
This five acre well established gravel pit fishery is square in shape and has depths varying from 6 to 16 feet. It contains roach, rudd, perch, tench to 6 lb., bream to 8 lb., and a modest head of common and mirror carp running into double figures. No night fishing. MEMBERS ONLY WATER of the Beccles Angling

Club. Anyone may join for a £20 yearly subscription. (For additional information Tel: 01502 716716.)

Route. From Norwich take the A146 Lowestoft road to the huge roundabout just outside Beccles. Turn left on to the A143 and proceed into Haddiscoe village. Turn right at the village hall and the lake is half a mile further on, on the right.

KINGFISHER FISHING CLUB LAKES, Lyng, Norfolk

For over 20 years a trout fishery, this interesting complex of four well matured gravel pits (plus a three-quarter mile stretch of the River Wensum) changed over to coarse fishing in 1994 when the Kingfisher Fishing Club was formed by the owners. In fact the three small lakes have always been coarse fisheries and contain a good stock of roach, perch, tench, bream and pike but it is the huge 26 acre ex trout water which has captured everyone's attention by producing at least two pike nudging 40 lb. A shoal of huge bream is also present and a 15 lb. 6 oz. monster was taken by R. Bedder in 2001. Depths vary from 5 to 14 feet in this prolific lake which is irregularly shaped with several islands. It also contains some quality roach and tench plus a tremendous head of carp to over 40 lb. The fishery record and a county record was caught by Dave Moore in 2001. It weighed 47 lb. 6 oz. The three-quarter mile stretch of the Wensum (see also River Wensum under 'Norfolk Rivers') skirts the big lake's northern shoreline and contains in addition to roach over 2 lb., chub to 6 lb., and pike to over 20 lb., plus small groups of specimen bream running into double figures. Closed in April and May. MEMBERS ONLY WATER. Contact Cyril or Paul Rogers of Walsis Farm, Lenwade, Norfolk (Tel: 01603 873333 or 01603 870400). Yearly (Jan – Dec) subscription costs £250 which also entitles members to the bar and restaurant facilities at the adjacent Leisure Complex.

Route. Take the A1067 Fakenham Road from Norwich to around two miles beyond Lenwade and turn left following the Lyng signpost. Proceed over the bridge spanning the River Wensum and in the middle of the village turn right down quarry lane at crossroads following signpost to the fishery.

LYNG PIT, Lyng village, Norfolk

This is a most attractive little pit of around four acres, which is wooded nearly all the way round with willow-clad peninsulas offering a variety of sheltered swims. The depth varies between 3 and 8 feet and the water is invariably well coloured. There is a good stock of roach, rudd and bream in all sizes. Though most are small there are a few bream up to 4 lb. The tench average around 4 lb., and there are a few pike plus a very small stock of large mirror carp. Dereham and District A.C. who control the fishing do in fact only have swims on about half the lake, along the river bank – about 20 swims in all. MEMBERS ONLY WATER of the Dereham and District A.C. Membership costs £30 yearly (£15 for senior citizens, ladies, juniors and disabled anglers) from the membership secretary, Mr. D. Appleby, 6 Rump Close, Swanton Morley, Norfolk (Tel: 01362 637591). Membership cards also available from Myhill's Tackle Shop of Church Street, Dereham (Tel: 01362 692975). Membership includes fishing on other local pits and on the River Wensum in choice locations (see also River Wensum under 'Norfolk Rivers').

Route. Leave Norwich on the A1067 Fakenham road, turning left at the Lyng signpost. At the village of Lyng take the right arm of the crossroads, signposted to sports club (which is in fact a track) and the pit is 50 yards on the right through a gate.

MANOR FARM LAKE, Battisford, Suffolk

Two small oval-shaped man-made lakes of around an acre apiece, with depths to 6 feet. They hold a stock of roach, rudd, perch, skimmer bream and crucian carp. Ideal pole and waggler fishing. MEMBERS ONLY WATER of the Gipping Valley Angling Club. Membership costs £26 from Bosmere Tackle, Needham Market (Tel: 01449 721808) and covers sport on two other pits and three pieces of river.

Route. From Needham Market take the B1078 (towards Wattisham Airfield). Turn right at the Barking Forge, signposted Battisford, and continue on this road past the church until you reach a concrete pad with an adjoining pair of houses on your left. Park on the concrete making sure all field exits and entrances are kept clear at all times.

MANOR LAKES FISHERY, nr Attleborough, Norfolk

This fishery comprises of two lakes situated a few hundred yards apart in quiet farmland.

'**Peck Meadow Pond**' is an extremely well coloured, well established pond of about three-quarters of an acre with depths varying between 3 and 5 feet. It contains a prolific stock of crucian carp to over 2 lb., rudd, perch, the odd large eel and both common and mirror carp to 20 lb. Ideal stalking on the float.

'**Manor Lake**' covers around three acres with depths fluctuating between 5 and 15 feet and is most irregular in shape. Stocks include rudd, perch, crucian carp,

Peck Meadow Pond, part of The Manor Lakes Fishery near Attleborough

tench to 7 lb., and a good head of common and mirror carp (plus some ghosties) to over 25 lb. The fishery opens 1 February and closes 15 October. This is a MEMBERS ONLY fishery controlled by Mr. Stephen Burroughs of Rockland Manor (Tel: 01953 483226). Season permits cost £90 of which only 30 are issued.

Route. The fishery is situated off the B1077 Attleborough to Watton Road at Rocklands.

MARSH COTTAGE LAKES, Thwaite, Suffolk

There are three man-made lakes here all about one and a half acres in size with depths varying from 2 to 4 feet. '**The Top Lake**' contains carp to 20 lb., barbel to 5 lb., and chub to 6 lb., plus rudd and a few skimmers. The '**Middle Lake**' varies from 2 to 6 feet and contains a good head of skimmer bream, small tench and crucian carp to 2 lb. The **'New Lake'**, recently excavated, has depths to 6 feet and holds a mixed stock of roach, rudd and skimmers. MEMBERS ONLY WATERS of Fishery Management Services Limited. Season permits cost £75 from Mr. Vic Green of Viscount Tackle in Ipswich (Tel: 01473 728179). Waiting list in force.

Route. Take the A140 from Norwich and in Thwaite look out on the left for the Bucks Head Public House. The fishery is immediately behind the pub with access via Marsh Cottage Lane.

MAYHEW'S, nr Waldringfield, Ipswich

This attractive half an acre man-made pond is reed-lined with depths varying between 2 and 7 feet. It holds roach, rudd and tench averaging 3 lb. No night fishing. MEMBERS ONLY WATER of the Framlingham and District A.C. Yearly membership cards cost £26 from Markhams Tackle in Ipswich (Tel: 01473 727841).

Route. From Woodbridge on the A12 proceed to Martlesham and take the Felixstowe road. Go half a mile past BT Laboratories and at the next roundabout turn left for Waldringfield. After one mile turn right at crossroads towards Newbourne; 300 yards further on take track on the right and after 500 yards the pond is then on the left.

MAYPOLE FARM LAKE, Buxhall, Suffolk

This three-quarter acre man-made lake contains just 12 swims. Depths vary between 3 and 7 feet and species include roach, rudd, tench, crucian carp and perch to specimen proportions. MEMBERS ONLY WATER of the Gipping Valley Angling Club. Club membership

costs £26 from Bosmere Tackle, Needham Market (Tel: 01449 721808) and entitles members to fish three other pits and three stretches of river.

Route. From Stowmarket take the B1115 to Great Finborough. About three-quarters of a mile out of Stowmarket turn right into Lower Road. Follow this past the golf course then take first left into Buxhall. The lake is then about half a mile on the left opposite Granary Craft Museum.

NAR VALLEY FISHERIES, Pentney, Norfolk

This thoughtfully landscaped fishery comprises a lovely winding piece of the River Nar (famous for its dace, roach and chub) and five interesting pits varying in size from just two to close on 40 acres, all set in over 400 acres. On each lake there is at least one wheelchair swim for

A 7 lb tench for John from Nar Valley Fisheries at Pentney near King's Lynn

disabled anglers with concrete ramps and level fishing platforms directly from cars. Two other lakes are currently being excavated. Stocks vary from pit to pit and include specimen sized tench to over 9 lb., double figure bream, carp and pike to over 30 lb., plus roach, perch and rudd. I chose the fishery for one of my television programmes in Series 13 of *Go Fishing* screened in 1999 and caught tench to over 7 lb. from the lakes and a superb 5 lb. plus chub using stalking tactics along the diminutive River Nar. MEMBERS ONLY WATER – fishing costs £40 for a dawn until dusk permit, or £70 for a 24 hour ticket. These are available from Mr. Chris Newell (Tel: 01553 841690). Members are issued with own keys.

Route. Take the A47 Norwich to King's Lynn road and turn off left in East Winch (opposite Carpenters Arms Public House) on to the Pentney Road. Continue past gate to Pentney Coarse Lakes which is on the left, following signs for Wimpey's and Middleton Aggregates whose entrance gate to the fishery is then on the right. Parking is adjacent to the lakes.

PARHAM LAKES, nr Great Glemham, Suffolk

Two man-made square-shaped lakes of around an acre apiece. Depth varies between 4 and 6 feet in each and the water is usually well coloured. They contain crucian carp, roach, tench, bream and carp into double figures. Ideal youngster's waters. MEMBERS ONLY WATER of the Saxmundham Angling Club. Contact secretary Mrs. B. Wilson (Tel: 01986 784317). Membership costs £25 yearly and entitles members to fish two other lakes.

Route. From Saxmundham take the A12 to just beyond Farnham. Look for garage on right at Stratford St. Andrew and turn right towards Great Glemham, just before garage. After a mile and a half turn left at crossroads. Lakes are then half a mile further on, on the left in old airfield.

PEDMARSH LAKE, nr Sudbury, Suffolk

Due to the enormous costs involved estate lakes are rarely made these days. Pedmarsh Lake, however, is an exception and has been created by damming a valley to provide some 20 acres of water. Depth varies from just 18 inches at the shallow end which has been designated a nature reserve, to around 16 feet at the dam end. Stocks include roach, perch, tench, bream plus a strong population of carp to 30 lb. MEMBERS ONLY WATER of the Colchester Angling Preservation Society who issue season permits costing £57 from Angling Essentials Tackle Shop in Witham (Tel: 01376 512255). This permit covers a wealth of local fishing in several stillwaters including famous Layer Pits and several miles of the Suffolk Stour (see 'Suffolk Rivers'). Anyone may join the club.

Route. From Sudbury take the A131 Halstead Road following signs for Pedmarsh and turning left three miles out of Sudbury. At Pedmarsh village turn right towards White Colne. Continue for one mile and the entrance to the lake is then via a track on the right and well signposted.

PLAYINGFIELD LAKES, Brandon, Suffolk

These two small man-made lakes of one acre and half an acre respectively are ideal float waters. Both are around 5 feet deep, nicely coloured with patches of lilies. Species include eels, perch, chub, roach, bream and pike with tench averaging over 4 lb., and carp to over 20 lb. MEMBERS ONLY WATERS of the Brandon and District A.C. who issue permits through the Leisure Centre in Brandon (Tel: 01842 813748). These cost £15 adults, £10 senior citizens and £5 juniors. Also available from Paul Macloughlin (Tel: 01842 812979). Fishing also covers a mile of the Little Ouse.

Route. From Thetford take the A11 to Brandon. Go into the town and turn right at Tesco's supermarket; 200 yards further along on the right are the playing fields with the fishery at the end of the lane adjacent to the Little Ouse.

REYDON NO. 2 AND 3 PITS, Southwold, Suffolk

No. 2 (Kingfisher Lake) is a one acre pit with depths to over 20 feet and holds specimen tench, odd chub, plus rudd, bream, roach, carp and perch to 2½ lb. The banks are reed fringed with just 15 swims available along on bank only.

No. 3 pit (Paisleys Pond) opened for the first time in 1989 having been dug specifically for fishing. It varies between 4 and 6 feet deep and is just half an acre in size. It provides easy fishing, especially for youngsters and contains a variety of species including roach, rudd, perch and tench, plus mirror and crucian carp. Both fisheries allow one rod only and NO NIGHT FISHING. MEMBERS ONLY WATER of the Southwold and District Freshwater Angling Preservation Society. A waiting list is in force. Apply to membership secretary, Mrs. B. Reid, 24 Royal Avenue, Lowestoft (Tel: 01502 518198).

Route. From Southwold take the A1095 and after going over road bridge spanning Buss Creek, look for Lakeside Park development on left. The estate road leads to the car parking area close to

No. 2 pit. Walk from park to no. 3 pit via footpath.

REYDON NO. 4 PIT (DENNY LAKE), Southwold, Suffolk

This two acre man-made fishery varies between 4 and 7 feet deep and has a centre island. It was dug as part of the 'Buss Creek' development specifically as a carp water and contains a strong head of commons and mirrors into high double figures, with specimens to 25 lb. MEMBERS ONLY WATER of the Southwold and District Angling Preservation Society. Subscriptions include an £8 joining fee plus £20 yearly, juniors £6. Apply to secretary, Mrs. B. Reid, 24 Royal Avenue, Lowestoft (Tel: 01502 518198).

Route. From Southwold take the A1095 and after going over a bridge spanning Buss Creek look for Lakeside Park development on the left. The estate road leads to the car parking area.

ROUGHAM LAKE, Bury St. Edmunds, Suffolk

A lake of about three acres with 8 feet of water at the dam end and shallows at the opposite end. Contains a nice stock of quality roach, some bream and tench, plus carp to over 20 lb. NO NIGHT FISHING. MEMBERS ONLY WATER of the Bury St. Edmunds Angling Association. Yearly membership costs £38 (£15 juniors) from general manager, John Easdown (Tel: 01284 753602), or from Baitmait tackle shop in Hardwick Industrial Estate, Bury St. Edmunds (Tel: 01284 750889). Membership also allows the holder to fish five other 'members only' lakes and sections of the Little Ouse.

Route. From Bury take the A14 Ipswich Road. Two miles out of Bury turn right at the AA box and then second right, signposted Whelnetham. The lake is then on the left at the bottom of the hill.

SCOTTOW POND, Scottow, Norfolk
This attractive five acre shallow lake contains an excellent head of tench. Scottow Pond's banks are heavily reed fringed and the water crystal clear. The bottom is silty and daphnia abound which is possibly the reason why the tench average over 4½ lb. – with specimens to 7 lb. There is also a head of pike, eels and some nice rudd to over the pound. MEMBERS ONLY WATER. Season permits cost £12 from Mr. Dunn (Tel: 01692 538662).

Route. Take the B1150 from Norwich passing through Coltishall, Buxton Lamas and on to Swanton Abbot. The lake is in the wood of Mr. Shaw's estate at Scottow.

SHEPHERDS PORT FISHERY,
Snettisham, Norfolk
This fishery comprises of three man-made clay pits. '**Shepherds Lake**' is oval in shape with an open aspect and covers four acres varying between 3 and 7 feet deep. It contains a mixed stock of roach, rudd, bream and tench. '**Bear Lake**' is around half an acre (17 pegs), doughnut in shape with a centre island and reed fringed. Depth varies between 2 and 7 feet and there is a prolific stock of crucian carp, common carp and mirror carp to over 10 lb. '**Stantons Lake**' is the largest at around eight acres with an open aspect. Depth varies between 3 and 6 feet and the stock comprises of rudd, roach, tench and bream. MEMBERS ONLY FISHERY of the King's Lynn A.A. Anyone can join however through local tackle shops or the secretary, Mr. M. Grief, 67 Peckover Way, South Wootton, King's Lynn, PE30 3UE (Tel: 01553 671545). Membership cards cost £28 (£14 senior citizens and £5 juniors).

Route. From King's Lynn take the A149 going towards Hunstanton. At Snettisham turn left into Beech Road and follow the RSPB signs to the fishery and adjacent parking.

SHROPHAM PIT, Shropham, Norfolk
A large irregular shaped pit of around six acres which has three reed clad islands and is heavily fringed in beds of lilies. Depth varies from 5 to over 10 feet and the stock includes a good head of bream to 7 lb., plus tench, roach, rudd, eels and pike into double figures. There is also a small wily stock of carp to over 20 lb. MEMBERS ONLY WATER of the Wymondham and District A.C. which issues club permits costing £25 from the secretary, Mr. T. Binks of 25 Rosemary Road, Norwich (Tel: 01603 405341) and through Myhill's Tackle Shops in Attleborough and in Wymondham.

Route. Take the A11 from Norwich and at the end of the Attleborough by-pass look on the left for the Breckland Lodge. One mile further on take Shropham turn off. One and a half miles further on proceed over bridge spanning River Thet and turn left immediately after the carrot factory. The pit is then 300 yards on the left down an apparent dead end called Bradcarr Road.

SIBTON LAKE, Sibton Park, Suffolk
This really shallow (2 – 3 feet deep) three acre man-made lake has three islands and the water is always thickly coloured. It contains rudd, tench, skimmer bream and a prolific stock of carp into double figures. MEMBERS ONLY WATER of the Saxmundham Angling Club. Contact secretary, Mrs. B. Wilson (Tel: 01986 784317). Membership costs £25 yearly and entitles members to fish three other lakes.

Route. From Yoxford take the A1120 towards Peasenhall. The lake is then in the grounds of Sibton Park around one and a half miles further on, on the right.

SNETTERTON PITS, nr Attleborough, Norfolk

Formerly known as Bert Wrights Pits, the complex comprises of seven nicely matured and quite deep gravel pits separated by spits and islands varying in size from just one to 12 acres nestled beside the River Thet and holding a variety of species. There is a good head of both roach and rudd, including large shoals of rudd over 2 lb., plus perch of the same weight. There are also tench to 7 lb., and bream running into double figures plus plenty of pike. Specimens over the 20 lb. mark come out each winter, mainly to deadbaits and there is a very healthy stock of 'doubles'. Other species include eels and mirror carp into double figures. Specimens to 34 lb. have in fact been taken. MEMBERS ONLY FISHERY. Season permits are available costing £150 for a 24 hour ticket and £100 for a dawn until dusk ticket. Also available are special match bookings. Additional information from Mrs. Cook (Tel: 01953 498289).

Route. From Norwich take the A11 to about three miles past Attleborough and at Snetterton Circuit (motor racing fame) proceed into Snetterton village. Then turn left and take second turning on the right which leads directly to the fishery.

SPARHAM POOL, Lyng, Norfolk

This extremely attractive well matured and heavily wooded ex gravel pit is a nature reserve shared with the Norfolk Naturalists Trust. It is irregular in shape and covers around 14 acres with a variation in depth from 3 to over 15 feet. Stocks include a strong head of roach to the pound, plus perch, rudd, eels and a good head of tench averaging around 4 lb. There are also pike including specimens over 20 lb.

A beautiful brace of double figure bream from Stradsett Lake

142

John Stevens took a 30 lb. specimen here in 1999. MEMBERS ONLY WATER of the Norfolk Anglers Conservation Association (N.A.C.A.) who issue just four tickets daily to members. These cost £4 and must be booked in advance. They are available only to N.A.C.A. members through the Fox and Hounds Public House in Lyng and from Tom Boulton/Angling Direct in Norwich (Tel: 01603 426834). A strict no keep net ban exists. To join N.A.C.A. contact Mr. Malcolm Hitchens, Woodside House, 5 The Meadows, Aylsham, NR11 6HP (Tel: 01263 732752).

Route. From Norwich take the A1067 Fakenham Road and turn left following the Lyng signpost one mile beyond Lenwade. At the bottom of the hill 100 yards before bridge spanning River Wensum turn left along track which leads to the N.A.C.A. car park.

STRADSETT LAKE, nr King's Lynn, Norfolk

A 20 acre triangular-shaped picturesque estate lake with three islands and an average depth of around 5 feet. This rich fishery contains a strong head of tench to over 5 lb., roach to 2 lb., and pike to over 20 lb. There is also a shoal of double figure bream and a handful of carp. I featured pike fishing on this beautiful estate lake in my 14th series of *Go Fishing* television programmes screened in 2000 on Anglia and Meridian Television and took six pike into high double figures, on both wobbled and static deadbaits. MEMBERS ONLY WATER. Contact the Estate Office (Tel: 01366 347642) who issue £80 full season tickets and £45 pike only – January until April tickets. The lake is open from January until September. Members may bank fish only. No boat fishing.

SWAFIELD FISHERY, Swafield, Norfolk

This reed lined, third of an acre fruit farm irrigation reservoir has depths to 20 feet and contains a stock of roach, tench and carp into double figures. MEMBERS ONLY WATER. Season permits cost £20 from Country Pursuits in North Walsham (Tel: 01692 403162).

Route. Take the A149 from North Walsham and as you come into Swafield village look for Tasty Tavern on the right. Park behind shop and proceed through fruit farm to the reservoir.

THE CLAY PIT, outskirts of Downham Market, Norfolk

An oval-shaped, reed lined pit of around three-quarters of an acre with patches of lilies and depths ranging from 6 to 12 feet. Contains roach, rudd, tench and carp running into double figures. There are also some crucian carp to 1½ lb. MEMBERS ONLY WATER of the Downham Market A.C. who issue membership cards costing £15 (£5 juniors) from Howletts Cycles and Fishing in the High Street, Downham Market (Tel: 01366 386067).

Route. From King's Lynn take the A10 road through to the Bexwall roundabout in Downham Market. Go over roundabout and after half a mile branch right on to Denver Road. At the T-junction turn left opposite Post Office. After 20 yards turn left just before church and the pit is then 200 yards ahead with adjacent car park.

THE FEN LAKES, Carleton Rode, Norfolk

A collection of six small lakes interspersed with islands and bars, set in deeply wooded countryside. Depths vary between 2 and 6 feet and stocks include roach, rudd, chub, tench, bream and a prolific head of king carp plus a few koi running into double figures. Open all year round. MEMBERS ONLY WATERS of The Fen Angling Club. Yearly tickets cost £60 available from Mr. Robin Ford (Tel: 01953 605514) or Mr. Andrew Ford (Tel: 01953 789947). There is also a junior yearly ticket costing £15.

Route. From Norwich take the B1113 Mulbarton road and proceed through Tacolneston and on to Bunwell, taking left fork at car sales and garage into Fen Road. After half a mile look on the right for entrance gates to fishery. There are two. First entrance is opposite cottage immediately before a sharp right hand bend.

THE IRRIGATION LAGOON, Beccles, Suffolk

A man-made, horseshoe-shaped fishery with depths ranging between 2 and 4 feet situated adjacent to the River Waveney which is the borderline between Norfolk and Suffolk. The lagoon can prove rather weedy but contains a fine stock of bream running to 6 lb., plus tench in the 2 – 3 lb. bracket. Other species include roach, rudd, perch and pike into double figures. MEMBERS ONLY WATER of the Southwold and District Freshwater Angling Preservation Society. Subscriptions include £8 joining fee plus £20 yearly. Juniors £6. Apply to Membership Secretary, Mrs. B. Reid, 24 Royal Avenue, Lowestoft (Tel: 01502 518198).

Route. From Norwich take the A146 road to just before Beccles and turn right at the large roundabout going under the footbridge and turning right again. Then take the second right just before public house and turn left down King's Dam, which leads to the fishery, via a dirt track at sharp right-hand bend.

THE MIDDLE RESERVOIR, Great Welnetham, Suffolk

A rather barren looking man-made irrigation reservoir of three acres. Depths shelve to 12 feet and species include roach, bream, tench and a stock of common and mirror carp into double figures. MEMBERS ONLY WATER of the Bury St. Edmunds Angling Association. Yearly membership costs £38, £15 for juniors, from General Manager, John Easdown (Tel: 01284 753602) or from 'Baitmait' tackle shop in Hardwick Industrial Estate, Bury St. Edmunds (Tel: 01284 750889). Membership includes fishing on five other 'members only' lakes and sections of the Little Ouse.

Route. From Bury St. Edmunds take A134 Sudbury Road to beyond Sicklemere. The lake is then on the left and can be seen from the road 50 yards beyond the speed restriction sign on the outskirts of Bradfield Combust. Follow the entrance road in front of a house and behind some cottages. The reservoir is then immediately on the left.

THORNHAM LAKES, nr Thwaite, Suffolk

There are three small lakes here varying in size from half an acre to three-quarters of an acre. Depths vary between 3 and 5 feet and each contains a mixed stock of small to medium sized roach, rudd, crucian carp, tench, mirror and common carp. MEMBERS ONLY WATERS of Fishery Management Services Limited. Season permits cost £75 from Mr. Vic Green of Viscount Tackle in Ipswich (Tel: 01473 728179). Waiting list in force.

Route. Take the A140 from Norwich to the village of Thornham. The lakes are then situated in Thornham Estate which is well signposted.

TOTTENHILL PIT, King's Lynn, Norfolk

A large pit varying in depth between 5 and 8 feet. Generally the water is clear with a little weed. The pit holds a good mix of roach, rudd, bream, specimen tench, crucians, pike and carp to over 20 lb. MEMBERS ONLY WATER controlled by King's Lynn A.A. Open membership with club cards costing £28 (£14 senior citizens and £5 juniors) from all local tackle shops and from the secretary, Mr. M. Grief, 67 Peckover Way, South Wootton, King's Lynn, PE30 3UE (Tel: 01553 671545).

Route. Take the A47 from Norwich branching on to the A1122 Downham road. In Stradsett turn right on to the A134 towards King's Lynn. Four miles on turn left to Tottenhill and the pit is then situated (rather well hidden from view) half a mile further on behind a housing estate which is diagonally across the common.

UNIVERSITY BROAD, Norwich, Norfolk

This is really a nicely landscaped and well matured gravel pit of around 10 acres and is the only large fishable stillwater within the city boundaries. Depths fluctuate between 4 and over 20 feet with at least 10 feet of water close in around much of the perimeter. It offers comfortable float fishing for roach, rudd, tench to 8 lb., and bream in the 7 – 9 lb. range, plus perch over 2 lb. There is also a good head of carp with specimen to nearly 30 lb. There are a few eels and a strong head of pike. Each winter several fish in the 20 – 26 lb. range are taken, usually on static deadbaits. There is in fact a 'no livebaiting' rule on the water. Closed for the months of April and May. MEMBERS ONLY WATER controlled by the University of East Anglia. Yearly permits cost £25 for a 12 hour yearly permit or £45 for a 24 hour yearly permit. Half price for concessionary tickets, from Mr. Ron

Alan Pearce nets a large perch from Water Lane Reservoir in Suffolk

Ashby of the Biology Department, U.E.A., Norwich, Norfolk. Apply in writing with stamped addressed envelope or telephone 01603 592238.

Route. Keep to the B1108 Watton Road from Norwich centre and turn left on to Bluebell Road in Earlham village. The university and broad are then seen down in the Yare Valley on the right.

WALPOLE LAKE, nr Halesworth, Suffolk

A one and a half acre rectangular-shaped man-made lake with depths varying from 6 to 12 feet. Contains roach, rudd, perch to 3 lb., and a few mirror carp into double figures. An excellent crucian carp water with specimens up to 2 lb. Open all year round. MEMBERS ONLY WATER of the Saxmundham Angling Club. Contact the secretary, Mrs. B. Wilson (Tel: 01986 784317). Membership costs £25 yearly and entitles members to fish three other lakes.

Route. Take the B1117 road from Halesworth to the village of Walpole.

Just before leaving the village turn right down lane with school on the left. The lake is then on the right 50 yards further along with adjacent parking.

WATER LANE RESERVOIR, Little Welnetham, Suffolk

A man-made irrigation reservoir of around three acres with a tree clad central island. This moat-like fishery has depths fluctuating between 4 and 9 feet, and contains bream, crucian carp, roach, common and mirror carp into double figures, plus a nice head of perch in all size ranges. Specimens to over 4 lb. have been caught in past seasons. MEMBERS ONLY WATER of the Bury St. Edmunds Angling Association. Yearly membership costs £38, £15 for juniors, from the General Manager, John Easdown (Tel: 01284 753602) or from 'Baitmait' tackle shop in Hardwick Industrial Estate, Bury St. Edmunds (Tel: 01284 750889). Membership includes fishing on five other 'members only

Water Lane Reservoir, Little Welnetham in Suffolk

lakes' and on the Little Ouse.

Route. From Bury St. Edmunds take the A134 Sudbury road and at Sicklemere take the left fork to Little Welnetham, signposted to Bradfields, Claire and Cockfield Green. The lake is then on the left, well elevated above road height, with adjacent parking beside a low building.

WENSUM FISHERIES, Costessey, Norfolk

Three well established old gravel workings beautifully set in wooded countryside in the Wensum Valley. These super fisheries vary between two and ten acres with depths to 14 feet. The largest (called the Back Lake) holds a prolific stock of roach and rudd with specimens to over 2 lb., plus shoals of bream in the 5 – 10 lb. range. A big pike is also not unlikely. Clear Water Lake holds the best stock of tench, averaging over 5 lb., plus a few bream to 10 lb., and carp to over 30 lb. Rainbow Pool contains roach, bream, tench and a few carp. There are three more (recently excavated) pits within the Wensum Fisheries Complex that will no doubt provide good fishing once they have matured. Also included is a three-quarter mile length of the River Wensum containing good chub and a few roach. NO NIGHT FISHING. Members have own keys. MEMBERS ONLY WATER of the Norwich and District A.A. 'Wensum Fishery' permits available from the secretary, Mr. C. Wigg, 3 Coppice Avenue, Norwich (Tel: 01603 423625).

Route. Take the A47 from Norwich and two miles from the city turn right by the Roundwell Public House down Longwater Lane. At the T-junction turn left and half a mile on take the right fork. The fisheries are then just 200 yards on the right behind iron gates.

WICKHAM MARKET RESERVOIRS, Suffolk

Two irrigation reservoirs of around one and a half acres apiece. One is 6 feet deep and weedy, the other has depths to 14 feet. Both contain a variety of species including roach, perch, rudd, bream and tench. NO NIGHT FISHING. MEMBERS ONLY WATER of the Fakenham and District A.C. Anyone may join for £26 (£13 for disabled, juniors and senior citizens) which covers several other local ponds and a stretch of the River Deben. Apply to Saxmunham Angling Centre (Tel: 01728 603443) or Stuart Clay Traps Limited in Melton (Tel: 01394 385567).

Route. From Norwich take the A140 turning on to the B1134 at Pulham Market to Harleston. Then take the B1116 Framlingham Road on to Wickham Market. Just before the town look on the right for the Easton Road (ignore previous signs) and the reservoirs are then on the left just 300 yards further on visible from the road.

THE WILLOWS (formerly TATTS PIT), Downham Market, Norfolk

A nicely coloured tree lined pit of one acre holding a strong head of tench to 4 lb., perch, roach, skimmer bream, plus some crucians and mirror carp into double figures. Ideal youngster's and beginner's water, on the float. MEMBERS ONLY WATER of the Downham Market A.C. who issue membership cards at £15 (£5 juniors) from Howletts Cycles and Fishing of the High Street in Downham Market (Tel: 01366 386067).

Route. From Norwich take the A47 Dereham Road branching on to the A1122 to Downham Market. In the town follow the route for Wisbech through the one-way system and look out on the left for a sub post office just before railway station. Turn left following track and the pit is just 100 yards along on the left behind trees.

WORTHING FISHERIES, Worthing, Norfolk

This excellent fishery with open membership, comprises of an 11 acre well established ex gravel pit varying in depth between 8 and 16 feet, plus half a mile of the adjacent River Wensum's southern bank, plus three-quarters of a mile of the diminutive Blackwater Stream, a tributary of the Wensum. Both contain chub, roach, dace, trout and barbel (See 'Norfolk Rivers' chapter). Most specialist anglers join the syndicate, however, for Worthing Pit's prolific stock of specimen fish. From nicely secluded swims with deep water close in carp have been caught to over 30 lb., pike to 34 lb., and tench into double figures. There is also a strong head of double figure bream which have been caught to over 15 lb. Other species include roach, perch and eels. MEMBERS ONLY WATER. Anyone may join by contacting Mr. T. Houseago (Tel: 01362 869122).

Route. Take the A1067 from Norwich to Bawdeswell then the B1145 going past Billingford village and over the River Wensum. Turn left 300 yards past the bridge and left again immediately after crossing a bridge over a small stream. The pit is then 600 yards along on the left.

John Mills cradles a 21 lb. carp from Worthing Fisheries, renowned also for its head of specimen sized bream and large pike

STILLWATERS — CAMPERS AND TOURING CARAVANNERS

GATTON WATERS, nr Sandringham, Norfolk

Eight acre well stocked lake containing a variety of species including roach, rudd, perch, tench, carp, available to both touring caravanners and campers with day tickets from the office costing £3.50. Telephone 01485 600643 for more information. Fishing from 8.00 a.m. until dusk only. Bar, food and toilet facilities on site.

GUNSSONS LAKE, White House Farm, Sibton, Suffolk

A one acre, shallow heavily coloured pond containing a prolific head of carp into double figures plus the odd larger specimen plus eels and bream to 2 lb. Day tickets cost £2 or £10 weekly to caravanners only (no camping) on top of overnight charges. For additional information Tel: Mr. Kitson on 01728 660260.

HAVERINGLAND LAKE, Norfolk

A 14 acre estate lake holding roach, perch, tench, bream and pike. Telephone the office on 01603 871302. Day ticket fishing costs £5 from the reception office. Both campers and touring caravanners welcome. Static holiday homes available for hire. Open all year round.

LAKESIDE LAKE, Denver, Norfolk

This small gravel pit fishery has two islands providing excellent fishing in around one and a half acres adjacent to parking. Holds a prolific stock of roach, perch and rudd plus some barbel, quality tench and bream with some carp to close on 30 lb. Touring caravanners

only. Fishing is dawn until dusk only. Open all year round. Day tickets cost £4 in addition to touring caravan charges. Apply to Mr. Bob Riches, 15 Sandy Lane, Denver (Tel: 01366 383291). Static caravan accommodation available to rent.

Route. From King's Lynn take the A10 to Denver and at the church follow signs to the Windmill. Then proceed ahead from the Windmill following signs to Lakeside Caravan Park and Fishery.

LAKESIDE LEISURE PARK, nr Saxmundham, Suffolk

Two attractive lakes of four acres and two acres set in wooded parklands are the attraction here. The larger lake contains a prolific head of carp into double figures with specimens to over 26 lb., whilst the smaller lake is a mixed fishery containing roach, bream, perch and tench. These are only available to campers who pitch their own tents and to touring caravanners for which there are some 400 spaces available. There is an outdoor pool, bar and restaurant facilities. Fishing costs £5 (per rod) daily on top of overnight camping or caravan charges. Tel: 01728 603344.

LITTLE LAKELAND, Wortwell, Norfolk

A half acre nicely wooded lake with depths to 12 feet containing roach, perch, bream, tench and a stock of carp into double figures with specimens to 25 lb. plus. Available to caravanners only. Fishing is from dawn until dusk and included in the caravan charges. Contact Mr. P. Leatherbarrow on 01986 788646.

ORBEN BECK, Sheringham, Norfolk
Available only to campers and caravanners this tiny pond holds roach, tench, crucian carp, rudd, bream and eels. Depth varies from 6 to 12 feet and the water is usually quite coloured with patches of lilies.

Nice fun fishing on the float and an ideal youngsters' camping location for the summer months. There is a shop on site, plus toilet and shower facilities. Day tickets to campers only cost £3 from Beeston Regis site office (Tel: 01263 823614).

STILLWATERS — MATCH FISHING ONLY

ABBEY WATERS, nr Old Buckenham, Norfolk
A triangular-shaped man-made one and three quarter acre 30 peg lake containing carp to 6 lb., plus tench, roach, rudd and chub. Depth averages between 4 and 9 feet and the fishery is surrounded by reeds and trees. Used for match fishing only. Club Secretaries should contact Barford Lakes on 01603 759624 for bookings. Open all year round.

COLTON LAKE, nr Barford, Norfolk
A two acre rectangular 40 peg lake with depths varying between 3 and 15 feet. The banks are reed lined and the fishery (an old irrigation reservoir) is open all year. Species include common and mirror carp between 4 and 12 lb., plus roach and rudd. The fisheries record catch for a six hour match was a staggering 328 lb., taken by Mick Mantle in 2001. Match fishing only. Club Secretaries should contact Barford Lakes on 01603 759624 for bookings.

RAILWAY LAKES, Thuxton, Norfolk
Two lakes of two acres and five acres and 60 and 40 pegs respectively. Depths vary between 4 and 6 feet in both lakes and the stocks include small carp, roach, rudd, chub, perch and tench. Club Secretaries should contact Barford Lakes on 01603 759624 for bookings. Match fishing only.

THE PONDS, Great Melton, nr Norwich, Norfolk
These three small lakes each of around an acre in size and each with a centre island average between 4 and 7 feet in depth and can in total accommodate 32 pegs. They are used for match fishing only and Club Secretaries should contact Mr. Bush on 01603 811135 for bookings and all additional information. The lakes are exceptionally well stocked with a variety of species including roach, rudd, perch, crucian carp, chub, both common and mirror carp plus some ghost koi.

STILLWATERS — SYNDICATE WATERS

BRIDGE LAKES, Lenwade, Norfolk
These are gravel pits, two small, one large, holding roach, rudd, bream, tench, carp to over 30 lb., and big pike. Limited number of yearly permits available from City of Norwich Angling Club. Secretary, Mr. Robert Watts (Tel: 01603 415984). Waiting list in force.

BROOKE PARK LAKES, Brooke, Norfolk
Two inter-connected mature well wooded estate lakes totalling some seven acres holding stocks of roach, rudd, tench, pike and carp to nearly 30 lb. Limited number of yearly permits available from Mr. M. Holl of Hillside Farm, Brooke, Norfolk (Tel: 01508 550260).

COLSTON HALL LAKES, nr Framlingham, Suffolk
Two well stocked lakes holding a mixed stock of rudd, tench, bream, carp, and ghost koi. Season permits available from Gerry Powell of Fishing Management Services, 19 Sirdar Road, Ipswich, Suffolk, IP1 2LD (Tel: 01473 40324).

GAYTON ROAD FISHERIES, Norfolk
A one and three quarter acre clay pit, dug and landscaped specifically for angling containing a stock of specimen roach, rudd, tench and carp with depths to 12 feet. Limited amount of season permits available by writing to Chris Newell, 'Field Fayre', School Lane, Middleton, King's Lynn, Norfolk. Waiting list currently in force.

THE NUNNERY FISHERY, Thetford, Norfolk
This extremely interesting and fast developing fishery comprises six pits ranging in size from one to ten acres and

Jason Davies caught this superb 25 lb. pike from the famous Nunnery Fishery near Thetford

in depth from 2 to over 20 feet situated beside the charming River Little Ouse on the outskirts of Thetford. Owned by the British Trust for Ornithology, who have organised a generous and continuous stocking policy for the future, these lakes offer superlative sport. Based to a large extent on carp fishing, three of these lakes regularly produce specimen mirrors, leathers and commons over 20 lb., plus a host of double figure fish, along with tench, rudd, roach, big perch and specimen pike. The largest carp to be taken weighed 41¼ lb., and fell to the rod of G. Maulkerson in 1999.

SNAKES MEADOW FISHERY,
Stokesby, Norfolk
This is a one and a half acre lake, well stocked with common and mirror carp to over 20 lb., plus roach, tench and crucian carp. Limited amount of season permits from Ray Chapman (Tel: 01493 369757). Waiting list in force.

THREE BRIDGES FARM LAKES,
Elsing, Norfolk
These three lakes of four, seven and 12 acres respectively, are in fact extremely well established ex gravel workings. Depths vary between 3 and 15 feet and

the water is usually quite clear. Stocks include specimen tench to 9 lb., plus good concentrations of double figure bream to 14 lb. plus and both common and mirror carp to over 30 lb. Other species include eels, roach and pike. Syndicate members also have access to around one mile of the adjacent River Wensum's southern bank. Species include dace, roach, pike and a prolific stock of specimen chub to over 6 lb. Due to the estate's wildfowling season, fishing on the lakes starts on 1 February and ends on 31 July. Syndicate tickets cost £200. Telephone Mr. David Baker on 01362 637883 for additional information.

WEST STOW COUNTRY PARK LAKE,
Bury St. Edmunds, Suffolk
This 18 acre well established gravel pit is situated in a bird sanctuary where depths fluctuate around three islands offering between 3 and 25 feet of water. It holds a good head of double figure bream, together with a stock of tench running to over 7 lb., plus king carp to well in excess of 30 lb. There are also a few specimen pike. For syndicate details (there is a waiting list in force) send stamped addressed envelope to Mr. Paul Taylor, 20 Swaffham Road, Watton, Norfolk, IP25 6LA.

STILLWATERS – HOLIDAY COTTAGES

COLSTON HALL, nr Framlingham,
Suffolk
Staying in 16th century cottage and fishing two lakes. Pond close to house averages over 10 feet deep and contains bream, golden orfe, ghost koi, rudd and tench etc. Second lake contains good stock of mirror carp running into double

figures in depths to 8 feet. Bed and breakfast accommodation in farmhouse also available. Contact John and Liz Bellefontaine, Colston Hall, Badingham, near Framlingham, Woodbridge, Suffolk, IP13 8LB (Tel: 01728 638375). Guests are charged £5 per day for the fishing. Touring caravans also welcome.

STILLWATERS — HOTEL ACCOMMODATION

GUNTON HALL LAKE, nr Lowestoft, Suffolk

An attractive weedy lake of around two acres. The water averages around 5 feet deep, is invariably well coloured and stocks include tench averaging around the 3½ lb. mark, pike, roach, rudd and mirror carp into double figures, plus specimens to 25 lb. The fishing is a facility open to hotel guests only. Open all year round. Gunton Hall is in fact a holiday centre with facilities such as golf, tennis and archery available to resident guests. For additional information telephone 01502 730288. Matches (20 peg) can be arranged at Gunton Hall Lake. Club Secretaries should contact Mr. Tony Cater on the above number.

Route. From Lowestoft take the A12 towards Great Yarmouth and Gunton Hall is on the right before the turn off to Corton.

LENWADE COUNTRY HOUSE HOTEL, LAKE AND RIVER, Lenwade, Norfolk

Fishing here, set in 18 acres of woodland, is available to guests only and comprises of a one acre lake with centre island holding a mixed stock of coarse species, plus one mile of the picturesque and winding River Wensum which holds dace, roach, chub and pike. Other facilities available to hotel guests include lawn tennis, a gymnasium, croquet, squash, sauna and an outdoor pool. For additional information telephone 01603 872288. Hotel guests on special holiday angling breaks have access to upgrade, which provides superlative extra sport at the famous Kingfisher Club lakes at nearby Lyng.

Route. From Norwich take the A1067 Fakenham road to Lenwade where the entrance to the hotel is on the left just before leaving the village.

STILLWATERS — FARMHOUSE HOLIDAY ACCOMMODATION

BROOKE PARK LAKES, Brooke, Norfolk

Two inter-connected mature well wooded estate lakes totalling some seven acres holding stocks of roach, rudd, tench, pike and carp to nearly 30 lb. Contact Mr. Holl of Hillside Farm, Brooke, Norfolk (Tel: 01508 550260).

Trout Fishing – Day Ticket (River – Fly Only)

RIVER WENSUM, Fakenham, Norfolk
One of the prettiest, streamiest parts of the River Wensum is immediately above and below the town of Fakenham where both day ticket and even free trout fishing is available. The upper Wensum in these parts is generally quite fast and shallow with odd pools and during the summer months very weedy. It produces well to the wet fly fished down and across, during the early season when fly fishing commences on 1 April and then to the upstream nymph and dry fly as soon as the weed comes up. The Fakenham Angling Club controls around two miles of the river here and issues day tickets costing £5 for a two fish limit through Dave's Tackle Shop, Millers Walk, Fakenham (Tel: 01328 862543).

The fishery is split up into several parcels above the mill and there are regular stockings of brown trout. There are also a few 'escapee rainbows' from adjacent fisheries in addition to a few dace and roach for those wishing also to try their fly outfits on coarse fish. Much of the banks are also free fishing (see map), particularly downstream of the mill and the polite enquiring angler will no doubt enjoy free fishing along other parts of the Wensum. Anglers living within a 10 mile radius of Fakenham and ONLY those can apply to join the Fakenham Angling Club through Dave's Tackle Shop. There is a first year entry fee of £3 plus £15 per season thereafter (£7.50 senior citizens and juniors) which covers all the club's holdings on the River Wensum and two local stillwater coarse fisheries. Day tickets are also available from Dave's Tackle Shop to fish the Railway Lake and Willsmore Water (see 'Stillwaters – Day ticket').

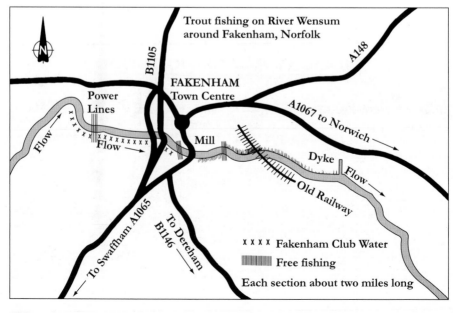

Trout fishing on River Wensum around Fakenham, Norfolk

x x x x Fakenham Club Water

||||||||| Free fishing

Each section about two miles long

TROUT FISHING – DAY TICKET (STILLWATERS)

COSTON TROUT FISHERY, Barnham Broom, Norfolk

This three lake well established fishery of three, four and 12 acres respectively nestles beside the upper reaches of the diminutive River Yare and is regularly stocked with rainbows and brown trout from 2 lb., upwards to the occasional double figure specimen. Depths here vary between 10 and 30 feet and the banks are nicely tree lined. Fishing is from 8.00 a.m. until dusk, 1 April through until end of October. Day tickets should be booked in advance. These cost £20 for a four fish limit from Mr. Phillip Gill (Tel: 01603 759253 or mobile 07860 238030). Toilet on site and summerhouse. Season rods are also available.

Route. Take the A47 from Norwich towards King's Lynn and turn off left at Barnham Broom signpost. Go through village and proceed over crossroads. Just out of village take first turning right to Coston. At T-junction turn right and the fishery is then straight ahead on the right, just past the church.

CROSS GREEN FLY FISHERIES, nr Bury St. Edmunds, Suffolk

This fishery comprises of four man-made and nicely landscaped lakes ranging in size from half an acre to two acres with depths to 20 feet. Two are oblong in shape, one triangular and one circular. Stocking includes varying sized rainbow trout from 1½ up to 6 lb. Brownies to 8 lb. are also stocked but the management asks these to be carefully unhooked and returned. A day ticket to fish the lakes costs £16. Eight fish can be caught but only two killed. Season rods also available at £300 comprising of 30 days fishing and a total of 60 fish to be taken. A half season rod at £160 is also available.

Pete Stacey waits for cousin Richard to net a nice rainbow trout at Coston Trout Fishery

These are purchased from the Fishing Office (Tel: Mr. Ken Steward on 01284 828323 for additional information). Fishing is from dawn until dusk. Open all year round.

Route. From Norwich take the A11 to the Thetford by-pass and then the A134 to Bury. Proceed around Bury on the A14 ring road and join the A134 again going towards Sudbury. Turn left on to the A1141 to Lavenham and some 400 yards along on the left is the fishery entrance which is well signposted.

EAST TUDDENHAM FISHERY, nr Norwich, Norfolk

This superb well established and attractive fishery comprises of two spring-fed and dammed lakes. The upper lake which flows into and feeds the lower lake varies between 5 and 8 feet deep and is around three acres with a centre island from which anglers may fish with access via a bridge. The lower lake shelves to 12 feet at the dam end and is around four acres also with a centre island. A very consistent fishery from lures in the early season to plenty of scope through the summer for the nymph and dry fly enthusiast. When the weed is up the lakes can fish well during the last hour of daylight. The stock includes both brownies and rainbow trout to over 8 lb. Open from early March to late October. Day tickets cost £15 for a four fish limit and are available from John's Tackle Den, 16 Bridewell Alley, Norwich (Tel: 01603 614114) or from Gallyons Tackle, Bedford Street, Norwich (Tel: 01603 622845) and from Tom Boulton's in Drayton Road, Norwich (Tel: 01603 426834). Controlled by the Norfolk and Suffolk Fly Fishers Society. Membership costs £20 from Mr. D. Armes, 100 Cozens Hardy Road, Norwich (Tel: 01603 423169). Members can take out a 'full rod' on the lakes (any day) for £223 yearly or a half rod for £125 (any day once a fortnight). The club has a

Tony Smith, the bailiff at Grove Water Trout Fishery, helps John display a superb rainbow caught during the filming of John's Anglia TV programme Go Fishing

busy social calendar with monthly meetings including well known guest speakers and other functions.

Route. Follow the A47 Dereham road from Norwich and take the Honingham turn off on the left through to East Tuddenham. In the village turn right at the crossroads (goes through a farm) and the lakes are then on the left, 500 yards further on.

GROVE WATER TROUT FISHERY, Newton Flotman, Norfolk

This fascinating and well managed fishery comprises around three-quarters of a mile of the diminutive and charming, ever twisting River Tas, and a most thoughtfully landscaped man-made three acre clearwater lake. The fishery is open from 1 April to 31 October and day tickets cost £20 for a limit bag of four rainbows. Fishing in the river for brown trout is catch and release only. The lake is regularly stocked with rainbows only, from 2 lb. upwards with a surprise in the form of a big fish always on the cards. I chose to feature Grove Water in my 2002 *Go Fishing* series for Anglia Television and enjoyed a thrilling day with rainbows to over 8 lb., on both damsel fly and gold head hare's ear nymphs. The occasional quality roach to a pound plus is not unlikely when presenting tiny patterns. An ideal fishery for brook rod enthusiasts. Limited to just five anglers a day. To book a day's fishing telephone the bailiff/gamekeeper, Tony Smith on 01508 471786 (mobile 07767 811007).

HATCHERY HOUSE TROUT FISHERY, Bury St. Edmunds, Suffolk

There are two oval-shaped interconnected lakes here, each of an acre plus. The water is clear and well weeded and fishes consistently all summer through. Depth varies between 6 and 10 feet. Well stocked with rainbow trout to over 3 lb. Day tickets cost £14 for a four fish limit or £9 for an evening ticket (two fish). Bookings in advance by telephone during office hours only 9.30 a.m. – 4.00 p.m. Monday to Friday (Tel: 01384 810300). Lakes open 1 April and close 1 October, sunrise to sunset.

Route. From Norwich to Thetford on the A11 and take the A134 to Bury St. Edmunds. From Bury take the A14 Newmarket road and four miles out look for the Willow Public House. Take the next turn on the left down Mill Lane in Barrow, which leads to Hatchery House and the fishery.

LARKWOOD TROUT FISHERY, West Stow, Suffolk

This attractive interesting fishery with a reputation for quality trout comprises of two lakes, each of around two and a half acres apiece, with depths to 20 feet. Both lakes are regularly stocked with rainbow trout from 1½ lb. upwards. The largest on record here being a specimen weighing 12 lb. 8 oz. Day tickets costing £16 for a four fish limit are available from the fishery's lodge, with reductions for juniors and senior citizens. Telephone the Manager, Mr. Ian McGregor on 01284 728612 for additional information. The fishery opens all year 9.00 a.m. until dusk. There is a tackle shop and new lodge where anglers can relax and enjoy tea or coffee. Beginners' courses available.

Route. From Bury St. Edmunds take the A1101 Mildenhall road turning right by Flempton church and proceed over the River Lark to West Stow village. Then turn left and left again on to the Icklingham road and the fishery lies between the road and the River Lark, a short distance along on the left.

NARBOROUGH TROUT AND COARSE LAKES, Narborough, Norfolk

A series of three nicely landscaped, stream-fed lakes varying between one and one and a half acres with depths from 3 to 10 feet. The density of fish and size in each varies considerably so that, depending on individual skill, one may plan the day accordingly. There are excellent stagings and facilities on level ground for wheelchair anglers. Also included is a fast flowing narrow feeder stream of the River Nar several hundred yards long which flows between the lakes. There is also a nature walk for non fishing members of the family through beautiful woodlands (see also 'Stillwaters – Day ticket'). These three trout lakes contain a prolific stock of rainbows (some triploids) of all sizes from 12 oz. upwards into high double figures. Best fish in recent years was caught in 2001 by Karl Miller and weighed 19 lb. On the following day one of 19 lb. 1 oz. was landed by Fergus Flynn. I featured this prolific trout fishery in series 14 of my *Go Fishing* television programmes in 2000 and accounted for several nice rainbows up to double figures. Good reason for rating Narborough by far the best location to stalk jumbo-sized rainbows in the whole of Norfolk and Suffolk.

The gates open at 9.00 a.m. all year round (depending upon weather) and day tickets cost £7. From May until September there is also an evening ticket costing £6 from 4.30 p.m. until 8.00 p.m. Trout caught are then charged at £1.70 per pound. All fish caught must be killed, weighed in and purchased. No fish to be returned. For additional information telephone 01760 338005. Tackle is for hire from the fishing lodge and casting tuition is available. The shop sells flies and tackle plus coffee and snacks. Toilet on site.
Route. From Norwich take the A47

Dereham Road and follow the signs into the village of Narborough. The fishery is then on the right and well signposted.

VALLEY FISHERIES, Walpole, Suffolk

This attractive two and a half acre spring-fed man-made lake offers depths between 3 and 18 feet. It is well established and nicely reeded around the perimeter. Stocked with both rainbow and brown trout triploids from 1½ lb. upwards and day tickets cost £20 for a five fish limit. Also available are 8.00 a.m. until 2.00 p.m. and 2.00 p.m. until sunset session tickets at £13.50 for a three fish limit. An evening ticket costs £10 for a two fish limit. Open all year round. Tickets must be purchased in advance from the adjacent fishery lodge. Tea and coffee always available. For additional information telephone Paul or Henry Murphy on 01986 784488. Corporate days can also be arranged and there is lakeside accommodation available.
Route. From Ipswich take the A12 (heading towards Gt. Yarmouth) and turn left at Yoxford on to the Peasenhall Road. Just before Walpole village look on the right for water tower and fishery entrance (well signposted) is half a mile further along on the right.

WHINBURGH TROUT LAKES, nr Dereham, Norfolk

This delightful fishery consists of two interconnecting man-made lakes of around one and three acres respectively. Depths vary between 3 and 8 feet and there is invariably a good hatch during the early evening throughout the summer months. A great buzzer water. Prolific stock of rainbows and brown trout of between 1 and over 8 lb. with rainbows predominating. The lake's record rainbow stands at 11¼ lb. caught in 1994. Day tickets are available at the fishery which encourages catch and release. Barbless hooks only. Anglers

158

wishing to purchase their catches instead of releasing them may do so at a cost of £1.70 per pound. There is also an experienced casting instructor at the lakes. For additional information telephone Mr. D. Potter on 07990 955859 or 01362 850188. Open all year dawn until dusk.

Route. From Norwich take the B1108 Watton road, forking on to the B1135 towards Dereham around 10 miles from the City. Go through Garvestone and half a mile further on at the bottom of the hill (where stream passes beneath rod) turn right just before white railings. Fishery is then at the end of the track.

WILLOW LAKES TROUT FISHERY, Ash Farm, Chediston, Suffolk
The fishery comprises of two superb extremely clear man-made lakes of one and a half and two and a half acres respectively. Both are oblong in shape and shelve down to over 12 feet deep. The larger has an island at one end. The lakes are stocked with brown and rainbow trout to 3 lb. and the record for the fishery is a rainbow of over 9 lb. Day tickets cost £16 for a four fish limit or £9 for a two fish limit and should be purchased prior to fishing from Ash Farm which is just 400 yards from the lakes, (Tel: 01986 785392 for additional information). The fishery opens on 15 March and closes at the end of October, from dawn until dusk. I featured this most picturesque fishery in my Anglia Television programmes, *Go Fishing*, back in 1996 in the 10th series. The fishing was relaxed and simply superb. A great nymphing – dryline fishery. Season permits are also available at £330 for up to two days a week, with a bag limit per week of four fish. A half rod is £170.

Route. From Halesworth take the B1123 Harleston road and take the first right turn (about one and a half miles out of Halesworth) signposted to Chediston Green. Ash Farm is then on the right about half a mile further on.

TROUT FISHING — SYNDICATE WATERS

RIVER BURE, Norfolk
This charming, twisting half a mile beat of the diminutive upper River Bure containing a natural head of wild brown trout is a stalker's paradise. Wonderful at mayfly time. For syndicate details contact Geoff Cooper or Chris Smith (Tel: 01263 587666).

NORFOLK FLY FISHERS' LAKE, Swanton Morley, Norfolk
A 20 acre gravel pit well stocked with rainbow trout (waiting list in force). Apply to the Treasurer, Mr. David Brookes (Tel: 01603 715431).

THE RIVER LARK, nr Bury St. Edmunds, Suffolk
River trouting controlled by the Lark Angling and Preservation Society. A delightful twisting section of this little river, switching from bank to bank and covering almost four miles from Lackford down to the A11 road bridge at Barton Mills. It is regularly stocked with browns and a rod for the season costs £100 which covers two fish per visit. Anyone may join the Lark Club for a £10 yearly subscription which also covers good coarse fishing on the River Lark starting at Barton Mills, for roach, dace and bream. Apply to the Secretary, Mr. E.

West, 8 Arrowhead Drive, Lakenheath (Tel: 01842 861369).

RIVER GLAVEN FISHERY ASSOCIATION, North Norfolk

About one mile of delightful small river fishing stocked mainly with browns in the Glandford Mill area, plus a stillwater fishery of around five acres. There is a waiting list in force, but interested parties may contact Secretary, Gordon Brook (Tel: 01692 581315).

SPRING LAKE TROUT FISHERY CLUB, Beccles, Suffolk

The club controls fly fishing on six acres of lakes comprising one large spring-fed lake and a collection of long and narrow waters, all stocked with rainbow trout between 1 and 7 lb. There is a waiting list in force. Apply to the Secretary, Mr. M. Venn of Brookfield, West End, Geldeston, Beccles, Suffolk, NR34 0LT (Tel: 01508 518295).

SALMON AND TROUT ASSOCIATION WATERS – OPEN MEMBERSHIP

For membership apply to Mr. N. Hammond, The Old Barn, Dereham Road, Scarning, Dereham, NR19 2PT (Tel: 01362 691510). This costs £35 yearly. Members may then enjoy any of the following four stocked fisheries at varying prices.

RIVERS
RIVER BURE, Ingworth

Two and a half miles stocked with browns only. Season rods cost £100 and day tickets cost £15 (for a two fish limit) from Simon Dodsworth (Tel: 01263 733471).

RIVER NAR, Narborough, West Norfolk

This lovely little river is fairly narrow in parts, flows swiftly and is generally quite shallow. It contains both rainbow and brown trout and is particularly suitable to the upstream nymph. From the road bridge in Narborough the beat stretches for one and a half miles on both banks to the waterworks at Marham. Season rods cost £110 and day tickets cost £12 (for a two fish limit) from Mr. D.E. Burrows

(Tel: 01760 337222), plus a £25 joining fee for new fishery members.

RIVER WENSUM, Bintry Mill, Norfolk

Delightful two and a half mile winding stretch of Upper Wensum. Stocked with brown trout. Excellent upstream nymphing. Season rods cost £125 from Mr. Terry Lawton (01603 872393). Day tickets (lower beat only) cost £10 (for a two fish limit).

STILLWATERS
ROOSTING HILLS, nr Dereham, Norfolk

One six acre lake and a two acre lake both stocked with rainbows and browns. Season rods cost £160 and day tickets cost £10 (for a three fish limit) from Mr. R. Bunning (Tel: 01362 860352). A family rod is also available at £240. Opens April, ends November.

Right: Russel Coulson displays an 18 lb. 1 oz. rainbow trout he caught from Narborough Trout Fisheries

SEA FISHING

The Norfolk and Suffolk coastline offers the angler over 100 miles of fishing from Hunstanton in the north to Felixstowe in the south. The coastline has a bonus attraction in the form of long sandy beaches with safe swimming, picturesque fishing villages and staithes much loved by photographers and several tip top holiday resorts led by Great Yarmouth, the second largest in England.

HUNSTANTON. Although on the east coast, Hunstanton looks out across the famous 'Wash' from a westerly aspect. Once renowned for its prolific tope fishing, the area is now relatively under fished, yet on the right day can still produce catches of tope, smooth hound, dog fish and stingrays. The best tope on record here is a 62 ½ lb. fish way back in 1964 by Mr. Guy Morton. As a rule the largest tope are taken by boat fishing offshore. Generally the beaches produce eels and flatties, although in recent years good numbers of bass have shown when onshore winds create a good surf, or smooth hounds when it is calm. The British boat record for the common smooth hound was caught offshore from nearby Heacham by Mr. A. Chilvers in 1969. It weighed 28 lb. exactly. The immediate area around the town also offers a plentiful bait supply with lugworm and ragworm being the

easiest to collect but razor fish and peeler crab are there for the finding. Hunstanton Sea Life Sanctuary along the southern promenade is well worth a visit. It is open all year round (Tel: 01485 533576).

HOLME NEXT THE SEA. Now a National Trust area which offers only limited beach fishing but offshore lies Thornham Hole, a good tope and skate mark. A tope of 70 lb. is said to have been taken here in 1956 but was not officially recorded. Robert Howell caught a 54 lb. tope off Thornham in 2000.

BRANCASTER beach offers dabs, flounders, soles and eels to visitors, who may actually drive their cars to within a stone's throw of the sea. Around the harbour much visited by tourists, mullet, bass and sea trout inhabit the various creeks and inlets, but are rarely fished for. Those willing to put in the effort will find that the mullet can be tempted with float fished bread paste or the tiny harbour ragworm. And the sea trout which are netted commercially locally will sometimes strike at a spinner or worm bait. There is some great if not rather spasmodic tope fishing to be enjoyed offshore from Brancaster as I featured in series 10 of my *Go Fishing* television programmes on board *Northern Princess*, skippered by Paul Bray and crewed by Steve Bale. On the day we accounted for several tope getting on for 40 lb., though Paul and Steve had on previous trips taken very much larger specimens. Unfortunately Paul no longer runs sports fishing charter trips. However, Brian Riches, skipper of *Tilley* specialises in tope trips over the

Top Left: The beautiful Willow Lakes Trout Fishery at Ash Farm near Chediston in Suffolk. A great 'nymphing' fishery

Bottom Left: Grove Water Fishery bailiff Tony Smith stalks wild brown trout in the habitat-rich waters of the tiny River Tas which is adjacent to a picturesque lake

same grounds from April to September (Tel: 01485 570921 for information), working out of nearby Thornham Harbour. Tope to 62 lb. were taken during the summer of 2001 by Brian's boat.

BURNHAM OVERY is a delightful little Norfolk fishing village full of charm and character. Close by, the village of Burnham Thorpe has the distinction of being the birthplace of Lord Nelson. Down by Overy Staithe, which is much used by holidaymakers at weekends, there is some swimming, good shrimping at low tide, and lugworm digging. Anglers may also launch their own craft from the staithe. Flatties, bass, mullet and the occasional largish sea trout run through Burnham Harbour and up the creeks with the flood tide. Local netsmen sometimes take specimen sized sea trout in their nets but it would take considerable effort to catch these on rod and line.

HOLKHAM offers beach anglers some flatties, including soles when the tide is up. At low tide there is some good bait collecting in the form of gathering cockles and digging for lugworm.

WELLS-NEXT-THE-SEA was once famous for its smuggling activities but now its quaint narrow streets are walked by tourists. The main shipping channel runs into Wells and is used by reasonable size vessels. Although subject to fairly strong tidal flows it offers good potential for flatfish, eels, bass, sea trout, and some very large mullet. A visit at low tide would reveal the route of gullies and positions of sandbanks to locate a good spot to fish as the tide floods.

STIFFKEY has the same name as the little river which flows through the town and under the A149 coast road. The river spills its water into the estuary via a sluice gate south of Blakeney Point. Sea trout, flounders and big mullet are taken periodically in the creeks and channels which fill with the flood tide. A baited spoon is worth a try for the flounders and there is good lugworm digging along the salt marshes at low tide.

MORSTON AND BLAKENEY.
Although these towns are two miles apart, they can be classified as one entity as far as the angler is concerned. This is because boats which fish out from these spots actually share a permanent anchorage in the deep section of Blakeney Harbour, known as Blakeney Pit, which is in fact about the only deep water suitable for permanent mooring in the whole harbour. Anglers who have booked to fish offshore are then ferried out by tender from Morston Quay. Visitors who come to see the seals here can book a trip with Jimmy Temple (Tel: 01263 740791 for details) via the Anchor Public House at Morston. Newcomers to the area must beware of the tremendous fall and rise of the tides which affect the access of entrance in and out of the harbour at Blakeney. Local fishermen will give advice to those wishing to launch their own boats but extreme care must be taken.
The entire southern half of the harbour is good lug digging ground and anyone who digs for lugworm would do well to respect the future availability of this excellent bait by not taking immature worms.
Deep sea boat fishing out from Blakeney is from early April until the

beginning of October, the popular species sought among anglers being thornback skate known locally as 'roker'. These average around 8 – 10 lb., but specimens into double figures are taken regularly. There is also good offshore tope fishing at certain times of the year with specimens topping 40 lb., and always plenty of dabs with some dogfish and good mackerel in season. The skipper of the boat usually supplies fresh bait in the way of sandeels and lugworms, but for much of the summer the angler may catch his own fresh bait by feathering for mackerel, one of the supreme sea baits and very good eating too. Within the limits of Blakeney Harbour flat fish, eels, bass and good mullet can be caught with the chance of a sea trout if your luck is in. Boat fishing trips can be arranged through Barry Girling (Tel: 01263 740792 for details). For weather details contact Joe Reed, Warden of Blakeney Point (Tel: 01263 740480). Feathering in the vicinity of the harbour mouth will produce good numbers of mackerel from July to September and in the harbour itself, dabs, flounders and eels are taken on worm baits all the year round.

CLEY. Cley represents the first 'real' beach from Hunstanton as the area between is essentially a salt marsh. A steep shingle-sandy beach offers deep water close in at all stages of the tide, so it is ideal for anglers of all abilities. Favourite local hotspot is opposite the wreck situated to the right of the gap. Here good bass are to be found and at low tide the wreck is within casting distance. Lure fishing with plugs and spinners can be very successful for bass right through from Cley to Weybourne due to the steep nature of the beaches.

The bass come very close to the shoreline so carp/pike rod outfits are ideal. During summer dabs, plaice, flounders, eels plus the odd sole and dogfish can make fishing interesting with good catches of mackerel likely at high tide on a hot, humid evening in July and August. During December to March codling are caught, particularly after a period of northerly winds.

SALTHOUSE is renowned for its fine beach fishing where good dabs, flounders and soles may be taken along with bass during the summer months. The beach consists mostly of heavy shingle and sandy areas only 50 yards out from low tide mark. Expect codling from December onwards, on both flood and ebb tides. Fresh lugworms may be obtained from several houses along the main coast road at Salthouse.

KELLING. The beach here is similar to Weybourne, but there are only two access points from the coast road. The first is approximately half a mile Weybourne side of Salthouse beach road which goes across Salthouse Marshes. The second is about 100 yards on the Salthouse side of the police station. These lanes are extremely rough going and cars should be driven carefully. Species to be expected are flatties and bass during the summer months and particularly goodish soles at late evening on an ebbing tide. A number of codling appear from December onwards.

WEYBOURNE has a beach of shingle which shelves steeply into deepish water. The shingle gives way to sand just below the low tide mark and excellent dab fishing with some soles is to be had from the wreck towards

Kelling. The wreck becomes visible at low tide. Other species to be expected are dabs, flounders, eels and during the autumn whiting. Skate, tope, mackerel and bass are taken from boats. Really good bass are often found around the wreck. To the right of the gap under the cliffs the bottom is rough but many cod gather over this type of ground in the winter for the rich feed it harbours and fishing can be exceptional at times.

There is a little boat fishing available through local skippers but this is dependent on the wind and tide conditions. Bait is available from local diggers and signs are displayed outside their homes along the coast road. Almost the entire coast road from Weybourne to Cromer runs very close to the sea and fishing and picnic spots abound. Some favourite fishing locations for all the previously mentioned species will be found about one and a quarter miles north of Sheringham by turning towards the coast at the bridge to Spallow Gap – a noted cod spot during the winter which fishes best at high tide.

SHERINGHAM is a quite sizeable town where the main street runs right down to the beach. To the north the beach comprises of large shingle at high water offering deep water close in but the outgoing tide soon reveals the flat sand. This is interspersed with gullies particularly where the chalky areas show although casting into these often causes tackle losses. To the south, rougher areas of larger stones and kelp can be found which offer peeler crab in late spring when the weather is warm and settled. During onshore winds in May and June the bass fishing can be excellent with eels also evident. Flatfish can be caught during most times of the

year with good fishing for codling at high water from December through until March. The bass can be taken at high or low water with lure fishing from the stone sea defences particularly rewarding in the summer. Float fishing for mullet is also good off the sea wall, especially during calm summer evenings. The local tackle shop 'Brights, The Outdoor Man' in Sheringham (Tel: 01263 825858) sells fresh and frozen bait and will advise visitors.

WEST AND EAST RUNTON. These beaches offer a contrast between very rocky ground interspersed with sandy patches. Bass fishing can be excellent during the summer months for those willing to risk tackle losses in the rocks. However, another method is to run a floating plug over the rocks as the tide floods. Bass will be in the shallow water as soon as the rocks cover and hit the lure with venom. So hang on. The sandy patches produce flatties during the summer and cod from December onwards. Dinghies can be launched from the slope at West Runton and offshore fishing is good for skate, doggies and occasional tope during the warmer months.

CROMER is an ideal base for the family man who happens also to be an angler. For added to the obvious attractions there is also an excellent golf course. There is even some excellent freshwater fishing close by in the grounds of lovely Gunton Park, just five miles south of the town (see 'Stillwaters -- Day ticket'). Cromer is well known for its fine all year round fishing. One of the best spots is usually the pier (free fishing) which offers good mixed catches of flatties, eels, plus some good bass. Bass into double figures are caught every year here with squid and peeler crab fished under the pier the best method. Be sure to use strong tackle as these fish do not take prisoners around the rusted metalwork. During April and May some good smooth hounds sometimes show to peeler crab baits and there is always the chance of the occasional tope. In winter excellent codling and whiting fishing is had from November through until March. Good local baits are mussels, lugworms and squid heads. These and expert advice may be obtained from Marine Sports of New Street (Tel: 01263 513676).

OVERSTRAND to TRIMINGHAM

The area between these villages is very similar with the beaches being mainly flat sand interspersed with wooden groynes. Although the water is quite shallow even at high tide the fishing can be excellent. At Overstrand there is a sewer pipe at the bottom of the main access point to the beach and in the immediate area some very fine bass into double figures have been caught. Best times are around two hours before high or low tide, through to lack water and both peeler crab and squid will produce. The latter probably accounts for most of the specimens taken. The access to Trimingham is via the Sandy Gulls Caravan Site where a road leads down the cliffs to the beach. There is some parking here but the area can become crowded at peak times. Double figure smooth hounds can show in April and May, and bass fishing during the spring and autumn can prove exceptionally good with catches of codling from October onwards through until April, from two hours before to two hours after high water. Some lugworm can be dug during low water

springs, although a 'bait pump' is sometimes more productive for individual worms.

MUNDESLEY is another rather flat sandy beach but some deeper gullies show up at low tide. Flatfish, eels and bass are the expected summer species with both whiting and codling appearing from October through to April. Some of the finest sport here is to be had straight in front of the main access slope which leads from the car park. Best results usually come from two hours before and two hours after high water for the codling especially, but rough low water seas will produce the bass. Lugworm can be dug from the sand banks at low tide.

BACTON is similar to Mundesley in that basically it tends to fish well in the summer for dabs, flounders and the odd soles. etc., with whiting and codling showing up from late October onwards. But it has a bonus in the form of really excellent offshore boat fishing marks within Bacton Bay. Skate, or rather thornback ray, to give its correct name, are the prime target species here, but smooth hounds, spurdogs and tope are also taken here during the summer. Boats can be launched from the slipway at Walcott. The feature of the beach and in fact all the beaches down to Winterton is their flat, sandy nature over the initial 60 yards, dropping into a very wide gulley with a sandbank shelving up around 200 yards out from the low water mark. Long range casting, therefore, can really pay off over the high tide mark, so the bait is placed in the gulley. Paradoxically the ebb tide can also fish well, simply because towards low water most anglers can reach the gulley and a favourite period is three hours before to around an hour after low water.

WALCOTT. Offshore fishing is excellent here with easy access for small boats from the slipway on the coast road. Species are identical as for Bacton. Beach fishing is also very good with flatfish all year round, plus bass during the summer and codling from October through until March. Because the sea comes up to the concrete wall at high tide the three hours before and one hour after low water are most favoured.

HAPPISBURGH. The fishing is similar to that at Walcott and along the sandy beach to the right of the gap dabs and flounders are the usual customers to worm baits. Skate come inshore during the summer months and are occasionally taken by long casting from the beach. Smooth hounds also show in the spring and some really good bags of fish to double figures have been taken in recent years. From September onwards one can expect whiting and then numbers of cod between October and January. Best at high water. The coastguard station at Happisburgh can furnish visitors with useful information (Tel: 08706 006505).

LESSINGHAM AND ECCLES. There is easy access to a long sandy beach which fishes all the year through for dabs. Bass show well during rough weather in spring towards the reefs at Sea Palling on a flood tide. Codling are caught from September to April with high water and low water being productive.

SEA PALLING AND WAXHAM are just a five mile drive from Hickling Broad and Horsey Mere, both excellent coarse fishing venues. (See 'The Broads' chapter). For the sea angler offshore fishing in this area is excellent for thornbacks, spurdog, the occasional tope, plus flat fish, all during the summer months, with whiting and codling during the autumn and winter. Small boats can be launched via the gap in the sea wall but rollers are necessary for the haul over the beach. Shore fishing has changed significantly since the building of the stone reefs. These run through to Horsey and have been a haven for bass. Unfortunately heavy netting has caused a big reduction in the stocks and rod and line fishing has suffered. Boat anglers do well casting lures around the stone reefs and shore anglers within casting range have caught using peeler crab. The large deep pools that have formed behind the reefs hold plenty of flat fish with codling moving through during rough weather. Both high and low tides can be good for bass and flat fish but the codling prefer the deeper water at high tide. At low tide some lugworm can be dug, although a bait pump is invariably more successful. Access to the beach at Waxham is through the small lane behind Waxham church.

HORSEY. The beach at Horsey has built up considerably since the reefs were built and at high tide there is a good depth close in. Bass show during the spring to autumn with plenty of smooth hounds in April/May. This was once a skate 'hot spot' and in recent years they have started to show with more frequency to the few anglers using fish baits. Calm weather on a night tide from April to June offers the best chance. Flat fish show all year and codling from October to April.

WINTERTON is a continuation of Horsey's sandy beach. Good freshwater fishing is only three miles away at Martham Ferry on the tidal River Thurne and at Martham Pits (see 'Stillwaters'). So a holidaying all-round angler could hardly choose a better location. The beach here is quite flat and sandy with numerous small gullies. However, these are continually changing due to the very strong tides, especially around the 'Point'. At the north end the wooden groynes that have stretched down from Horsey finish and in the spring many good bass are caught from this location. A rough sea is favourite with two hours before and one hour after high water being the ideal time. Crab and squid both produce with numbers of fish falling to the former but those real specimens to the latter. In winter flat fish and codling are caught but very often strong tides bring heavy weed to spoil fishing.

HEMSBY – NEWPORT – SCRATBY. There is access to the beach at each end of these locations with a fair depth of water quite close in. High water favours the longer caster but low water allows the average caster to reach the best spots. Tides are strong here but the last three hours of both flood and ebb usually produce well. Flat fish, eels and the occasional large bass feature in the spring to summer period with good catches of cod taken throughout December and January. The deepest water is in fact at Scratby where a 32 lb. cod was caught by Ivan Smith in 1981.

CAISTER-ON-SEA has a fairly deep sand and shingle beach, where a fast tide runs at times. There are the usual flat fish from April onwards and excellent whiting and cod fishing from mid autumn to early spring, especially at night. Caister is a popular holiday resort and so the beaches become congested during high summer. Best sport is usually found on the last three hours of the ebb and over low water. A huge grey mullet of 8 lb. 6 oz. was taken here by John James in 1979.

GREAT YARMOUTH is the second largest seaside resort in Britain and it seems to become busier each year. But there is generally enough space even during the holiday season for the ardent angler to catch a few fish. The variety of fishing is split up somewhat, in as much as one may choose to fish the sandy beaches, the harbour and river, off the jetty or boat fish well offshore. In recent years the beach has built up and both the Britannia Pier and the Wellington Pier no longer project out to

A nice catch of cod for Paul Kerry from the south beach at Great Yarmouth

sea as far as they did. Anglers are now not allowed access to them anyway. In fact at low tide you would be just as far out on the beach. The jetty has always produced good flat fish and cod during the winter but can prove snaggy from lost tackle.

The north beach offers deep water close in and is noted for cod during the winter, with access available from several points off Marine Parade. Strong tides and weed can make fishing difficult but the results are often well worth the effort. Fishing from the south beach is also very good, particularly on the last three hours of the flood tide but responds best to long range casting. The area in front of the Pleasure Beach is particularly productive.

Offshore during the summer months skate, doggies, large dabs and tope are taken but the fishing really comes into its own from autumn through to spring when huge bags of sizeable cod are taken including many fish high into double figures. Best cod taken offshore was caught by Jim Patterson in 1979 and weighed 38½ lb. For boat fishing trips contact Mr. R. Green (skipper of *Blue Dawn*) Tel: 01493 601008; Mr. P. Dyble (skipper of MV *Sea Quest*) Tel: 01493 731305; or Mr. John Temple (a 50 foot lifeboat) Tel: 01493 858523.

The best bait by far is fresh lugworm and these are generally supplied by the skipper of the boat. Local tackle dealers 'Tackle 'N' Tide' in King Street, Great Yarmouth supply fresh bait all year round (Tel: 01493 852221) and will advise visiting anglers. Another Great Yarmouth tackle dealer is F. Pownall, Regent Road (Tel: 01493 843873).

GORLESTON-ON-SEA. As far as the fishing is concerned it would be as well to class Gorleston in the same league as Great Yarmouth. The species are the same, with excellent flatties, eels, bass and mullet within the harbours. There are some monster grey mullet found all the way upriver to Breydon Water and these receive very little angling attention. Bass are also found well upstream but the area immediately inside the harbour usually produces the bigger fish. Lures, peeler crab and squid all work well depending on conditions. South of the harbour the beaches fish well for whiting, codling and bass. The latter being particularly active whenever a fresh south-easterly wind creates a good surf on the area of beach adjacent to the harbour. On very low tides you can sometimes dig lugworm, although a bait pump is advisable in the wet sand. The area towards the wreck, about a mile down towards Hopton, is better for the whiting and codling with both flood and ebb tides fishing well. A large car park is adjacent to the harbour. Local advice and fresh bait may be obtained from Gorleston Tackle (Tel: 01493 662448) and from Greenstead Tackle Centre (Tel: 01493 602474). A massive cod of 43 lb. was caught two miles off shore here in 1973 by Cyril Easy. In recent years bass have appeared in large numbers. Boat trips can be arranged through Bishop Boat Services (*The Ellen Bee*) Tel: 01493 664739 and Mr. L. Read (*Florence L*) Tel: 01493 859653.

Top Right: Steve Bale and John display one of the many tope caught boat fishing out of Brancaster in north Norfolk

Bottom Right: Stewart Smalley, who specializes in small boat bassing off Orford in Suffolk, with proof of the pudding. A double figure bass caught on sand-eel

HOPTON. Access here is via Beach Road or by the cottages near the holiday camp. In both cases parking is restricted and a place can be difficult at peak times. However, this beach can fish very well and because it sits in a bay offers some protection from both strong northerly and southerly winds. The Corton end of the beach seems to fish better on the flood tide and the Gorleston end on the ebb but either are worth a try. September to May are the best months with dabs, whiting and codling the main species. The odd specimen bass also turns up during autumn. At the end of Beach Road there is a slipway and this is a popular dinghy launch spot when conditions allow.

CORTON offers deeper water than Hopton although the bottom tends to be snaggy in places due to areas of clay. Access is via the slipway in the village and although a dinghy club operated from here recent work has stopped this. The slipway is quite long and steep so a tractor to launch a dinghy was a must. Both flood and ebb tides fish well with the emphasis on winter fishing for whiting and codling. Some good bass and sole however are caught towards Lowestoft where the old broken concrete defences are in the sea. The ground is snaggy but peeler crab and squid can tempt a bass with the potential of fish into double figures.

LOWESTOFT. Sam Hook made this resort famous when he caught the, since beaten, shore record cod of 32 lb. way back in 1945 from the town's Claremont

Left: John displays a thickset double figure bass caught drift fishing out from Orford on board Stewart Smalley's boat Aldeborough Angler

Pier. A good family base with freshwater fishing on Oulton Broad close by, Lowestoft offers plenty for the sea angler all year round. The north beach has broken concrete sea defences in the water for much of its length but there are clear areas. However, these offer protection to the fish from small trawlers and the fishing is very good. During September to December there are plenty of whiting and codling and dabs are there through to April. In the summer there are plenty of eels, bass and sole. Lure fishing for bass can be good around the short jetty at Ness Point, the most easterly point of the British Isles. Beware though that this is a calm weather place and can be quite slippery. The harbour offers dabs, flounders, sole, bass and good mullet fishing with access to the harbour and seaward sides from the south pier.

The south beach is very shallow but can be good for flatties although bass show when the wind kicks up a surf. The Claremont Pier is situated here but unfortunately years of damage have closed it for fishing. Deep water wrecks way offshore from Lowestoft offer by far the best prospects for hooking into a big cod, as I experienced during the filming of series 11 of my Anglia Television *Go Fishing* programmes on board *Blue Waters* out of Lowestoft, skippered by Andy Fox. Unfortunately Andy and *Blue Waters* now no longer work out of Lowestoft but my arms still ache from the catch of double figure cod we hauled up from 150 feet down, including a 25 pounder for yours truly. Between May and August is usually the best time for drifting over these wrecks on neap tides.

For fresh bait visit Sam Hook's tackle shop in Bevan Street, Lowestoft (Tel: 01502 565821), or Lowestoft Angling

Centre (Tel: 01502 573392) in London Road South. Boat trips offshore can be arranged through local skippers, Mr. J. Woods (MFV *Hvita*) Tel: 01502 518000 and Mr. M. Kelly (MV *Freedom*) Tel: 07980 871731.

PAKEFIELD is one of the most popular and productive venues in the area. The sloping shingle-sandy beach is very easy to fish and offers a fair depth of water reasonably close in. The flood tide is best for the last three hours for all species but the long casters favour the last three hours of the ebb so they can clear the sandbank. A fair bit of inshore trawling is evident which limits summer sport but autumn and winter sees excellent fishing for cod, whiting and dabs. The dab fishing in January is superb both in terms of quality and quantity. Lug tipped with a small piece of sprat seems to tempt the larger flat fish. Fresh bait is available all year round from 'Ding-Its' Tackle Den of London Road, Pakefield (Tel: 01502 519483). Access is available where the boats are pulled up on the beach and fishing is good almost anywhere. A favourite spot is at the back of the rifle range which unfortunately requires a fair walk over rough ground.

KESSINGLAND has much to offer the angling addicted family man. There is good fishing from the local beach in a fair depth of water for dabs, flounders and soles in summer and cod and whiting for the keen beach angler from October onwards. Although involving a long walk the area around the 'Point' is a particular hotspot, even if fierce tides can make fishing difficult at times. A massive bass of 19 lb. was taken by commercial fishermen here in 1994.

BENACRE was very popular with beach anglers because the beach here shelves

deeply, affording excellent winter fishing. However, access is very difficult involving over a mile's hike from either Covehithe to the south or Kessingland to the north. The whiting arrive early, usually in late August, followed by cod during October including some double figure fish.

COVEHITHE. The sand cliffs are constantly being eroded by the sea which reaches their base at high tide, making fishing impossible at this time. More of the road which provides access disappears each year and whether you go to the left or right it is a fair walk to reach the beach. Results on the ebb tide are good although the inshore bank tends to favour the long casters for whiting and cod. During October through to December catches can be excellent especially following a south/south-west gale. During summer soles are caught here especially at night on or just over the bank using lug or ragworm bait.

SOUTHWOLD. Like Great Yarmouth and Lowestoft, Southwold has a harbour and offers varied sea fishing, both summer and winter. In the harbour likely catches are those ultra-shy grey mullet which can be so frustrating to catch and numbers of bass into double figures. The bass fall to both lure anglers and those who offer fresh bait. Lures are good for fish to 5 lb., but the real whoppers fall to peeler crab, squid and whole fish baits especially where the fishing boats unload upstream from the harbour mouth. The mouth tends to be the best area for lure anglers, though well upstream is worth trying also.

The beaches offer good cod and whiting during the winter and bass plus some soles during the summer. A hotspot for soles is usually the groynes to the north of the old pier. This has been rebuilt recently and is a good spot. However fishing is controlled by the local club and not generally available to the public. Dinghy owners may launch their own craft from the slipway close to the old pier and in the harbour but anglers are asked to check on local tides and weather forecasts before going offshore to fish. For fresh bait and local advice contact Southwold Angling Centre, High Street, Southwold (Tel: 01502 722085). For boat fishing trips, particularly deep water wrecking trips for big cod, ling, bass and even the occasional pollack, contact Nigel Hayters (*Mistress I*) (Tel: 01502 478581 – mobile 07885 316429); Colin Clarke (*Mistress II*) (Tel: 01502 741609) or David Wright (*Prospector III*) (Tel: 01501 711422).

In addition to numerous bass-prolific rips situated well offshore to the south of Southwold, there are some 150 First and Second World War deep water wrecks within reach of Southwold boats. Each holds extensive stocks of cod, plus odd ling and even pollack for which the best fishing period is between May and August. In series 16 of my *Go Fishing* television series screened in 2002 on Anglia TV, long time fishing buddy John (Jinx) Davey and I wreck fished for cod way offshore on board Nigel Hayters' 40 foot. boat *Mistress I*. Using 12 oz. pirks we filled several boxes with prime cod, many in the 14 – 16 lb. range, though fish over 20 lb. are regularly caught from these deep water wrecks.

WALBERSWICK is a little south of Southwold harbour and the fishing is much the same as that of Southwold. Good bass are taken periodically in summer on spinners and artificial rubber sandeels. At low tide lugworms and harbour ragworm may be dug from the estuary by the Bailey Bridge (the footbridge linking Southwold and Walberswick). Although shallow the

Wreck fishing for cod in deep water out of Southwold on board Nigel Hayters' boat Mistress I

beach does offer dabs, flounders, sole plus some good bass. In the winter the beach is sheltered from northerly winds and can fish very well for whiting and codling.

DUNWICH. Once the capital of East Anglia, Dunwich offers the angler some excellent cod fishing from the local beach which is shingle and shelves quite steeply into a fair depth of water all along Dunwich Bay. Top bait for the area is the lugworm and it was on this bait in April 1973 that Finningham angler, Derrick Dorling, surprised everyone in the sea angling world by producing from the beach here a mammoth turbot weighing 28½ lb. Derrick hooked into the fish at 2.30 in the morning after a fruitless night and put his name in the record book by landing the biggest British shore caught turbot of all time. This catch, creditable though it was, should not in any sense be considered a likely future occurrence. Although turbot may very occasionally be taken from the east coast beaches they are nonetheless a great rarity. Most people have to be content with the more usual mixed catches of flatties, which consist of dabs, flounders and in the spring some plaice. Good soles show in the summer along with bass. Lure fishing at high tide on a calm summer's evening can be very good although whole squid or Joey mackerel sorts out the largest specimens. From September whiting are plentiful and codling show from October to April on both flood and ebb tides, although locals favour the latter.

MINSMERE AND SIZEWELL. There are just four miles of beach between Dunwich and Sizewell known locally as Minsmere Haven. Access is through the nature reserve to the large car park at the end of the cliffs. Fishing during the summer can be particularly good for soles with the occasional bass to add interest. Although a fairly shallow beach, winter sees good numbers of whiting and codling and sport is good on the last three hours of both the flood or ebb tides. Behind the power station at Sizewell the warm water outlet attracts large numbers of 'school' bass. Unfortunately heavy netting has taken its toll but fair numbers of fish to 3 lb. can still be taken.

ALDEBURGH is one of the better fishing locations on the Suffolk coast. With its steeply shelving beach of coarse shingle and deep water it offers a wide choice of fishing. The best flattie fishing is generally up towards Thorpeness and for whiting and cod one should turn south towards the local hotspot of 'Dirty Wall'. Access here is now limited to a mile or so from the Martello Tower by a fence erected by the National Trust. However this steep beach produces superb catches virtually all year round with a few surprise species always on the cards. Lugworm and fish baits are usually favourite and either flood or ebb tides can produce good sport.

ORFORDNESS probably represents the very best in shore fishing along the entire Norfolk and Suffolk coastline. A very steep shingle beach with very deep water within easy casting distance. The tides are exceptionally strong and weights of at least 6 oz. may be needed to hold effectively. During summer sole, bass, eels, dogfish etc., are caught with both worm, crab and fish baits. In winter cod and whiting abound in numbers with a chance of hooking into a cod over that 20 lb. mark. Mr. Ellis of Diss landed a 43 lb. conger here in 1973 so you never quite know what the next bite may bring. The beach extends for several miles but access is rather difficult. It was once possible to drive from Aldeburgh with a four-wheel drive vehicle but the National Trust fence has stopped that. A boat from Orford Quay is the usual way of reaching the narrow spit of land known as Orford Island either on your own or on an organised trip. The latter, however, does rather dictate the fishing time but an excellent ferrying service for anglers is run by Peter Merin (Tel: mobile 07900 230579). Fishing at all points is likely to be productive and there are two drop off points for the ferry. The shortest is 'The Crouch' which is at the end of the old army camp fence line. From here it is a very long walk to the lighthouse which is considered a hot spot. The other is 'The Narrows' which is towards the estuary and is a longer journey. However, both can fish well although 'The Narrows' can be good for sole and bass during the summer. Thornbacks used to show in good numbers around the estuary where it is very deep but commercial fishing reduced stocks considerably. A few are still caught around April to June.

In recent years I have enjoyed some marvellous bass fishing some 20 miles off Orford during the summer on board Stewart Smalley's 20 foot. boat *Aldeburgh Angler*. Stewart specialises in drift fishing for bass over rips caused by the tide passing over shallow, steep-sided sandbanks. I featured his technique during series 14 of my *Go Fishing* TV programmes screened in 2000 and true to form Stewart obliged with a magnificent 12 lb. bass amongst a host of lesser fish between 4 and 8 lb. whilst the cameras were rolling. I have taken three double figure bass whilst out with Stewart, the best also scaling 12 lb. He takes only two anglers out at a time and interested parties should contact him on Tel/Fax 01728 453088.

Stewart Smalley (left) and John with part of a bass haul caught drifting over rips 20 miles offshore from Orford in Suffolk

SHINGLE STREET beach could hardly have been better named. It shelves sharply into deep water and in the winter months becomes the home to whiting and cod addicts. There is a lapse until around mid-April when thornback skate may be taken by beach anglers. Favourite baits are cuts from fresh herring or mackerel for the skate and lugworm for just about everything else. Peeler crab can be killing when available. Apart from the usual flatties and odd useful soles, good numbers of bass are found, especially around the river mouth at the north end of the beach. Crabs and worm baits on medium to light tackle are advisable here.

EAST LANE is really a continuation of Shingle Street beach and stretches down as far as the mouth of the River Deben where it is backed by the cliffs at Bawdsey. The beach is stony and deeply shelving into deepish water over a snaggy sea bed. Species include dabs, soles, bass, whiting, cod and a few skate in season. The approach to this beach is from the Woodbridge to Bawdsey road turning right at the Star Inn. Information concerning this area and fresh bait all year round is available from Stuart Clay Traps in Melton (Tel: 01394 385567).

BAWDSEY is an ideal area for codling, soles and bass. Fishing in the estuary of the River Deben is good for grey mullet and bass with the thought that one may be lucky enough to hook into a sea trout. Anglers should beware of the consistently heavy tide rip in the river mouth.

FELIXSTOWE. The town sits between two important river estuaries. The Deben, with Felixstowe's ferry on its southern bank, flows in from the north and to the south of the town lies spacious Harwich Harbour which drains the Suffolk Stour (see 'Suffolk Rivers') and the River Orwell. Angling between these estuaries from the shingle beaches is often rewarding with whiting and cod from late September onwards, especially at night. In summer bass are likely and there is always the chance of a double figure fish. The ex-British record bass of   18 lb. 2 oz. was caught here way back in 1943 by the late F.C. Borley. Plaice, doggies, turbot, garfish, sea trout etc., are all taken at various times from the estuary and beaches around Felixstowe but should not be considered common catches. Neither should the 90 lb. conger eel found washed up on the local beach in January 1974 by two local anglers.

The pier fishing here really comes into its own from late September onwards when good whiting and the cod arrive. There is no night fishing allowed and a small charge is made to anglers. During the warmer months there are plaice, soles, eels and bass to be taken as well as the proverbial dabs. Best baits are small rag and lugworms.

Offshore sport is excellent from Felixstowe and highly organised. Anglers may expect good numbers of whiting and big cod from late September until April. The two largest fish in past years are the 43 lb. cod taken by T. Marsh in 1968 and one of 40 lb. 2 oz. by A.C. Ashong in 1973. The general run of cod, however, is from 3 to 10 lb., with the occasional 20 lb. specimen. For the summer boat angler there is just about every species imaginable, with dabs, flounders, eels, plaice, skate, smooth hounds, and bass predominating. But almost anything can happen. In recent times specimen catches have included a huge bass weighing 18 ¼ lb. to the rod of

Mike Bradley in 1994 and a 20 lb. smooth hound caught by K. Hill in 2001. Additional information about the area may be obtained from 'Castaway' Tackle and Bait (Tel: 01394 278316) which is near the Ordnance Hotel in Felixstowe and Markhams Tackle of Woodbridge Road in Ipswich who have their own charter boats *Tracy Jane* and *Flirt*. For boat bookings or fresh bait telephone 01473 727841. Gordon Button, skipper of *Fast Lane*, also arranges offshore trips (Tel: 01394 282201). Anglers may also launch their own small craft from Felixstowe Ferry.

SEA BAITS

Obtaining fresh sea bait is not always easy, especially during the cod season from October to March when lugworms, which are considered 'the' bait by most Norfolk and Suffolk anglers, are in such great demand. However, there are other excellent baits which may be gathered without too much difficulty or purchased quite reasonably from commercial fishermen and fishmongers. These baits may be used all the year round and some will be found in the list below, with hints on how to obtain and use them.

NATURAL BAITS

Cockles are small bivalve molluscs with a most distinctive 'fluted' shell of about 1 inch across. They make excellent baits and are found mostly in north-west Norfolk along muddy, sandy beaches, especially at low tide. Commercially packed, pickled cockles may be used as a poor alternative.

Crabs – soft and peelers. There are several species of small crabs found close inshore which, in their soft or peeling stage as they shed their shell to grow a larger one, make really terrific baits.

They are usually found in this vulnerable state hiding from predators under boulders and large stones in the rock pools, particularly at low tide. Cod, skate, doggies and bass etc., will all avidly take a 'peeler' or 'softy'.

Hermit crab. The local name given to this small crab, which has made its home from the shell of a whelk is a 'Jack'. They can be bought cheaply from the whelk fishermen of north Norfolk. Jacks are a good all-round bait and are particularly liked by thornback skate and smoothhounds. To extract Mr. Hermit from his shell without crushing it, hold a lighted match under the shell or chip its rear end and tickle the tail. Either way he will soon pop out.

Harbour ragworm. These small cousins of the famous king ragworm are much paler in colour, being almost white, and rather thin for their length. They are found in the mud of estuaries and may be dug quite easily at low tide. All the flat fish will accept these small worms and so, too, will eels, bass and mullet, which are particularly fond of them.

Lugworms are the largest burrowing worms to be found along the Norfolk and Suffolk coastline and are without question the most popular of sea baits. They are dug at low tide from parts of most mud and sand beaches, after their distinctive 'worm casts' have been located. Lug can be kept for a few days if put into a shallow tray containing moist peat, or laid on a sheet of clean, dry newspaper and put into a cooler. Lug is the one bait that most coastal tackle dealers are likely to sell.

Mussels are bivalve molluscs and perhaps one of the most neglected sea baits. They are abundant around the piles of all piers and breakwaters, and can be gathered easily at low tide. Once the shell has been prized open with a strong bladed knife, the mussel should be used whole and the hook inserted into the firm part of the 'foot'. Just about every swimming creature will take this bait, including unfortunately crabs.

Sandeels, not to be confused with the common or conger eels, are a very popular bait with tope, bass and skate fishermen, especially in the early part of the season. They can be netted from the estuaries or purchased from professional fishermen and are best fished whole and preferably as fresh as possible on a large single hook.

Shrimps. The lowly shrimp can at times prove a very useful bait, especially when the sea is calm and it can be lightly fished on float tackle at harbour entrances or around pier stanchions, etc. Then one may expect such species as bass, garfish and mackerel, etc. Shrimps are easily gathered by net from the pools left in the estuaries or along sandy beaches at low tide. If you catch a surplus to bait requirements, then you can always eat them!

FISH BAITS

Mackerel, especially if freshly caught while out boat fishing, is the tope bait 'par excellence'. It should be used whole or, for skate, cut into large slices or chunks. Mackerel will also attract other smaller species if used in strip form and like the shrimp is excellent eating if freshly killed and cooked.

Herring are seldom caught by anglers and must be purchased either fresh or frozen from the fishmongers. They may be cast a very long distance from the beach, either whole or in slices while frozen, and for this reason they are an extremely popular bait. Thin strips of herring make a good all-round sea bait for the east coast.

Squid. Although the squid is actually a mollusc, it appears under the heading of fish bait because it may be purchased readily from the fishmongers and the smaller the better. The very tiny ones are used whole and with their flowing tentacles make a most desirable and deadly bait for most species of sea fish. Larger squid should be cut into suitable strips. Squid is an excellent cod bait and stays on the hook well when long casting.

Sprats are also obtained from the fishmonger and, if used whole, account for some good-sized cod. They are particularly suitable for pier fishing when short casting, because then the bait stays intact and attractive. Sprats can also be mounted on spinning tackle and used effectively around harbour entrances for bass and mackerel.

Other small sea fish and even small silver-coloured freshwater fish like dace and roach can be effectively used as sea baits. They work especially well if used whole and can be made more attractive if one injects pilchard or sardine oil into them. A hypodermic syringe can be purchased from tackle shops with a large bore needle, so that if armed with several different fish oils the angler is able to turn the unlikeliest of baits into something palatable.

176

THE TIDES

RIVERS

The tides on Broadland rivers ebb and flow twice in each lunar day of 24 hours 51 minutes. The flow, or rising, of the water is called the flood; and the reflux, or dropping, the ebb. When the moon is in the first and third quarter there is a smaller high tide than usual, known as the 'neap tide'. On the full moon the rise is greater and is called the 'spring tide'. On the Norfolk Broads and rivers the flood continues for about five hours and the ebb about seven hours. The tide runs at from a half-mile to five miles per hour according to the distance from the sea. With a north-west wind high tides can be expected and in winter they often bring up the 'salts' or salt water. Occasionally on very high tides the water will be found brackish far up the Thurne, as far as Ludham on the Ant, Cantley on the Yare and St. Olaves on the Waveney. Tides around the coast, moon stages, and barometer readings can be obtained daily from the local press.

SEA

Sea anglers should equip themselves with tide tables which can usually be obtained from tackle dealers and ships' stores. If none is available, however, consult one of the national daily newspapers where high water at London Bridge is given. From this the approximate time of high water around these coasts may be arrived at by consulting the following table.

High water at Hunstanton	add	4 hr. 40 min. to L.B. time
Wells-next-the-Sea	"	5 hr. 1 min. " " "
Cromer	"	5 hr. 5 min. " " "
Great Yarmouth	deduct	4 hr. 55 min. from L. B. time
Lowestoft	"	4 hr. 26 min. " " "
Southwold	"	3 hr. 48 min. " " "
Aldeburgh	"	3 hr. 23 min. " " "
Felixstowe	"	2 hr. 18 min. " " "
Harwich	"	2 hr. 18 min. " " "
Walton-on-Naze	"	2 hr. 15 min. " " "
Clacton-on-Sea	"	2 hr. 1 min. " " "

It is usual for Greenwich Mean Time to be quoted; in Summer Time add one hour.

LOCAL SPECIMEN FRESHWATER FISH

1870 – 2002

It should be noted with the following lists that obviously everyone's specimen catch is not recorded. Indeed many anglers do not want their catches and locations made public, while others catch so many large carp for instance, now that big carp are available to all, I could literally have filled the following pages with carp in excess of even that once magical 30 lb. figure. But rather than do this I have chosen to

provide the reader with a cross section of specimen catches that have occurred over a lengthy period of time from a diversity of freshwater locations within the counties of Norfolk and Suffolk. So if yours is not included and you want it to be I shall be only too pleased to accept the information for the next edition.

John Wilson

BARBEL

16 lb. 13 oz.	J. Fulton	River Wensum, Taverham	1998
16 lb. 9 oz.	D. Livermore	River Wensum, Taverham	1998
16 lb. 6 oz.	S. Keer	River Wensum, Taverham	1998
15 lb. 8 oz.	M. Patterson	River Wensum, Taverham	2001
15 lb. 6 oz.	A. Jubb	River Wensum, Taverham	1997
15 lb. 5 oz.	J. King	River Wensum, Taverham	1998
14 lb. 14 oz.	C. Basford	River Wensum, Taverham	2001
14 lb. 14 oz.	A. Brown	River Wensum	1998
14 lb. 12 oz.	C. Turnbull	River Wensum, Costessey	2001
14 lb. 8 oz.	S. Hunt	River Wensum, Costessey	1998
14 lb. 6 oz.	R. Bedder	River Wensum, Costessey	1999
14 lb. 2 oz.	B. Bradley	River Wensum	2001
14 lb. 1 oz.	J. Crameri	River Wensum, Drayton	2001
14 lb. 1 oz.	M. Rylands	River Wensum	1999
13 lb. 12 oz.	M. Burgess	River Wensum	2001
13 lb. 8 oz.	A. Alden	River Wensum	1998
13 lb. 6 oz.	D. Plummer	River Wensum, Costessey	1984
13 lb. 4 oz.	M. Clouser	River Wensum, Costessey	1993
13 lb. 2 oz.	M. Whipps	River Wensum	1995
13 lb. 1 oz.	S. Blackburn	River Wensum, Taverham	1994
12 lb. 12 oz.	J. Wilson	River Wensum, Drayton	1984
12 lb. 12 oz.	S. Earp	River Wensum, Taverham	1994
12 lb. 12 oz.	S. Allen	River Wensum, Costessey	1992
12 lb. 12 oz.	T. West	River Wensum, Costessey	1983
12 1bs. 11 oz.	A. Rawden	River Wensum, Drayton	1983
12 lb. 7 oz.	R. Westgate	River Wensum, Drayton	1988
12 lb. 5 oz.	R. Nudd	River Wensum	1984
12 lb. 4 oz.	A. Clarke	River Wensum, Drayton	1980
11 lb. 14 oz.	S. Harper	River Wensum, Costessey	1976

Most of the big Wensum barbel are repeat catches of the same 'known' fish. Some anglers have caught the same fish on more than one occasion, including myself. So this list simply records each angler's largest.

BREAM

18 lb. 15 oz.	T. Huntley	Bawburgh Lake	2001
18 lb. 8 oz.**	K. Walker	Bawburgh Lakes	2001
16 lb. 4 oz.	L. Cooper	Bawburgh Lakes	2001
15 lb. 11 oz.	M. Stewart	Bawburgh Lakes	2000
15 lb. 8 oz.	A. Brown	Norfolk lake	1996
15 lb. 6 oz.	R. Bedder	Kingfisher Lake, Lyng	1998
15 lb. 4 oz.	M. Davey	Kingfisher Lake, Lyng	2002
15 lb. 2 oz.	L. Grove	Worthing Fisheries	2001
14 lb. 10 oz.	R. Bedder	Kingfisher Lake, Lyng	1998
14 lb. 7 oz.	R. Bedder	Kingfisher Lake, Lyng	1996
14 lb. 2 oz.	R. Bedder	Kingfisher Lake, Lyng	1997
14 lb. 0 oz.	L. Grove	Worthing Fisheries	2001
14 lb. 0 oz.	D. Cross	Kingfisher Lake, Lyng	1994
13 lb. 14 oz.	J. Wilson	Norfolk lake	1995
13 lb. 13 oz.	L. Head	Norfolk lake	1994
13 lb. 12 oz.	J. Wilson	Norfolk lake	1994
13 lb. 11 oz.	L. Head	Norfolk lake	1994
13 lb. 10 oz.	J. Wilson	Norfolk lake	1994
13 lb. 9 oz.*	M. Davison	Beeston Lake	1982
13 lb. 8 oz.	D. Wilson	Norfolk lake	1996
13 lb. 7 oz.	L. Head	Norfolk lake	1994
13 lb. 6 oz.	J. Wilson	Norfolk lake	1994
13 lb. 4 oz.	D. Wilson	Norfolk lake	1996
13 lb. 4 oz.	P. Garner	Breakaway Pits, Suffolk	1999
13 lb. 2 oz.	S. Williams	Costessey Pits	2000
12 lb. 14 oz.*	G. Harper	Suffolk Stour	1971

Kerry Walker proudly displays his Britsh record bream of 18 lb. 8oz., caught from Bawburgh Lakes near Norwich

12 lb. 12 oz.	M. Shorting	Nar Valley Fisheries	2000
12 lb. 12 oz.	J. Davies	Norfolk lake	1994
12 lb. 12 oz.	G. Shipley	Norfolk lake	1994
12 lb. 10 oz.	A. Turrell	River Hundred	1994
12 lb. 9 oz.	M. Gabriel	Stradsett Lake	1995
12 lb. 8 oz.	M. Clowser	Stradsett Lake	1997
12 lb. 5 oz.	J. Wilson	Norfolk pit	1996
12 lb. 4 oz.	J. Harmer	Beeston Lake	1979
12 lb. 3 oz.	D. Cross	Kingfisher Lake, Lyng	1994
12 lb. 2 oz.	R. Dennison	Breakaway Pits, Suffolk	1999
11 lb. 8 oz.	R.W. Ketton-Cremer	Beeston Regis	1879

* Both of these bream held the British record for several years.
** The current British record bream.

CARP

47 lb. 6 oz.	D. Moore	Kingfisher Lakes, Lyng	2001
46 lb. 8 oz.	E. Head	River Gipping	1998
45 lb. 14 oz.	G. Turner	Kingfisher Lakes, Lyng	1999
44 lb. 8 oz.	A. Flint	Kingfisher Lakes, Lyng	1998
43 lb. 0 oz.	D. Amies	Alder Carr Lake	1999
42 lb. 12 oz.	R. Williams	Kingfisher Lakes, Lyng	1998
42 lb. 2 oz.	G. Roberts	Kingfisher Lakes, Lyng	2000
42 lb. 0 oz.	C. Pitelen	Suffolk lake	2000
42 lb. 0 oz.	A. Beasley	Kingfisher Lake, Lyng	2000
41 lb. 8 oz.	A. Tubby	Suffolk lake	2001
41 lb. 4 oz.	G. Maulkerson	Nunnery Fishery	1998
40 lb. 10 oz.	G. Roberts	Kingfisher Lakes, Lyng	1999
40 lb. 6 oz.	G. Turner	Kingfisher Lakes, Lyng	1999
40 lb. 4oz.	J. Deacon	Costessey Pits	2001
40 lb. 0 oz.	P. Reagan	Kingfisher Lakes, Lyng	2000
39 lb. 12 oz.	P. Sexton	Norfolk Estate lake	1993
39 lb. 12 oz.	G. Nobes	Kingfisher Lakes, Lyng	2000
39 lb. 1 oz.	S. Swan	Costessey Pits	1999
38 lb. 9 oz.	C. Richardson	Norfolk Estate lake	1992
38 lb. 8 oz.	A. Beasley	Kingfisher Lakes, Lyng	2000
38 lb. 4 oz.	G. Pezzotta	Alder Carr Lake	1994
38 lb. 4 oz.	T. Doyle	Waveney Valley Lakes	1996
37 lb. 10 oz.	A. Wores	Costessey Pits	2000
37 lb. 8 oz.	K. Norton	Bawburgh Lakes	2000
37 lb. 8 oz.	R. Bedder	Kingfisher Lakes, Lyng	2000
37 lb. 2 oz.	A. Edmonds	Waveney Valley Lakes	1999
36 lb. 12 oz.	M. Simmonds	Waveney Valley Lakes	1994
35 lb. 12 oz.	N. Wilson	Suffolk lake	1984
34 lb. 4 oz.	J. Dunn	Suffolk lake	1982
35 lb. 4 oz.	M. Jermy	Kingfisher Lakes, Lyng	2000
35 lb. 4 oz.	G. Maulkerson	Nunnery Lakes	1993
35 lb. 2 oz.	C. Turnbull	Norfolk Estate lake	1993
34 lb. 12 oz.	G. Wills	Waveney Valley Lakes	2001
34 lb. 12 oz.	B. Ward	Geens Pit	1984
34 lb. 8 oz.	J. Palmer	Suffolk lake	1981
34 lb. 6 oz.	J. Dunn	Costessey No. 3 Pit	1994
34 lb. 2 oz.	T. Houseago	Wensum Valley Pit	1994
34 lb. 0 oz.	R. Williams	Kingfisher Lakes, Lyng	1998
34 lb. 0 oz.	C. Richardson	Norfolk Estate lake	1992

34 lb. 0 oz.	J. Bailey	Geens Pit	1984
33 lb. 14 oz.	J. Hickleton	Bedingham Lake	2001
33 lb. 1 oz.	J. Wilson	Norfolk Estate lake	1992
33 lb. 1 oz.	R. Williams	Suffolk lake	1988
32 lb. 12 oz.	K. Howes	Gimmingham Lake	1984
32 lb. 10 oz.	P. Baker	Suffolk lake	1984
32 lb. 8 oz.	K. Norton	Lenwade Lakes	1977
32 lb. 8 oz.	C. Turnbull	Geens Pit	1985
32 lb. 8 oz.	R. Johnson	Swangey Lakes	2002
32 lb. 4 oz.	L. Grove	Worthing Fisheries	2001
32 lb. 0 oz.	D. Weale	Waveney Valley Lakes	1976
32 lb. 0 oz.	T. Harrison	Waveney Valley Lakes	1974

CATFISH (WELS)

57 lb. 8 oz.	K. Gardener	Yew Tree Lake	1999
51 lb. 0 oz.	C. Smith	Yew Tree Lake	1997
50 lb. 0 oz.	J. Carter	Lakeside Onehouse	2002
49 lb. 14 oz.*	S. Poyntz	Suffolk lake	1993
49 lb. 0 oz.	D. Caley	Lakeside Onehouse	2001
48 lb. 0 oz.	M. Banham	Suffolk lake	1994
42 lb. 8 oz.	M. Robinson	Swangey Lakes	2000
42 lb. 0 oz.	S. Leggart	Lakeside Onehouse	2001
40 lb. 8 oz.	V. Arminger	Swangey Lakes	2000
37 lb. 8 oz.	J. Shelley	Swangey Lakes	1998
37 lb. 1oz.	N. Conner	Lakeside Onehouse	2000
35 lb. 0 oz.	A. Tubby	Suffolk lake	2001
33 lb. 0 oz.	J. Murray	Cross Drove Fishery	2000
32 lb. 8 oz.	C. Pitelen	Suffolk lake	2001
32 lb. 5 oz.	M. Swatman	Swangey Lakes	1997
31 lb. 10 oz.	T. Warner	Yew Tree Lakes	2001
31 lb. 4 oz.	P. Howells	Swangey Lakes	1998
30 lb. 0 oz.	D. Farrington	River Waveney, Beccles	1998
20 lb. 2 oz.	S. Loades	Lake at Hevingham	1988

* once held the British record

CHUB

8 lb. 4 oz.	M.J. Roberts	River Wissey	1950
8 lb. 2 oz.	P. Heywood	River Waveney	1993
8 lb. 1½ oz.	M. Callaby	River Wensum	1998
7 lb. 9 oz.	S. Maddox	River Waveney	1974
7 lb. 0 oz.	S. Hunt	River Wensum	1997
6 lb. 14 oz.	C. Smith	River Yare	1994
6 lb. 10 oz.	C. Basford	River Waveney	2001
6 lb. 10 oz.	S. Loades	River Wensum	1998
6 lb. 8 oz.	R. Holmes	River Waveney	1977
6 lb. 7 oz.	J. Wilson	Wensum Valley Pit	1980
6 lb. 7 oz.	R. Williams	River Waveney	1993
6 lb. 6 oz.	S. Hunt	River Wensum	1997
6 lb. 5 oz.	R. Williams	River Waveney	1995
6 lb. 5 oz.	J. Wilson	River Wensum, Ringland	2001
6 lb. 5 oz.	J. Crameri	River Wensum, Ringland	1998
6 lb. 5 oz.	S. Hunt	River Wensum	1998
6 lb. 4 oz.	J. Humphries	River Wensum, Taverham	1999
6 lb. 3 oz.	J. Westwood	River Wensum, Ringland	2001

6 lb. 3 oz.	R. Nudd	Irrigation Reservoir	1985
6 lb. 2 oz.	M. Rouse	River Wensum	2001
6 lb. 2 oz.	T. Houseago	Lakeside, Lenwade	1994
6 lb. 2 oz.	M. Clouser	River Wensum, Ringland	1997
6 lb. 2 oz.	C. Stevens	River Wissey	1959
6 lb. 2 oz.	R. Harris	River Wensum, Drayton	1965
6 lb. 2 oz.	M. James	River Wensum, S. Morley	1982
6 lb. 2 oz.	G. Ellis	Suffolk Stour, Glemsford	2002
6 lb. 2 oz.	A. Rawden	River Waveney	1988
6 lb. 1 oz.	R. Nudd	Irrigation Reservoir	1987
6 lb. 1 oz.	J. Cameri	River Wensum, Ringland	2000
6 lb. 1 oz.	C. Smith	River Yare	1994
6 lb. 0 oz.	M. Harvey	River Waveney	1986
6 lb. 0 oz.	J. Wilson	River Wensum, Lenwade	1998
6 lb. 0 oz.	R. Cork	Lakeside, Lenwade	1988
6 lb. 0 oz.	G. Gifford	River Wensum, Hellesdon	1983
5 lb. 15 oz.	J. Wilson	River Wensum, Ringland	1978
5 lb. 14 oz.	C. Gooch	River Wensum, Costessey	1970
5 lb. 14 oz.	J. Wilson	River Wensum, Drayton	1984
5 lb. 14 oz.	K. Fuller	River Wensum, Ringland	1976
5 lb. 14 oz.	K. Fuller	River Wensum, Ringland	1976
5 lb. 14 oz.	T. West	River Wensum, Costessey	1983

CRUCIAN CARP

5 lb. 10 ½ oz.*	G. Halls	Bradmoor Lakes	1976
4 lb. 7½ oz.	G.T. Mills	Hevingham Lakes	1973
4 lb. 0 oz.	L. Freeman	Shallow Brook Lakes	1999
4 lb. 0 oz.	A. Huxtable	Weybread Pits	1981
3 lb. 13 oz.	B. Gibbs	Lake near Bury St. Edmunds	1973
3 lb. 8 oz.	J. Hickleton	Bedingham Lake	2000
3 lb. 8 oz.	S. Loades	Lenwade Common Lakes	1993
3 lb. 8 oz.	C. Turnbull	Lenwade Common Lakes	1992
3 lb. 6½ oz.	C. Turnbull	Lenwade Common Lakes	1992
3 lb. 4 oz.	R. Francis	Ringland Lakes	1997
3 lb. 3 oz.	C. Turnbull	Lenwade Common Lakes	1992
3 lb. 2 oz.	S. Allen	Bedingham Lake	1999
3 lb. 1 oz.	J. Norton	Hevingham Lakes	1972
3 lb. 1 oz.	B. Neave	Lenwade Lakes	1976
3 lb. 0 oz.	A. Hunt	Bedingham Lake	1996
2 lb. 14 oz.	D. Gladwell	Earsham Pit	1973

* Once the British record prior to being deleted.

DACE

1 lb. 4 ½ oz.*	J.L. Gasson	Little Ouse, Thetford	1960
1 lb. 4 oz.	D. Flack	Little Ouse, Thetford	1987
1 lb. 4 oz.	B. Kettell	River Wensum, Fakenham	1969
1 lb. 4 oz.	T. Cleere	River Wensum, Drayton	1958
1 lb. 4 oz.	K. Burlingham	River Wensum, Elsing	1981
1 lb. 3 ½ oz.	W.L. Comer	River Tas	1943
1 lb. 3 ¼ oz.	W. Clarke	River Ouse, Thetford	1972
1 lb. 2 ½ oz.	A. Davison	River Tud, Easton	1971
1 lb. 2 oz.	J. Hendry	River Wensum	1972
1 lb. 2 oz.	K. Burlingham	River Wensum, Fakenham	1975
1 lb. 2 oz.	W. Barton	River Wensum	1966
1 lb. 1 ½ oz.	A. Davidson	River Tud, Easton	1971

1 lb. 1 oz.	G. Parsons	River Wensum, Fakenham	1975
1 lb. 1 oz.	K. Gardner	River Wensum, S. Morley	1982
1 lb. 1 oz.	J. Wilson	River Tud, Easton	1963
1 lb. 1 oz.	K. Smith	River Tas	1995
1 lb. 1 oz.	A. Emden	River Yare, Bawburgh	1963
1 lb. ½ oz.	R.H. Clements	River Wensum, Drayton	1954
1 lb. 0 oz.	T. Cleere	River Wensum, Drayton	1956

* The Current British record dace

Almost beating the entire list above by himself comes the late Bill Clarke from Barnham, near Thetford, who from 1951 to 1985 took an incredible 44 dace of over the pound. Bill's largest weighed 1 lb. 3 ¼ oz. and all came from his local Rivers, the Thet and the Little Ouse. Bill's pal, Denis Flack, also regularly gets amongst the big dace of the Little Ouse. In 1987 he took a staggering haul of 11 dace, mostly just over or just on the pound, with the heaviest going 1 lb. 3 ½ oz. and 1 lb. 4 oz. This must surely rate as the best catch of dace ever. Denis did it again in 1994 by taking from a stretch of the Little Ouse, some nine miles from where he took the above catch, no less than 10 dace in a single haul averaging over the pound with the best tipping the scales at 1 lb. 3 oz. In 1998 Denis became king of the mini species record holders by catching a new British record bleak from the River Lark weighing 4 oz. 9 dr.

EEL

8 lb. 8 oz.	R. Gratton	Feltwell Pit	1994
7 lb. 8 oz.	A.J. Dewsnap	Oulton Broad	1953
6 lb. 12 oz.	Unknown angler	Lake at Welney	1983
6 lb. 11 oz.	Dodger Green	Fritton Lake	1975
6 lb. 4 oz.	G. Dixon	Lenwade Lakes	1977
6 lb. 2 oz.	J. Hickleton	Bedingham Lake	1996
6 lb. 2 oz.	I. Trevors	Filby Broad	1983
5 lb. 14 oz.	J. Holliman	Waveney Pit	1981
5 lb. 13 oz.	N. Saunders	Suffolk Moat	1982
5 lb. 12 oz.	E. Taylor	River Bure	2000
5 lb. 12 oz.	N. Saunders	Weybread Pits	1982
5 lb. 9 oz.	A. Gorham	Waveney Pit	1983
5 lb. 9 oz.	A. Huxtable	Suffolk Moat	1982
5 lb. 8 oz.	A. Gorham	Waveney Pit	1984
5 lb. 8 oz.	K. Whall	River Thurne	1954
5 lb. 4 oz.	R. Davis	Scoulton Pond	1973
5 lb. 4 oz.	L. Wilson	Lakeside Lenwade	1987
5 lb. 4 oz.	J. Knights	Lenwade Lakes	1973
5 lb. 1 oz.	K. Clarke	Taverham Pits	1970
5 lb. 1 oz.	T. Boulton	Weybread Pits	1974

GOLDEN ORFE

7 lb. 9 oz.	D. Wall	Norfolk Lake	1999
6 lb. 6 oz.	J. Wilson	Lakeside, Lenwade	1997
5 lb. 0 oz.	D. McKay	Bridge Farm Fisheries	2002
5 lb. 0 oz.	P. Wilson	Lakeside, Lenwade	1999
4 lb. 13 oz.	J. Crameri	Lakeside, Lenwade	2000

GRASS CARP

36 lb. 12 oz.	P. Howlett	Suffolk lake	1998
27 lb. 10 oz.	P. Spinks	Common Lakes, Lenwade	2001
24 lb. 12 oz.	C. Germaine	Taswood Lakes	2001
23 lb. 0 oz.	C. Brown	Taswood Lakes	2001
22 lb. 0 oz.	C. Brown	Taswood Lakes	2001

John displays a beautiful golden orfe of 6 lb. 6 oz. caught from Lakeside in Lenwade

21 lb. 12 oz.	S. Smithson	Taswood Lakes	2001
21 lb. 12 oz.	P. Howell	Taswood Lakes	2001
21 lb. 5 oz.	J. Wilson	Lakeside, Lenwade	1998
21 lb. 4 oz.	M. Plane	Taswood Lakes	2001
21 lb. 0 oz.	P. Dawson	Lakeside, Lenwade	2001
20 lb. 8 oz.	A. Sutton	Taswood Lakes	2001
19 lb. 6 oz.	B. Alexander	Lakeside, Lenwade	1997
18 lb. 4 oz.	P. Curtis	Lakeside, Lenwade	2001

PERCH

5 lb. 15 ½ oz.**	P. Clarke	Suffolk Stour	1949
5 lb. 4 ¾ oz.	H. Green	Stradsett Lake	1936
5 lb. 2 oz.	L. Gordon	River Waveney, Geldeston	1886
4 lb. 12 oz.*	S. Baker	Oulton Broad	1962
4 lb. 12 oz.	A. Hodges	River Bure, Upton	1959
4 lb. 9 oz.	L. Proudfoot	Oulton Broad	1963
4 lb. 9 oz.	A.J. Emden	Oulton Broad	1961
4 lb. 7 ½ oz.	W. Mason	Oulton Broad	1965
4 lb. 6 oz.	K. Matthews	River Wensum, Norwich	1999
4 lb. 5 oz.	A.J. Hodges	South Walsham Broad	1964
4 lb. 3 oz.	E. Allen	River Wensum, S. Morley	1964
4 lb. 2 ½ oz.	L. Proudfoot	Oulton Broad	1966
4 lb. 1 oz.	L. Head	Suffolk Irrigation Reservoir	1994
4 lb. 1 oz.	J. Davies	Suffolk Irrigation Reservoir	1997
4 lb. 1 oz.	S. Hunt	River Thurne	1999
4 lb. 1 oz.	K. Burlingham	River Wensum, Elsing	1963
4 lb. 1 oz.	I. Lambert	Selbrigg Pond	1984
4 lb. 1 oz.	N. Cooper	Decoy Broad	1937
3 lb. 14 oz.	J. Bailey	Norfolk pit	1987
3 lb. 11 oz.	L. Head	Suffolk Irrigation Reservoir	1992
3 lb. 10 oz.	P. Collins	Oulton Broad	1965

3 lb. 8 oz.	M. Curtis	River Wensum	1973
3 lb. 7 oz.	D. Flack	River Lark, Suffolk	1999
3 lb. 6 oz.	M. Edwards	River Thurne	1995
3 lb. 4 oz.	M. Flowerday	Oulton Broad	1966

** Once the British record before it was deleted
* Also held the British record for several years until eclipsed.

PIKE

42 lb. 2 oz.*	D. Amis	River Thurne, Martham	1986
42 lb. 0 oz.	J. Nudd	Wroxham Broad	1901
41 lb. 6 oz.*	N. Fickling	River Thurne, Martham	1985
40 lb. 1 oz.*	P. Hancock	Horsey Mere	1967
39 lb. 8 oz.	D. Leary	Kingfisher Lakes, Lyng	1984
39 lb. 8 oz.	R. Miller	Kingfisher Lakes, Lyng	1989
38 lb. 0 oz.	Angler from Bath	Somerton	1979
38 lb. 0 oz.	M. Wilkin	Swangey Lakes	1999
38 lb. 0 oz.	J. Watson	Horsey Mere	1988
37 lb. 10 oz.	P. Woodhouse	Thurne System	1984
37 lb. 8 oz.	A. Cottrell	Somerton	1982
37 lb. 8 oz.	D. Allen	Bure System	1972
37 lb. 0 oz.	B. Florey	Somerton	1981
36 lb. 6 oz.	D. Amies	Somerton	1982
36 lb. 0 oz.	M. Haliday	River Yare	1939
36 lb. 0 oz.	J. Bailey	Kingfisher Lakes, Lyng	1985
36 lb. 0 oz.	F. Thorns	Haveringland Lake	1880
35 lb. 13 oz.	P. Belton	Thurne system	1983
35 lb. 10 oz.	J. Henry	River Thurne	1998
35 lb. 8 oz.	A. Jackson	Heigham Sound	1948
35 lb. 6 oz.	R. Pownall	Somerton	1960
35 lb. 4 oz.	J. Goble	River Thurne	1998
35 lb. 0 oz.	D. Pond	Thurne system	1989
35 lb. 0 oz.	F. Wright	Horsey Mere	1968
34 lb. 12 oz.	P. Belton	Thurne system	1983
34 lb. 9 oz.	B. Cannell	Kingfisher Lakes, Lyng	1994
34 lb. 8 oz.	A. Goram	Hickling Broad	1994
34 lb. 5 oz.	R. Childs	River Yare	2001
34 lb. 2 oz.	D. Pye	Horsey Mere	1965
34 lb. 2 oz.	J. Davies	Swangey Lakes	1998
34 lb. 0 oz.	L. Spencer	Horsey Mere	1967
34 lb. 0 oz.	D. Bradley	Worthing Fisheries	2000
34 lb. 0 oz.	M. Swatman	Swangey Lakes	1997
34 lb. 0 oz.	D. Sutton	Bure Valley Lakes	1999
33 lb. 12 oz.	C. Warnes	Wensum Pit	1993
33 lb. 12 oz.	P. Cooper	River Bure	2000
33 lb. 8 oz.	D. Pye	Candle Dyke	1964
33 lb. 8 oz.	P. Coull	Somerton	1982
33 lb. 4 oz.	K. Cracknell	Horsey Mere	1994
33 lb. 0 oz.	R. Nelson	Somerton	1980
33 lb. 0 oz.	D. Pye	Horsey Mere	1963

* Each of these pike once held the British record.

ROACH

| 3 lb. 15 oz. | M. Page | Suffolk lake | 2001 |
| 3 lb. 10 oz. | C. Pitelen | Suffolk lake | 2000 |

3 lb. 10 oz.	J. Bailey	River Wensum	1987
3 lb. 6 oz.	F. Staples	Suffolk Stour	1955
3 lb. 5 oz.	M. Hudson	River Ant	1954
3 lb. 5 oz.	J. Bailey	River Wensum	1987
3 lb. 5 oz.	A.W. Howard	Salhouse Broad	1963
3 lb. 4 ¼ oz.	K. Fuller	River Wensum	1984
3 lb. 4 oz.	W.C. Bly	River Bure, Horning	1949
3 lb. 3 oz.	J. Nunn	River Bure	1984
3 lb. 3 oz.	M. Page	Suffolk lake	2001
3 lb. 2 oz.	N. Glover	River Wensum, S. Morley	1984
3 lb. 2 oz.	G. Harwin	River Bure, Coltishall	1959
3 lb. 2 oz.	D. Amies	Bure Valley Lakes	2002
3 lb. 2 oz.	J. Bailey	River Wensum, Elsing	1976
3 lb. 1 ½ oz.	D. Crisp	River Wensum, North Elmham	1975
3 lb. 1 ½ oz.	K. Redgrave	Weybread Pits	1999
3 lb. 1 oz.	R. Westgate	River Wensum	1984
3 lb. 0 oz.	G. Gamble	River Wensum	1997
3 lb. 0 oz.	M. Page	Suffolk lake	2001
3 lb. 0 oz.	L. Nobbs	River Bure, Horstead	1960
3 lb. 0 oz.	G. Canham	River Wensum, North Elmham	1974
3 lb. 0 oz.	M. Francis	River Yare, Trowse	1958
3 lb. 0 oz.	J. Mitchell	Taverham Pits	1956
2 lb. 15 ½ oz.	T. Appleton	River Wensum, Costessey	1979
2 lb. 15 oz.	J. Sapey	River Wensum, Lyng	1975
2 lb. 15 oz.	M. Bond	River Wensum, Hellesdon	1979
2 lb. 15 oz.	J. Tyree	River Wensum, Taverham	1988

RUDD

4 lb. 8 oz.*	Rev. L.E. Alston	Thetford Mere	1933
3 lb. 7 oz.	R. Clements	River Ant, Irstead	1958
3 lb. 6 oz.	A. Holdcroft	River Wensum, Elsing	1973
3 lb. 6 oz.	D. Plummer	Lenwade Lakes	1981
3 lb. 5 ½ oz.	C. Turnbull	Lenwade Lakes	1981
3 lb. 5 ½ oz.	J. Watson	Lenwade Lakes	1981
3 lb. 5 oz.	D. Pye	Horsey Mere	1965
3 lb. 4 oz.	D. Pye	Hickling Broad	1964
3 lb. 4 oz.	A. Clarke	Lenwade Lakes	1981
3 lb. 4 oz.	D. Pye	Hickling Broad	1962
3 lb. 3 oz.	B. Cannel	Wolterton Lake	1975
3 lb. 2 oz.	R. Springall	Taverham Mills Lake	1998
3 lb. 2 oz.	A. Towers	Lenwade Lakes	1975
3 lb. 1 oz.	D. Pye	River Thurne, Martham	1964
3 lb. 1 oz.	G. Tansley	Lenwade Lakes	1981

* This rudd held the British record for 68 years until eclipsed in 2001 by a 4 lb. 10 oz. rudd caught by S. Parry from Freshwwater Lake, Co. Armagh, Northern Ireland

TENCH

11 lb. 5 oz.	M. Burgess	Bawburgh Lakes	1998
11 lb. 2 oz.	C. Turnbull	Bawburgh Lakes	1998
11 lb. 2 oz.	J. Cranswick	Bawburgh Lakes	1999
11 lb. 1 oz.	R. Bedder	Kingfisher Lakes, Lyng	2001
10 lb. 14 oz.	K. Fuller	Bawburgh Lakes	2000
10 lb. 10 oz.	M. Burgess	Bawburgh Lakes	1998

10 lb. 10 oz.	S. Blyth	Bawburgh Lakes	2001
10 lb. 7 oz.	J. Issit	Bawburgh Lakes	1999
10 lb. 7 oz.	C. Turnbull	Bawburgh Lakes	2001
10 lb. 4 oz.	D. Gould	Bawburgh Lakes	2000
10 lb. 3 oz.	C. Turnbull	Bawburgh Lakes	2000
10 lb. 2 oz.	A. Bunn	Taverham Mills Lake	2000
10 lb. 1 oz.	C. Smith	Bawburgh Lakes	1998
10 lb. 1 oz.	C. Turnbull	Bawburgh Lakes	2000
10 lb. 0 oz.	T. Bidwell	Bawburgh Lakes	2000
9 lb. 12 oz.	K. Cant	Ringland Lakes	1995
9 lb. 12 oz.	J. Sapey	Worthing Fisheries	1990
9 lb. 11 oz.	R. Williams	Waveney Valley Pit	2000
9 lb. 10 oz.	C. Turnbull	Bawburgh Lakes	2001
9 lb. 7 oz.	R. Williams	Waveney Valley Pit	2001
9 lb. 6 oz.	C. Turnbull	Bawburgh Lakes	1999
9 lb. 5 oz.	J. Nunn	Bawburgh Lakes	1998
9 lb. 4 oz.	J. Wilson	Wensum Pit	2001
9 lb. 4 oz.	G. Vanderrin	Nar Valley Fisheries	2001
9 lb. 1 oz.	G. Humphries	Bawburgh Lakes	1999
8 lb. 14 oz.	C. Turnbull	Bawburgh Lakes	1999
8 lb. 12 oz.	R. Bedder	Kingfisher Lakes, Lyng	1999
8 lb. 9 oz.	C. Turnbull	Bawburgh Lakes	1999
8 lb. 8 oz.	G. Humphries	Bawburgh Lakes	1999
8 lb. 6 oz.	D. Gould	Upton Broad	1992
8 lb. 4 oz.	S. Challis	Suffolk Stour	1975
8 lb. 3 oz.	D. Stolworthy	Ringland Lakes	1998
8 lb. 2 oz.	L. Head	Bures Lake	1975
8 lb. 2 oz.	J. Haydon	Bures Lake	1973
8 lb. 2 oz.	D. Batten	Costessey Pits	1986

TROUT
R = RAINBOW TROUT
B = BROWN TROUT

R 22 lb. 3 oz.	M. Turner	Narborough Trout Fisheries	1977
R 19 lb. 1 oz.	F. Flynn	Narborough Trout Fisheries	2001
R 19 lb. 0 oz.	K. Miller	Narborough Trout Fisheries	2001
R 17 lb. 8 ½ oz.	M. Webster	Narborough Trout Fisheries	1989
R 17 lb. 8 oz.	J. Millar	Narborough Trout Fisheries	1988
R 16 lb. 8 oz.	R. Lucas	Narborough Trout Fisheries	2001
R 16 lb. 6 oz.	R. Smith	Narborough Trout Fisheries	2001
R 16 lb. 1 ½ oz.	J. Tomlinson	Narborough Trout Fisheries	2001
R 15 lb. 12 oz.	J. Millar	Narborough Trout Fisheries	1988
R 14 lb. 14 oz.	J. Bilner	Narborough Trout Fisheries	2001
R 14 lb. 10 oz.	K. Woolsey	Narborough Trout Fisheries	2002
R 13 lb. 9 oz.	J. Holliman	Narborough Trout Fisheries	1989
R 13 lb. 2 oz.	J. Tyree	Narborough Trout Fisheries	1989
B 12 lb. 14 oz.	G. Mays	River Wissey, Wissington	1959
R 12 lb. 8 oz.	J. Wilson	Narborough Trout Fisheries	2000
R 12 lb. 4 oz.	J. Tyree	Narborough Trout Fisheries	1989
R 11 lb. 1 oz.	R. Horne	Whinburgh	1994
R 10 lb. 12 oz.	L. Tebbs	Narborough Trout Fisheries	1983
R 10 lb. 5 oz.	L. Desuza	Whinburgh	1994
R 10 lb. 4 oz.	M. Palmer	Narborough Trout Fisheries	1994

R 10 lb. 4 oz.	C. Skeggs	River Wissey, Wissington	1970
R 10 lb. 3 oz.	C. Bishop	Narborough Trout Fisheries	1984
B 10 lb. 2 oz.	M. Clouser	Cut Off Channel	1993
B 9 lb. 12 oz.	M. Sayer	River Wensum, Lenwade	1964
R 9 lb. 4 oz.	R. Williams	Valley Fisheries	1994
R 9 lb. 2 oz.	Mr. Allday	Reepham Trout Fisheries	1983
B 9 lb. 0 oz.	C. Horsley	River Wensum, Fakenham	1980
R 8 lb. 7 oz.	A. Varnava	Reepham Trout Fisheries	1982
B 8 lb. 3 oz.	D. Davey	River Wissey	1972
B 8 lb. 2 oz.	C. Clay	Lyng Trout Lake	1987
R 8 lb. 0 oz.	W. Bailey	Lyng Trout Lake	1983
B 7 lb. 15 oz.	J. Sapey	River Wensum, Lyng	1971
B 6 lb. 4 oz.	Joker Norton	River Wensum, Ringland	1968
B 6 lb. 2 oz.	J. Wilson	River Wensum, Ringland	1999
B 6 lb. 0 oz.	C. Bullard	River Wensum, Ringland	1960
B 5 lb. 4 oz.	D. Hewett	River Wensum, Hellesdon	1971
B 5 lb. 4 oz.	H.B. Waters	River Wensum, Helleson	1985

ZANDER

19 lb. 5 ½ oz.**	D. Lavender	Fen Drain	1998
18 lb. 9 oz.	D. Lavender	Fen Drain	1998
18 lb. 8 oz.	B. Meadows	Roswell Pit	1988
18 lb. 6 oz.	D. Gaunt	Fenland Drain	1993
18 lb. 2 oz.	R. Hughes	Fenland Drain	1993
18 lb. 2 oz.	T. Ward	Middle Level	1994
18 lb. 2 oz.	D. Gaunt	Fenland Drain	1993
18 lb. 0 oz.	A. Wood	Fenland Drain	1993
17 lb. 12 oz.*	D. Litton	Relief Channel	1977
17 lb. 8 oz.	L. Brown	Fenland Drain	1992
17 lb. 5 oz.	D. Lavender	Middle Level	1994
17 lb. 4 oz.	C. Bloy	Middle Level	1994
17 lb. 4 oz.	W. Gaunt	Middle Level	1994
17 lb. 1 oz.	D. Lavender	Middle Level	1994
17 lb. 1 oz.	D. Gaunt	Fen Drain	1993
16 lb. 14 oz.	N. Jones	Middle Level	1995
16 lb. 13 oz.	I. Weatherall	Middle Level	1993
16 lb. 11 oz.	J. Crameri	Middle Level	2001
16 lb. 9 oz.	I. Weatherall	Middle Level	1993
16 lb. 6 oz.	S. Smith	Cut Off Channel	1976
16 lb. 2 oz.	M. Vials	Fen Drain	1994
16 lb. 2 oz.	C. Mapp	Middle Level	1996
16 lb. 2 oz.	J. Davis	Fen Drain	1996
16 lb. 2 oz.	C. Brown	Fen Drain	1996
16 lb. 1 oz.	J. Watson	Middle Level	1996
16 lb. 0 oz.	G. Arnold	Fen Drain	1994
16 lb. 0 oz.	A. Prime	Middle Level	1996
15 lb. 13 oz.	P. Woodford	Relief Channel	1994
15 lb. 6 ¼ oz.	R. Young	Relief Channel	1977
15 lb. 5 oz.*	B. Chillingworth	Relief Channel	1971
15 lb. 3 oz.	K. Jeary	Cut Off Channel	2001

* Both of these zander once held the British record.
** The current British record zander.

INDEX